AFGHANISTAN a window on the tragedy

ISBN: 978-0-9819891-7-4
Published January 2011

Printed and bound in Malaysia

Photography by
Alen Silva
www.alensilva.com

Translated by
Patrick Doyle & Tobias Doyle

Designed by
Pedro Neto
www.pedroneto.eu

Presented by
The Oliver Arts & Open Press
www.oliveropenpress.com

Texts by
Alan Rachins
Bahman Ghobadi
Bernardo Atxaga
Ezzat Goushegir
Gillian Anderson
John Sistiaga
Malalai Joya
Michael Ratner
Mike Farrell
Suheir Hammad
Susan Kelly-DeWitt
Toti Martinez de Lezea
Yasmina Khadra

dedicated to my mother,
Magari

INTRO

Alen Silva

The exuberance of infinite dust, flowing through oceans of legend, enveloped the landscape retained in some mystical nook of memory, embraced the splendour of the soul and created the perfect atmosphere of thousands of years of history.

This is how I might define my encounter with this country of sturdy, friendly people, I thought — concealed by an obscure recent past and the ghostly "burka" desolately adorning its women and the horizon of a hopeful peace.

I didn't go to Afghanistan to write a story. It was a journey conceived in an unconscious outpouring of escapism, a youthful insolence in the face of destiny, an unmistakable piece in the puzzle of tolerance.

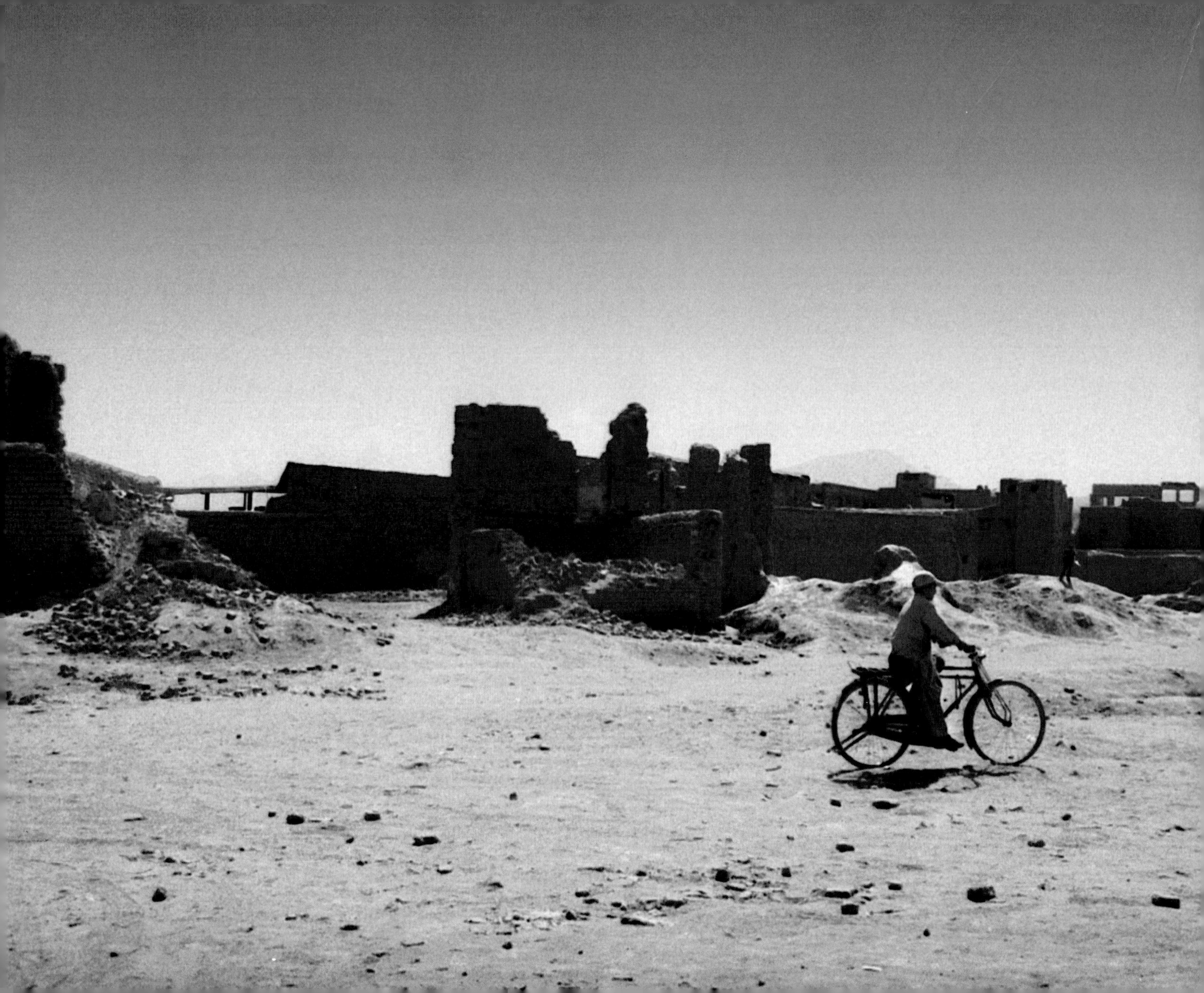

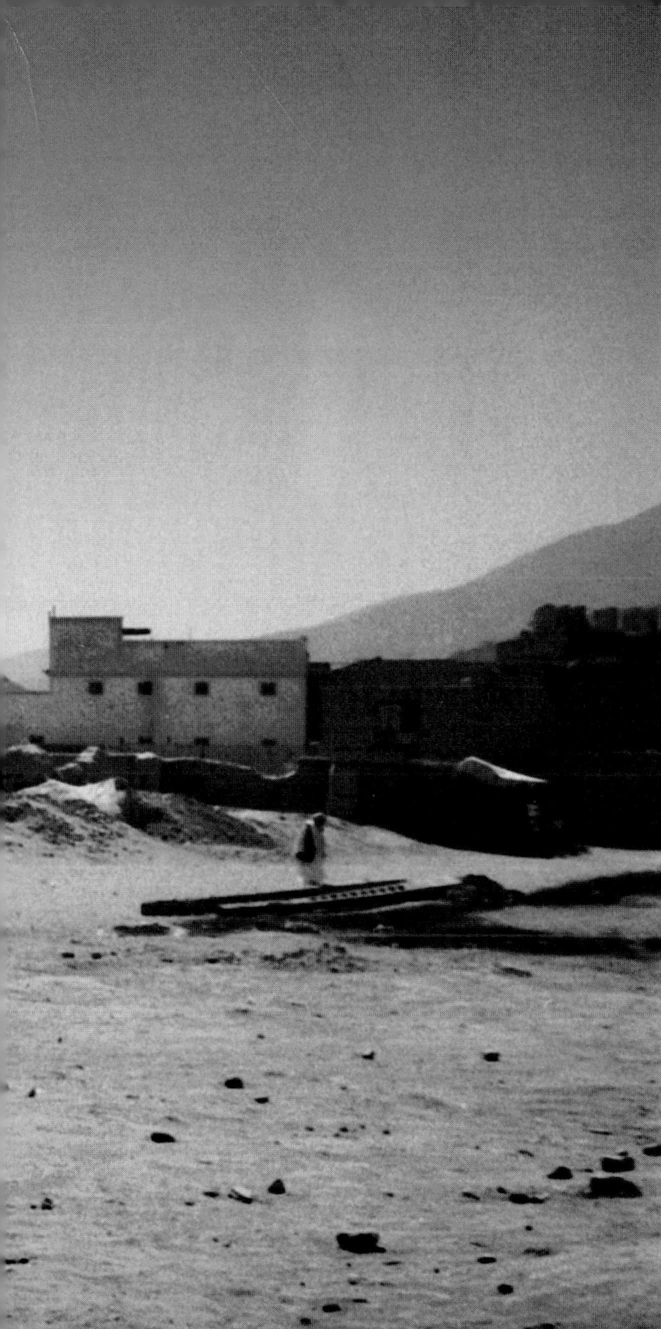

The quarter of Shar-e kohna, in the center of Kabul, is the capital's most badly damaged, by the bitter battles to gain control over it.

Next page
A woman in a burka on her way to a voting place on election day.
Women are obliged to uncover their faces to exercise their right to vote.

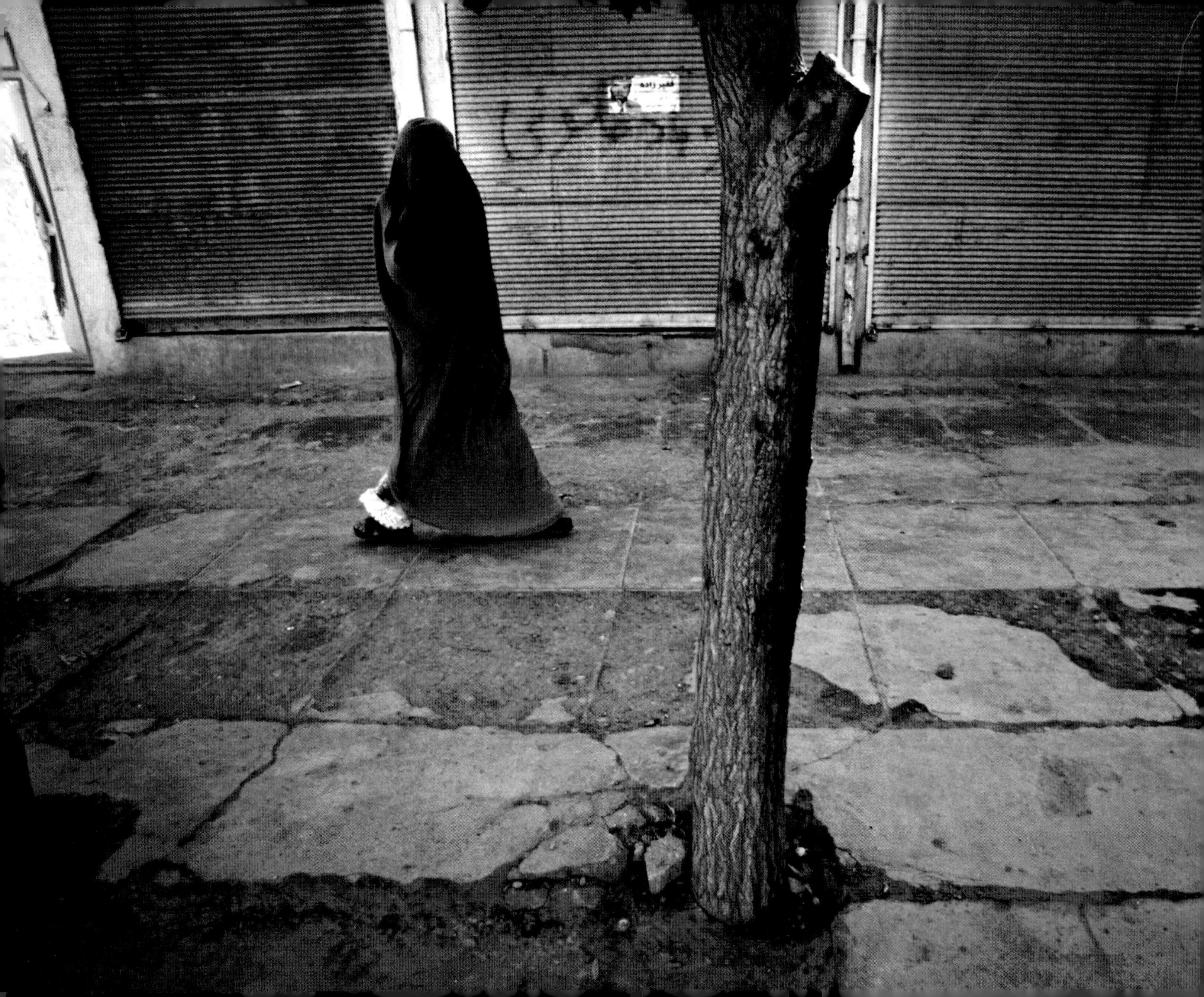

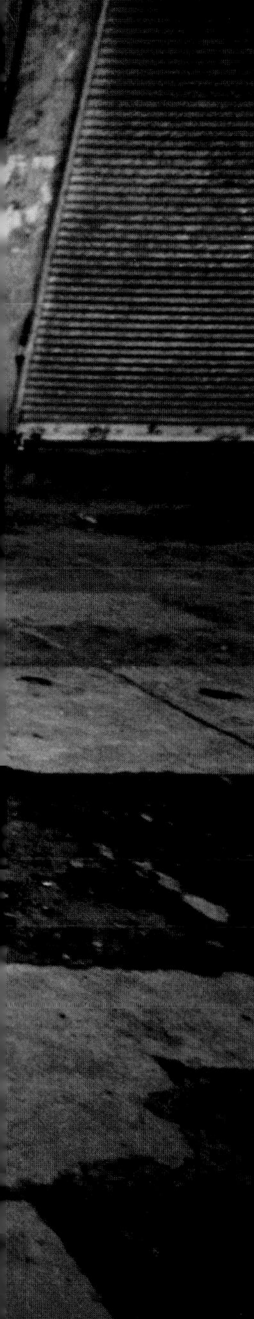

PROLOGUE

Malalai Joya

It was December 2003. I rehearsed my speech, looking out the window into a dusty street of Kabul where children played. The blood of more than 65,000 people had literally stained this city red in the early 90's. Girls were raped, kidnapped, murdered or forced into marriage to commanders. Many committed suicide to escape such fates. Houses and shops were looted on a daily basis. Rockets exchanged between different factions killed more civilians than rivals. Armed factions killed defenceless people of other tribes, like warlord Rasul Sayyaf's Pashtun men who burned Hazara people in containers. In revenge, the Hazara faction of Abdul Ali Mazari pulled out the eyes of Pashtun people. Thousands of other horrendous crimes overwhelmed the people. No film-maker or story writer can possibly express the tyrannies of those days. The warlords did not stop at that. They killed intellectuals and freedom-fighters. Gulbuddin Hekmatyar, the most powerful of all the warlords, killed Saydal Sukhundan, a young, democratic-minded poet in the Kabul University. Hekmatyar's band was behind the assassination of Meena, leader of the Revolutionary Association of the Women of Afghanistan (RAWA) in Pakistan, along with many other democratic-minded and peace-loving Afghans.

The next day, on December 17, 2003, I stood in the queue waiting for my turn in the hall of the Grand Assembly. It was packed with the criminals who had committed all those crimes, and many more. The criminal parties and their hangers-on were there to decide the future of Afghanistan. I had a flashback to the horrendous stories that refugees in Pakistan had told me, describing the wars under fundamentalist rule from 1992-96; I remembered the photos of Kabul that resembled the destruction of World War II. I relived seeing the balcony of an apartment where a young girl had jumped to her death, to escape some warlords who wanted to kidnap her. Many other such memories swirled around in my mind.

Finally I had got my chance to face the real causes of Afghanistan's tragedy. There were no second thoughts now, no turning back. As Zapata, the great hero of Mexico, famously said, "It's better to die on your feet than live on your knees." I had got the chance to speak on behalf of all the unfortunate people of my burnt-out land. I was going to make my voice be heard, despite the taboo I knew I was breaking in Afghanistan, and despite the extreme danger, as these people only talk with the language of the gun, and do not believe in freedom of speech and democracy. I started and my heart swelled with the pain of my people, hatred against the war criminals and the desire to keep on speaking against them. Suddenly I realized that my microphone had been cut off, and I was being attacked on all sides by fundamentalist men with slogans and abuse. I was nearly expelled from

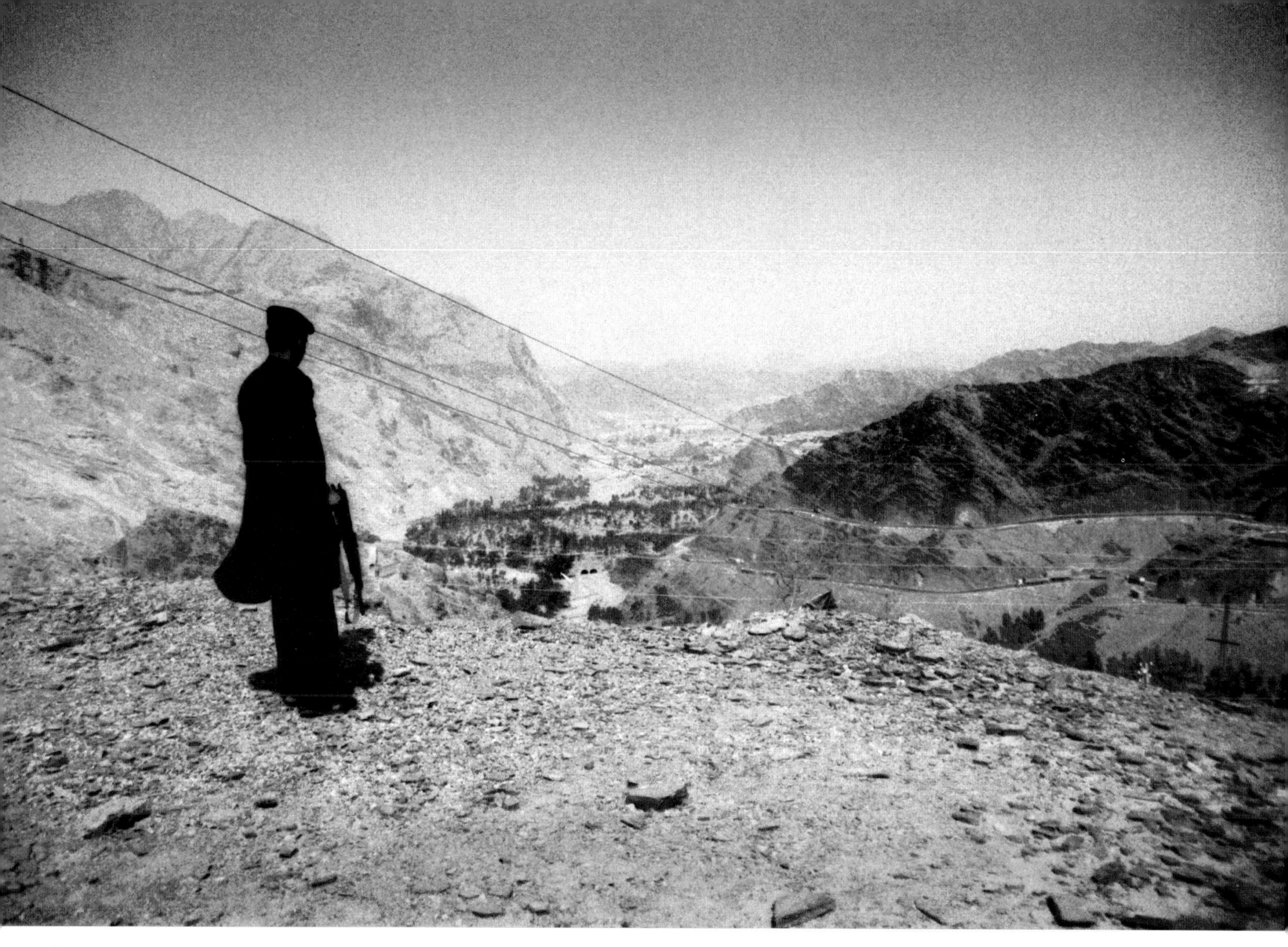

A policeman from Pakistan looking toward the border of Afghanistan, on the horizon.
This is a tribal area, which I reached by crossing the Khyber Pass. Foreigners are not allowed here without a police escort.

the assembly, although I was an elected representative of Farah province. This was the start of my harder and more decisive fight with the enemies of my people, the fundamentalists. They were now once again in power, generously supported by the US government, but on behalf of my suffering people, I asked for their prosecution in the national and international courts.

After this speech, my name reached to the faraway villages of Afghanistan, and many poor people came to meet me and to congratulate me. They strongly supported me, expressing their sympathy and backing, which give me more courage, determination and power to challenge their blood-thirsty enemies publicly.

A year later, due to the requests of many people, I decided to stand in the elections for the new parliament of Afghanistan, which was finally due to convene again after 30 years. Although it was predictable that a parliament under the shadow of the gun and foreign invasion will be a laughingstock and a fraud, I was happy to enter that new arena, to challenge the killers of my people where it may have more impact.

"You are our only hope, Joya," one of the pained women said to me with a tear-stained face during my election campaign. Though they had been threatened by their husbands, the three women had voted for me—and later they were beaten for it by their husbands. These people empowered me in my mission against the criminals who had demanded an apology after my speech, which I refused.

I had found my way into the parliament filled with drug kingpins, thieves of millions of dollars of aid, lackeys of foreign countries and war criminals. There was no hope for the legislature of Afghanistan, as it was composed of the brethren-in-creed of the Taliban. The most important people in the government were warlords and war criminals whose hands were stained with the blood of our people. Men like Khalili, Fahim, Ismael Khan, Dostum, Sayyaf, Haji Almas, Haji Farid, Mohaqiq and many more, and they all had the backing of the US government and the so-called "international

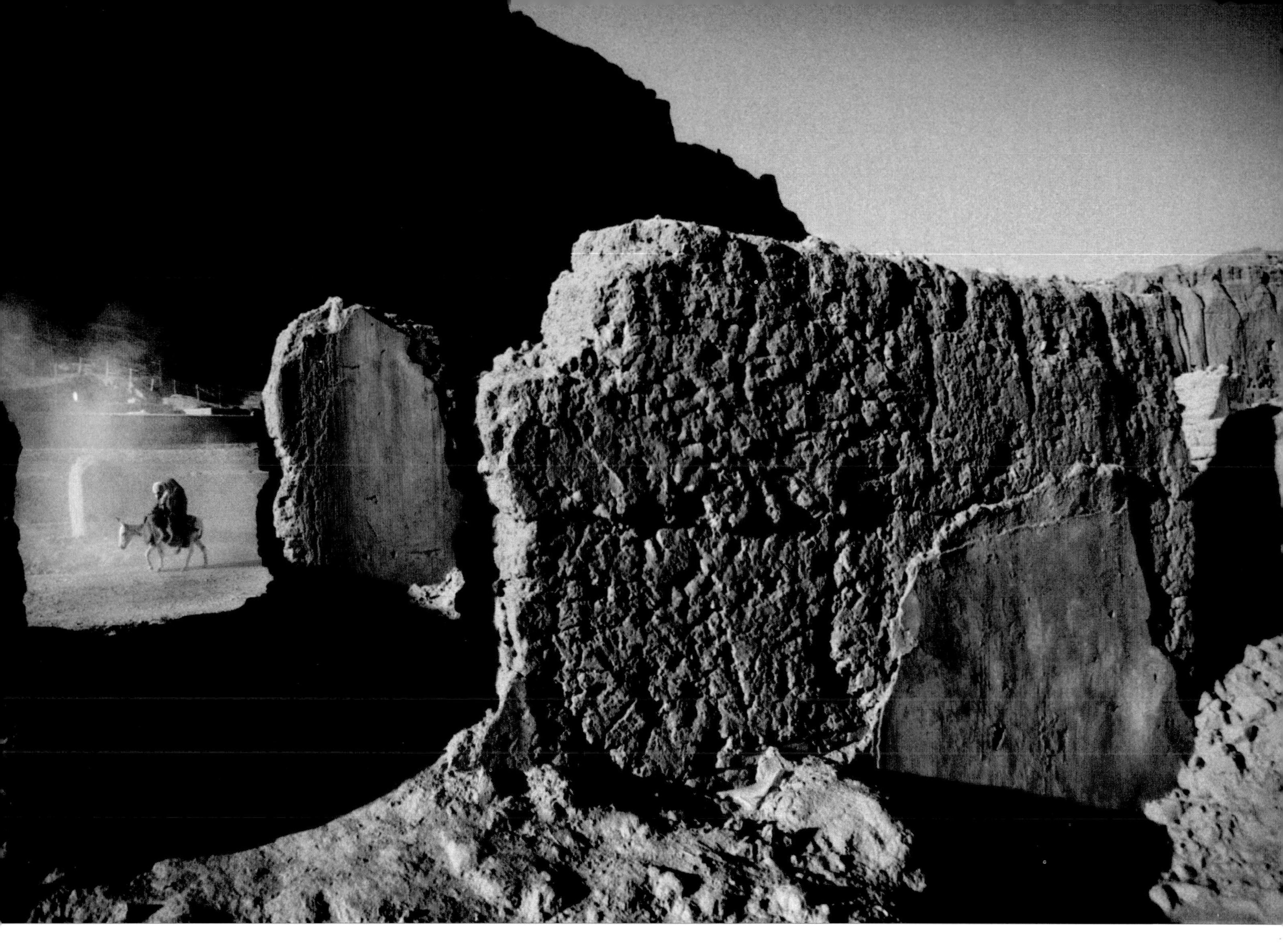

Covered by a thick screen of dust, surrounded by buildings ruined by endless warfare, two Hazara children riding a donkey in Bamiyan, capital of the Hazarajat province. I wonder why, with more than 1,000 NGO's in Afghanistan, one never sees a foreigner outside the capital.

community". Some of them have even been called "war criminals" by Human Rights Watch.

And while the criminals are in charge of the system, they are trying to pass laws to block any efforts for their prosecution. In April 2007 both houses of the Afghan parliament approved an amnesty law, granting immunity from prosecution for all those accused of war crimes committed during the past 30 years. I and a few other MPs raised our voices against it, but as the fundamentalist warlords hold over 80% of the seats, the bill was easily passed, and even Mr. Karzai approved it. This law will now provide amnesty to all criminals.

When I had seen the reaction of the warlords in the Grand Assembly, I was more sure than ever that peace, democracy, human rights and women's rights can only be established in Afghanistan after fundamentalists of every kind are removed from our political scenario.

Our nation is living under the shadow of war, and the crimes and brutalities of the fundamentalists, and women are the primary and silent sacrifice of this situation. Justice doesn't exist in Afghanistan. I came to know about cases of rape and kidnap of young girls by commanders in rural areas. But the police and judiciary did not detain or punish any of the criminals, as they were more powerful than the government itself. A young girl named Bashira was gang-raped by a 17-year old son of an MP with his friends, in the north. His father, Haji Payinda, the member of parliament, is also a powerful commander in the area, so the police ignored the case, and his son walked about with impunity. I can't forget Bashira crying on television demanding for justice.

The most famous case of Sayed Parwiz Kambaksh showed clearly what kind of judiciary exists under the dark-minded, evil fundamentalists. Kambakhsh, a young journalism student, was sentenced to death after he downloaded and shared an article from the Internet which the court termed "anti-Islamic".

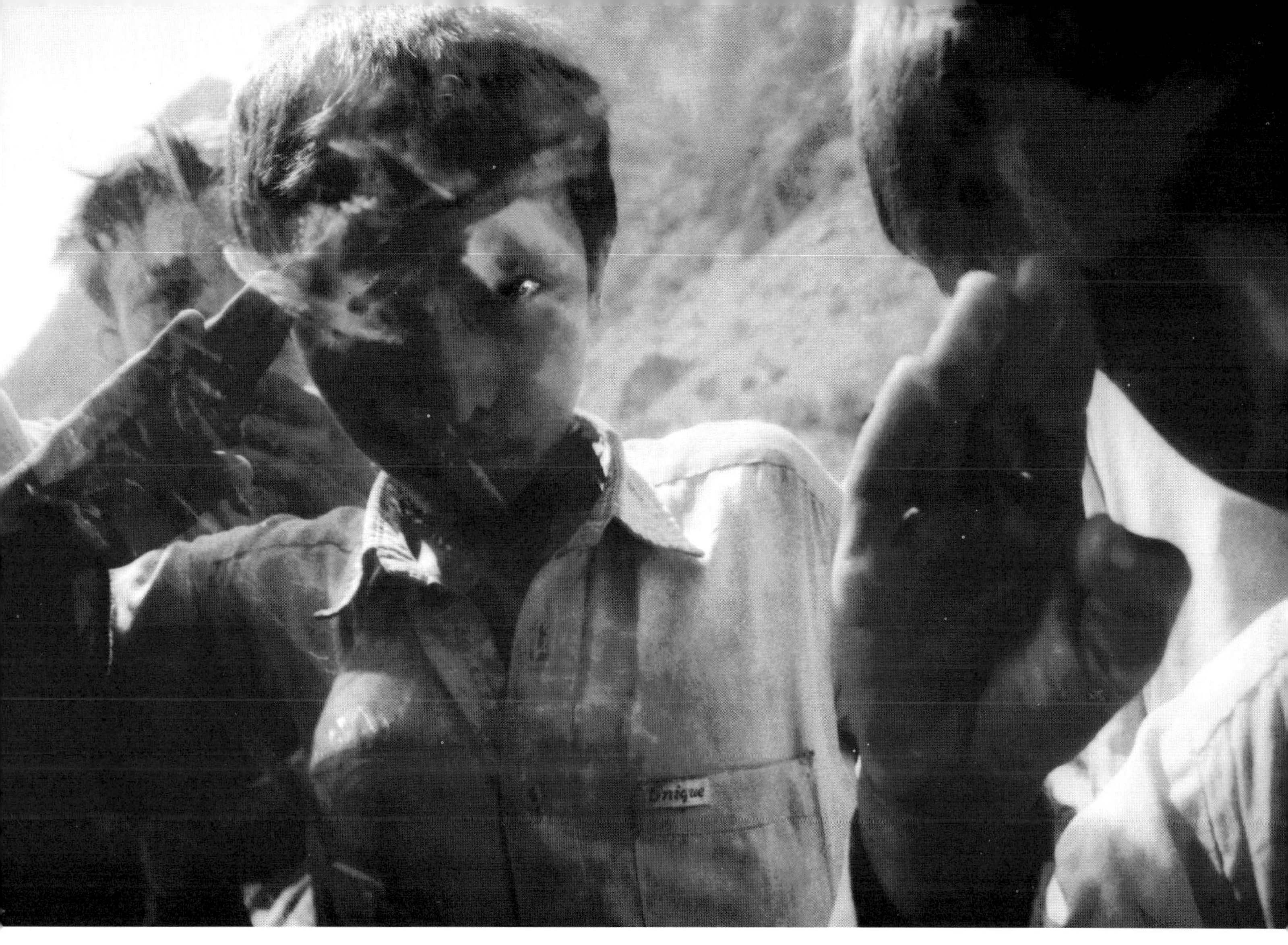

I took this photo in Torkham, on the border with Pakistan, where some boys gave me the salute I would see again and again, the whole time I spent in the country. I was surprised how spontaneous it was. It must be something they were very used to seeing.

Other horrible cases of women's rights violations hit the news from time to time. The rates of self-immolation and suicide due to domestic violence and poverty, forced marriages and violence against women are higher than ever. Most of the cases are not even reported to the media, due to traditional complexities. Afghanistan is deeply suffering from a health scourge caused mainly by lack of facilities. Death of mothers during childbirth is incredibly high, as are rates of dangerous diseases like tuberculosis and other health problems.

In addition, America trumpets its propaganda to the world about liberating Afghanistan and women, and fighting against terrorists. I believe that no nation can donate liberty to another nation. Democracy, human rights, women's rights are not something that someone gives to us. We must ourselves fight to achieve these values. The condition of women has not improved, but gotten worse than ever since the US invasion of Afghanistan in October 2001.

It is a heart-wrenching fact that Afghanistan has received 15 billion dollars in aid, but up to 70% of my people live on less than $2 a day. Corruption and poverty have made life a torture for millions of Afghans. Afghanistan is at the top in the drug trade, contributing 93% of the world's opium, and has pinned itself in the bottom places in the indices of corruption and human development. The country is actually gripped in the claws of warlords with their "independent governments" in rural areas; One high-ranking U.S. official remarked that only 30% of the country is in control of the Afghan government, the rest being under the dominance of local warlords and Taliban.

Although the so-called liberation of Afghan women was the main reason given for invading Afghanistan in 2001, women are suppressed and live under disastrous conditions today more than ever. Instead of going into many details of the women's rights catastrophe in Afghanistan, let me give you a few shocking examples to describe the terrible conditions of Afghan women:

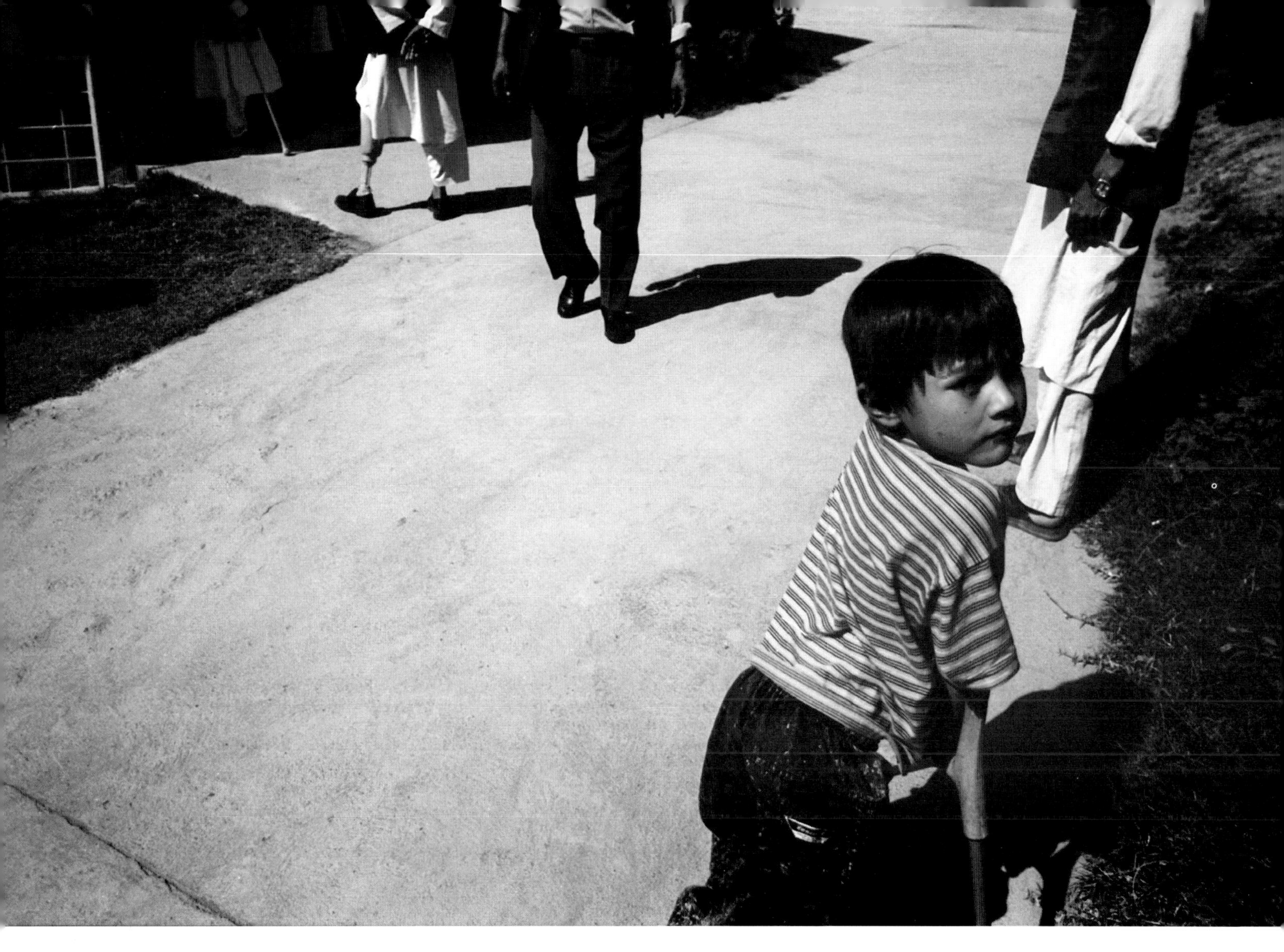

Little Ahmed learning to walk on artificial limbs in the Orthopedic Center of Kabul, after his legs were blown off by land mines. The hospital has a workshop that makes orthopedic limbs, but the waiting list at this time is enormously long.

A WomenKind report on Feb.28, 2008 about the conditions of Afghan women says: "Violent attacks against females, usually domestic, are at epidemic proportions, with 87 per cent of females complaining of such abuse—half of it sexual…"

According to official figures by the Health Ministry of Afghanistan, around 6,500 women die of childbirth complications every year in the Badakhshan province of Afghanistan, the highest rate in the world.

Eight-year old Bibi Fatima was raped by three men and then murdered and buried.

UNIFEM survey suggests that violence affects 80 percent of Afghan women at some time in their lives.

The number of suicide cases among Afghan women as a result of destitution and non-existence of justice was never so high in Afghanistan as it is today. And most suicides are not reported in the statistics at all.

22-year-old Fatima's husband cut off her toes and burned her by hot water. In a similar case the nose and ear of Nafisa were cut off by her husband.

18-year-old Samiya hung herself by a rope because she was to be sold to a sixty-year-old man. Another woman called Bibi Gul locked herself up in the animals' stable and committed self-immolation. Later her family found nothing except her bones.

According to UNIFEM, 65 percent of the 50,000 widows in Kabul and thousands of women all over the country see suicide as the only option to get rid of their miseries and desolation.

Over 95% of Afghan women suffer from depression.

Every 28 minutes a woman dies in Afghanistan during childbirth.

The life expectancy of Afghan women is only 44 years.

Girls are still traded like currency in Afghanistan. Surveys say that 80% marriages are forced.

Commanders of the Northern Alliance rule with a reign of terror, and abduct and rape girls and women in areas of their control.

According to an OXFAM survey, just one in five girls is enrolled in primary education, and only one in 20 in secondary school. 200,000 children in the areas controlled by the Taliban are completely without education.

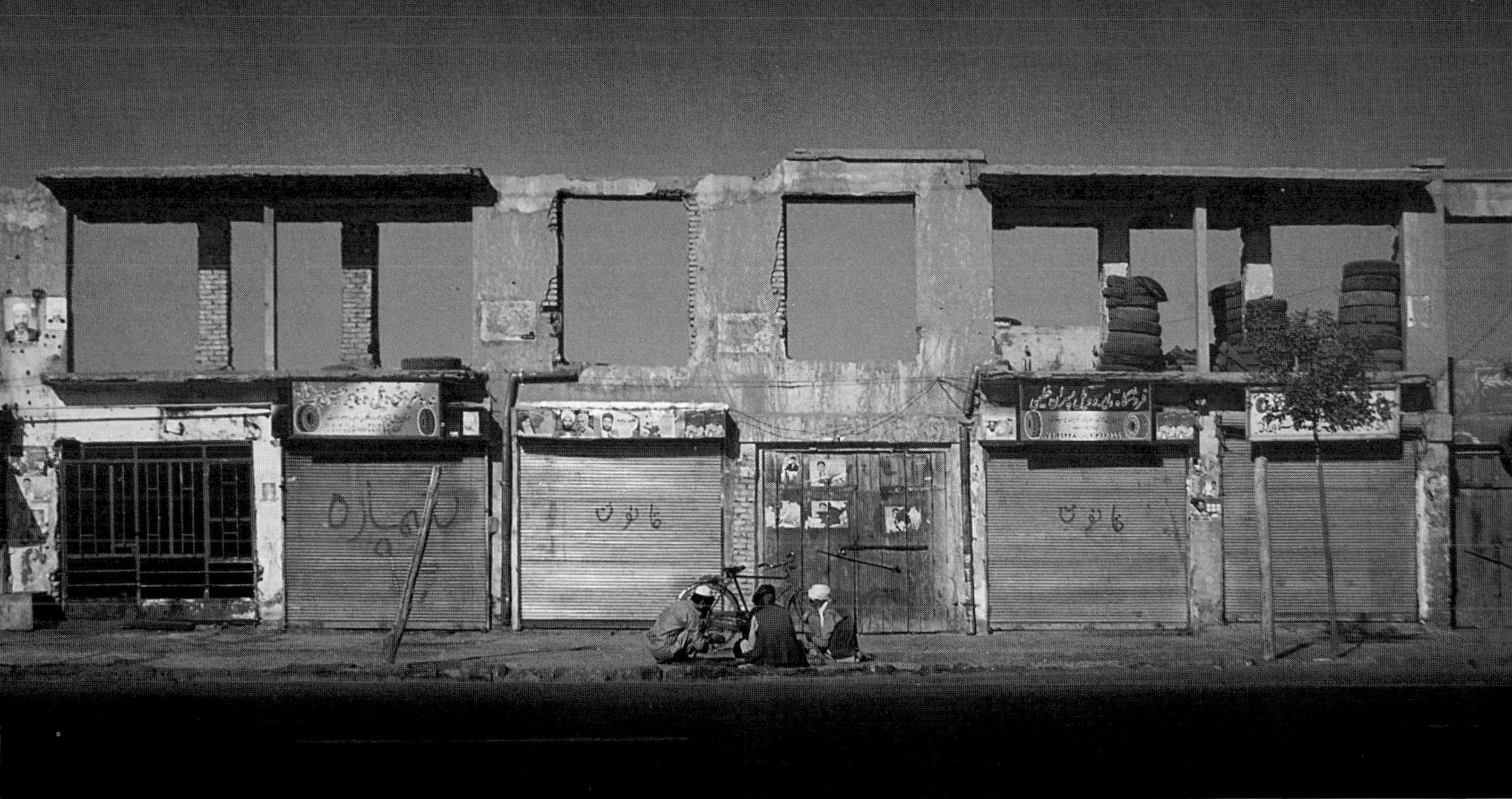

A group of men meet for mid-morning tea in a street of ruined buildings. Unfortunately, this is a common landscape in the cities of Afghanistán, where many buildings have been completely destroyed.

On July 6, 2008, US troops bombed a wedding party in Nengarhar province and killed 47 civilians, including the bride. In a similar tragic incident, 27 civilians perished in an attack by US-led NATO forces on a remote village of Nouristan. In both cases, the US troops refused even to apologize. On July 8, in a powerful suicide bombing in Kabul, around 200 civilians were killed or injured; most of the victims were women and children. I know a two-year-old child who lost her mother and a family who lost five members.

For my outspokenness against the corruption of land-grabbers such as Sayyaf and drug kingpins like Qanooni, I earned the serious threats from the most medieval-minded MPs in the world. I was abused, threatened to be killed and raped, called non-Muslim and other such things. Once, in one of my interviews the interviewer promised not to censor my speeches as was the normal practice. I called the parliamentarians 'worse than animals in the stable'. The next day I was voted out of the parliament for violating some law. I was truly sorry for the words I had said, but there was no chance of apologizing—to the useful, kind animals. I had truly insulted them by comparing them to the war criminals.

On my last visit to a hospital in Kabul, and learning about the stories of the girls and women who had attempted suicide by self-immolation, seeing the city resembling a graveyard, raising my eyes to stare at the tall buildings of the warlords, reading the news of the deaths of families from hunger—I see only one solution. My suffering people have been well and truly betrayed over many years by the US and allies, who invited themselves and bombed our country in the name of democracy, human rights and women's rights, but the most infamous enemies of these values were supported and installed into the power. They relied on the Northern Alliance bandits, who have a history full of bloodshed, treason and crimes against our people.

The US talks of human rights, but so far has killed more innocent civilians than the Taliban or Al-Qaeda. According to

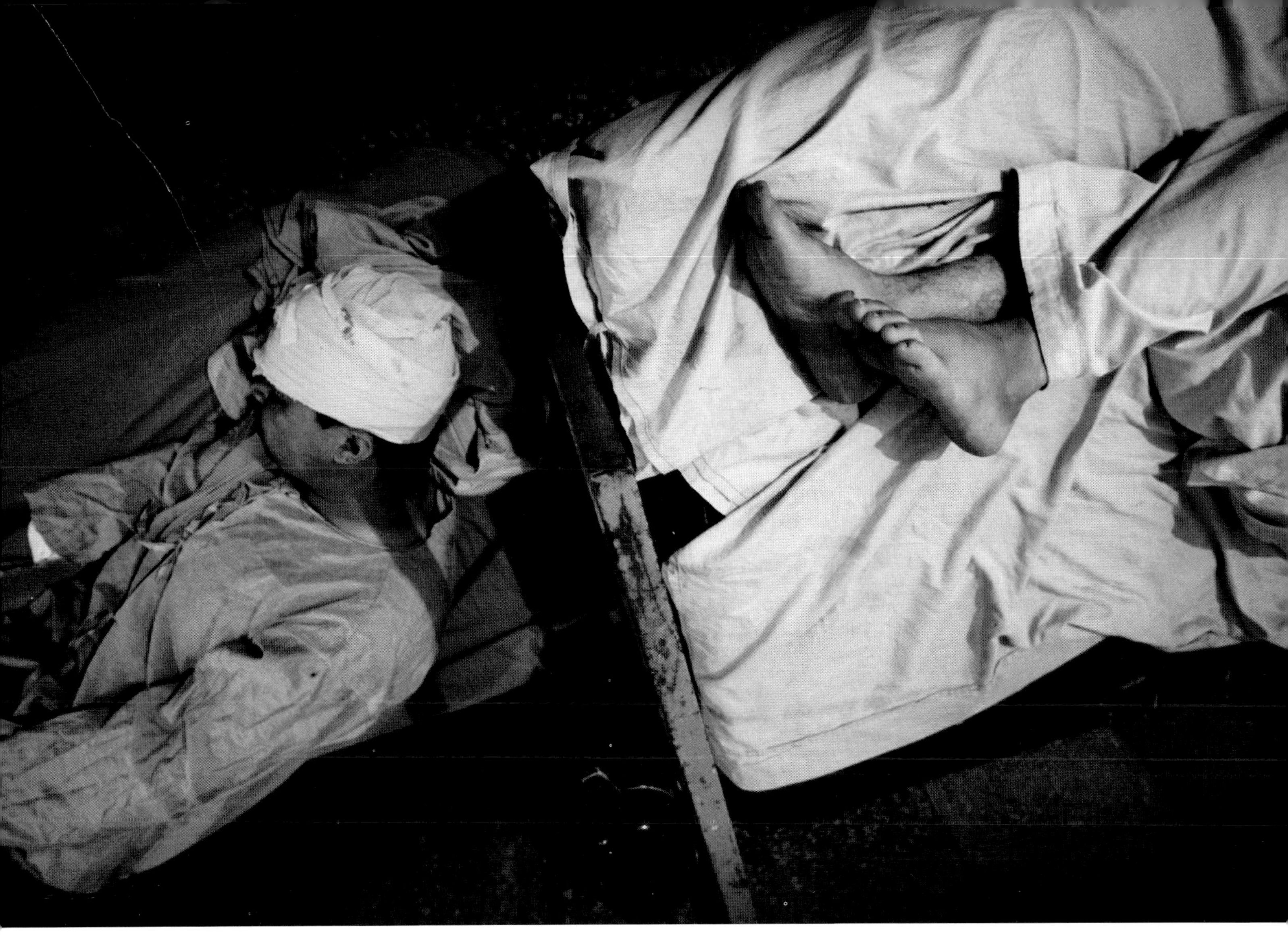

Patients on the floor of the hospital.

a survey by Prof. Marc Herold, around 8,000 innocent people have been killed so far by the US troops.

The US is not concerned with the suffering and disastrous conditions of our people. To achieve their strategic and economic interests, US policymakers put our people in danger.

Many Afghans think the US wants to keep Afghanistan in its current state of chaos to legitimate their long presence in the region, and make Afghanistan their base for monitoring and controlling the Central Asian Republics, China, Iran and other Asian powers, besides controlling the drug business, which is the third biggest global commodity in cash terms, after oil and the arms trade.

Today the majority of our people have come to the conclusion that these troops must pull out of Afghanistan as soon as possible. I think if these troops do not pull out voluntarily, in the coming future they may face resistance from the people of Afghanistan. Right now anti-US sentiments are high among people, because years of conflict in Afghanistan have given political consciousness to our people, and they know the US has been responsible for pushing Afghanistan into its current tragedies. It was the US government which poured billions of dollars during the Cold War into the pockets of the dark-minded Islamist forces, and then helped the rise of the Taliban and al-Qaeda. Today they are once again supporting the Northern Alliance.

Unfortunately as we have witnessed in the past few months, Obama's foreign policies, especially regarding Afghanistan, are very similar to Bush's and worse, with even more war-mongering. He wants to send more troops to Afghanistan, which is synonymous with more war, more conflict and more killing of our innocent civilians.

While Obama is now the President of War in Iraq and Afghanistan and wants to impose war on Pakistan, it is really preposterous that he is given the Nobel Peace Prize. This once again exposes the travesty of the Nobel Peace Prize, and leaves no doubt that it is given out of political interests.

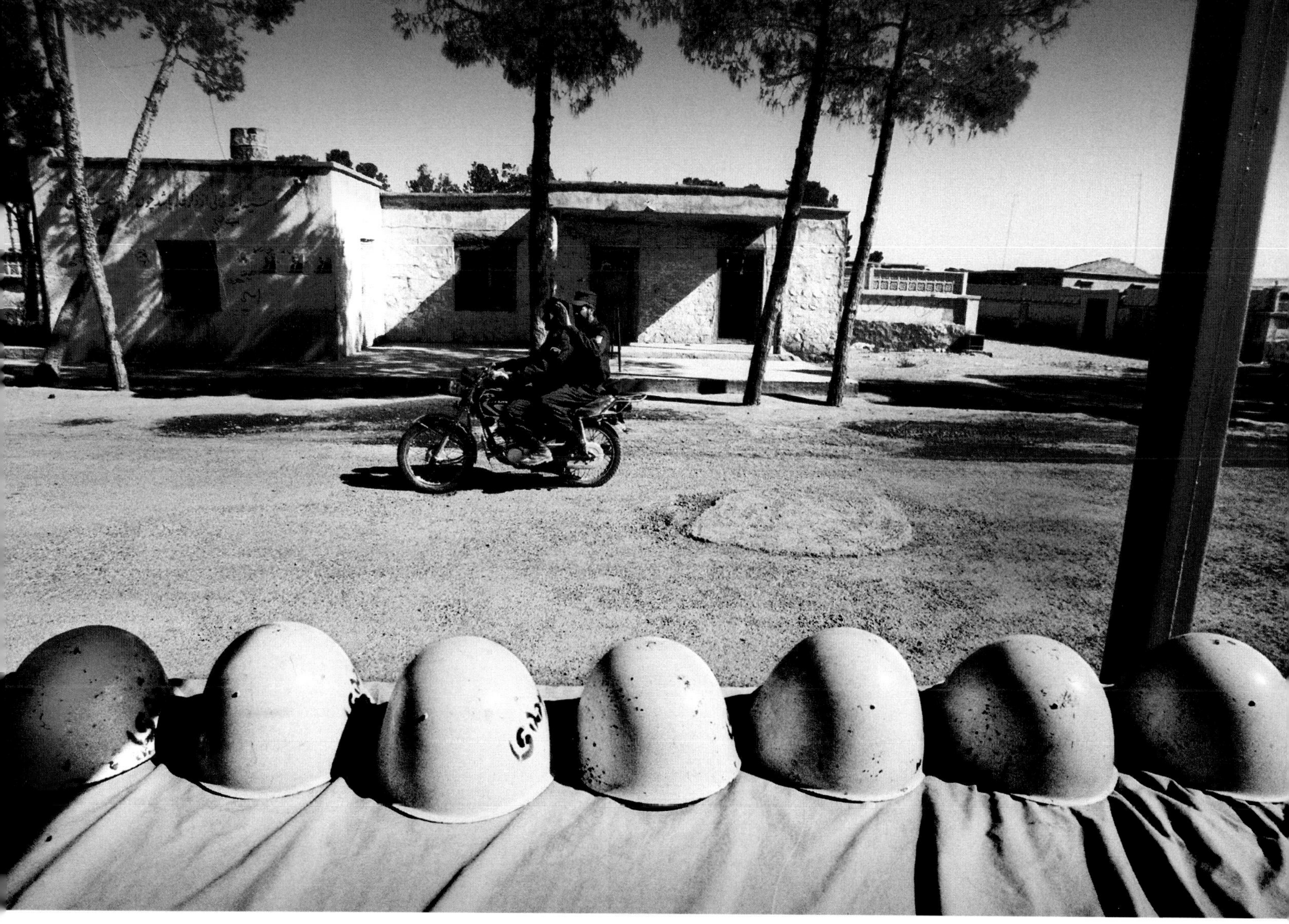

Guard station at Herat airport.

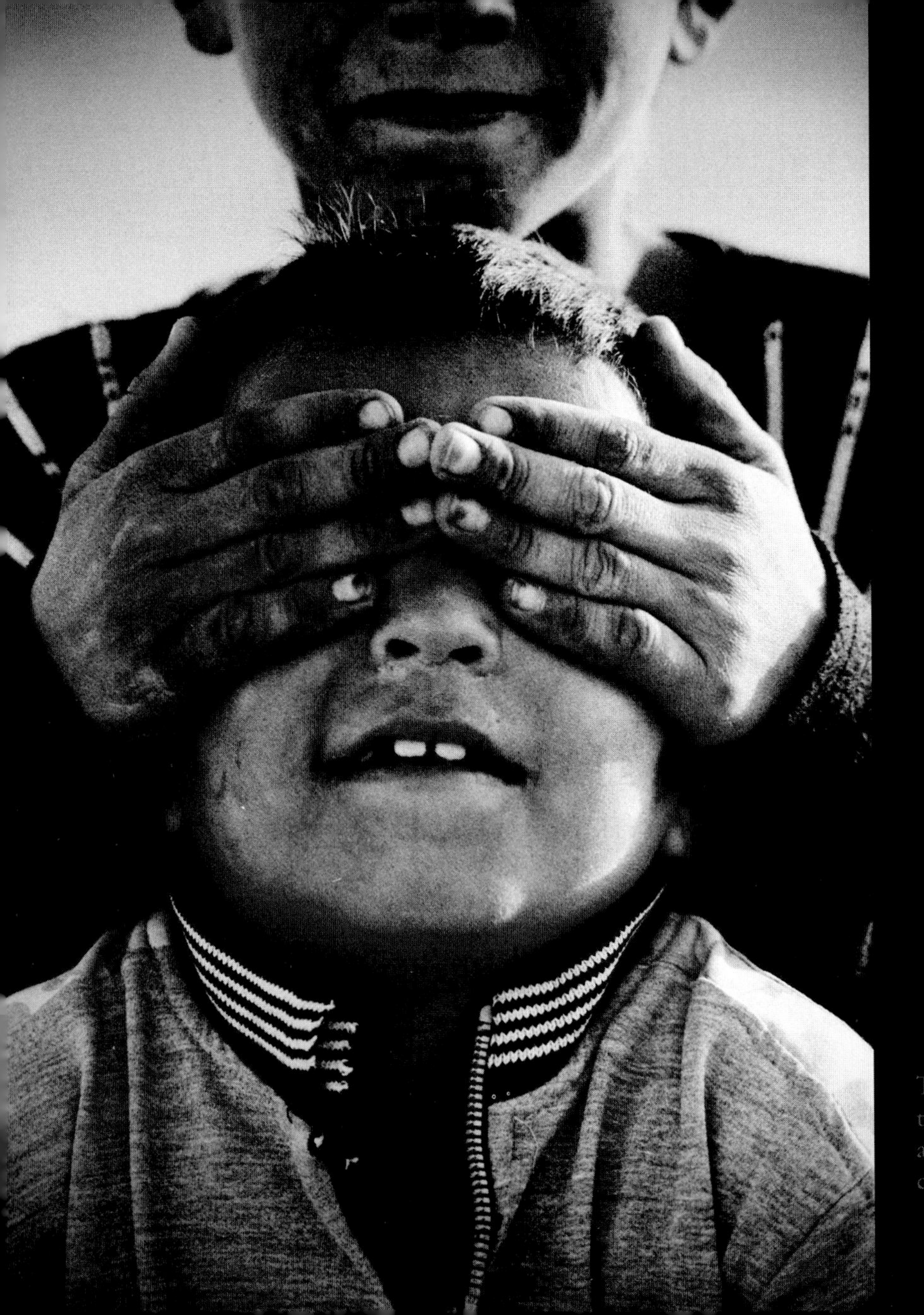

The future of Afghanistan's children seems to be symbolized by this photograph of a children's game. With an unpromising past and no hope of peace in sight, the struggle for power keeps the country in a state of perfect chaos.

Khan Agha lost an eye in the war with the Taliban when he was struck by a stray piece of shrapnel. He keeps at his job working in the post office of the Sharenow quarter of Kabul.

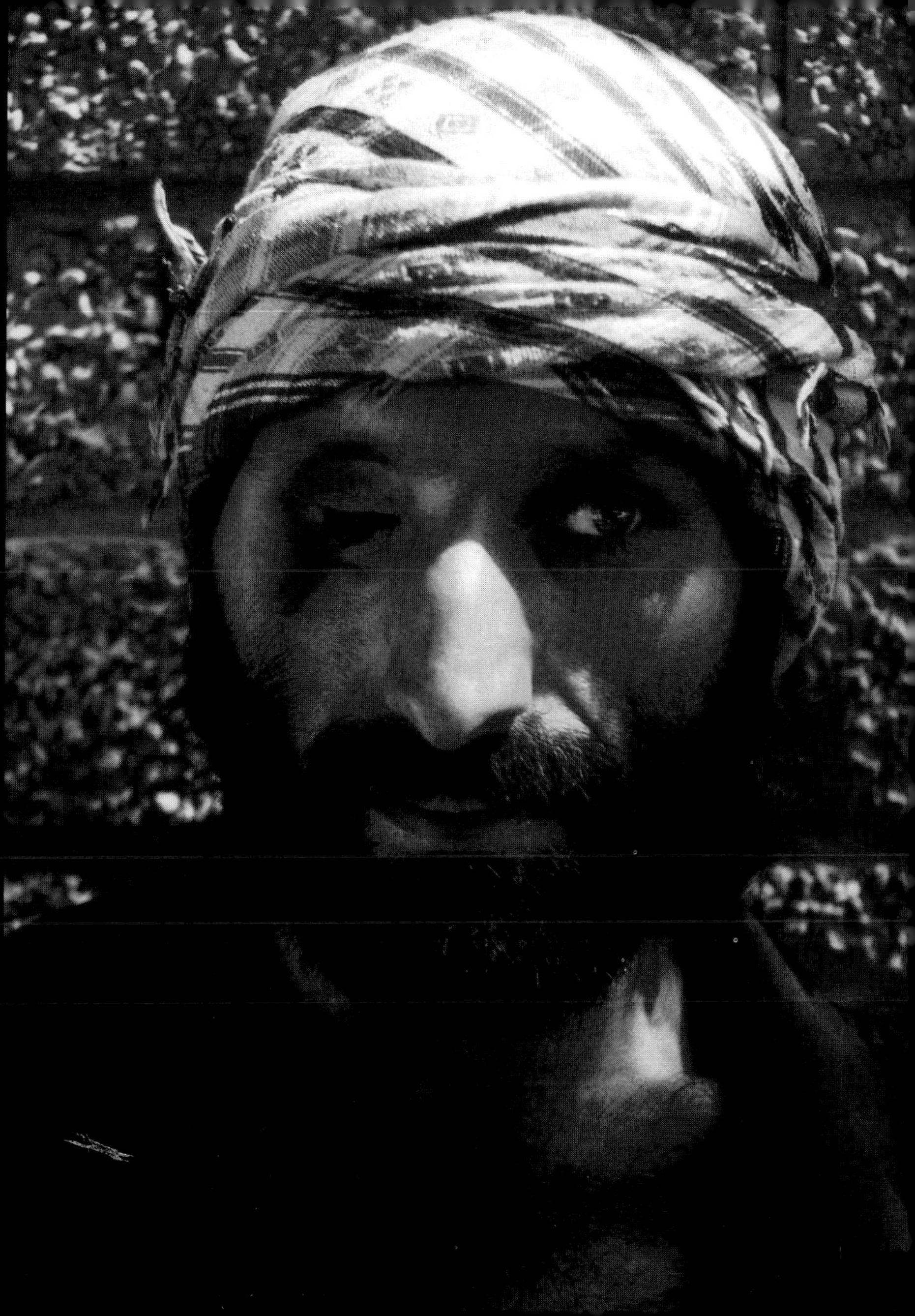

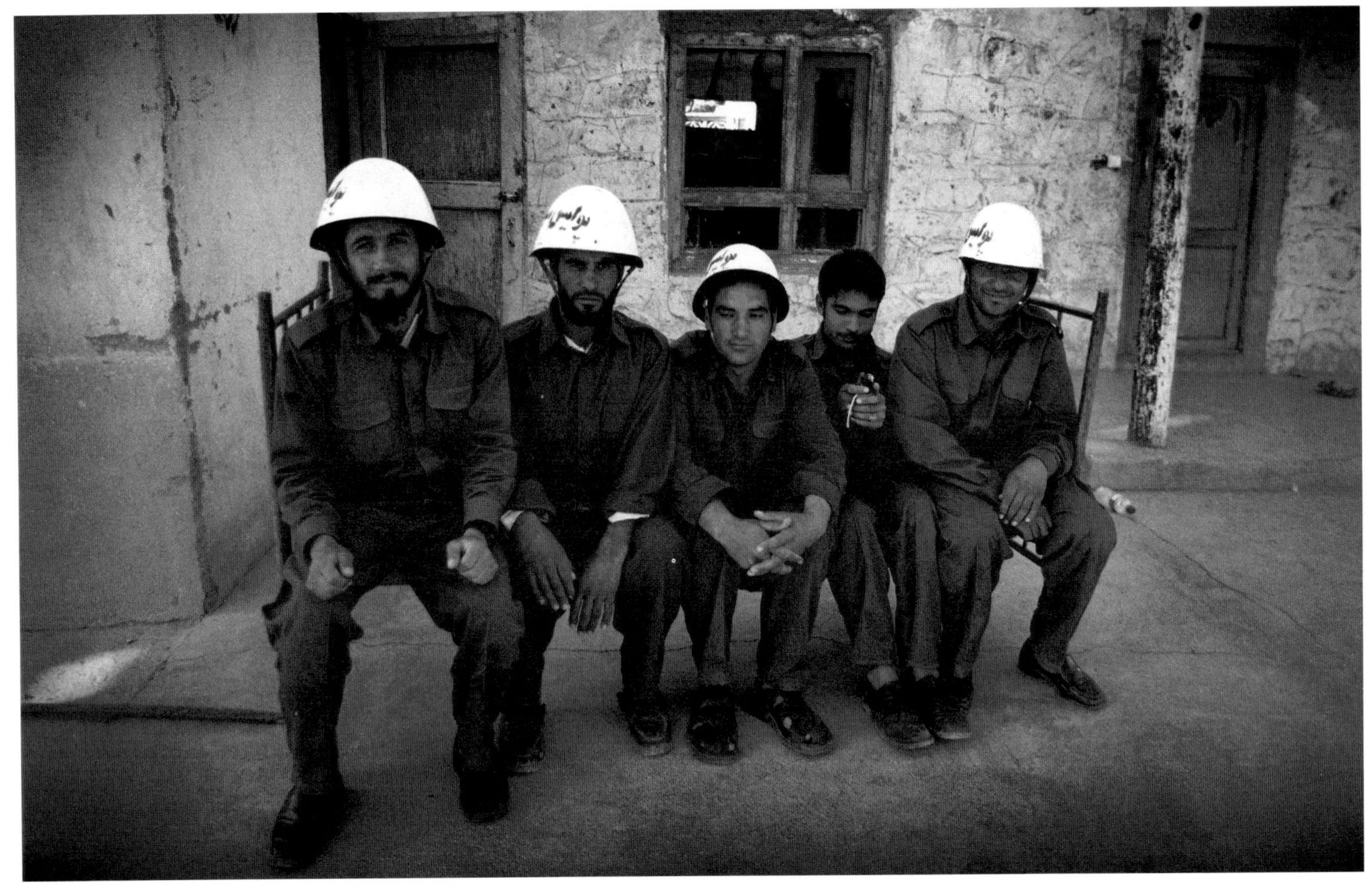

Near the Spanish military base in Herat, an Afghan army patrol sitting on the night watchman's bed.

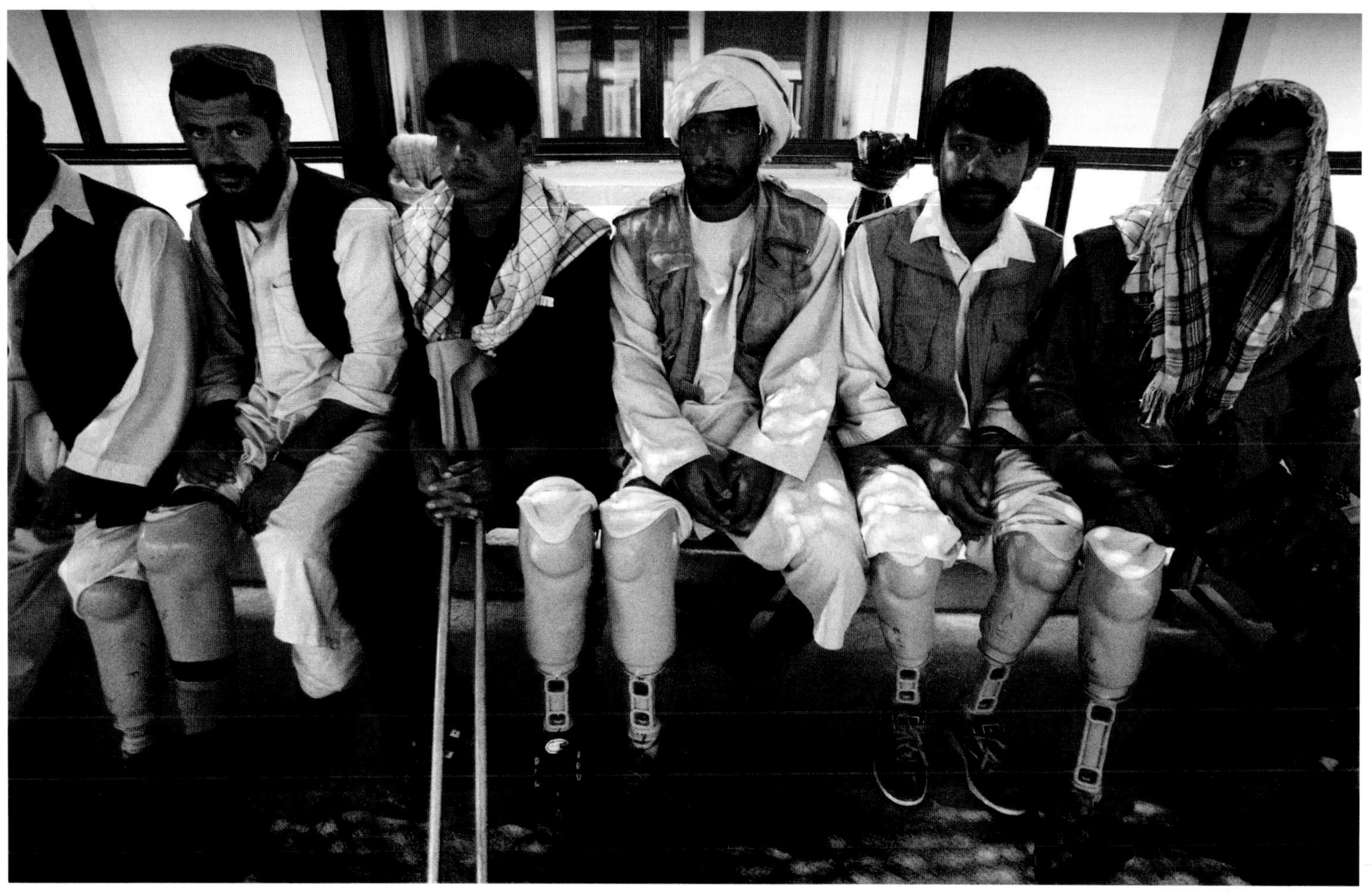

Land-mine victims resting after doing their rehabilitation exercises. They come from all parts of the country, as there are very few centers that can help those who have lost a leg. The unluckiest ones are those who have no money to go to the hospital. Often they die of infections.

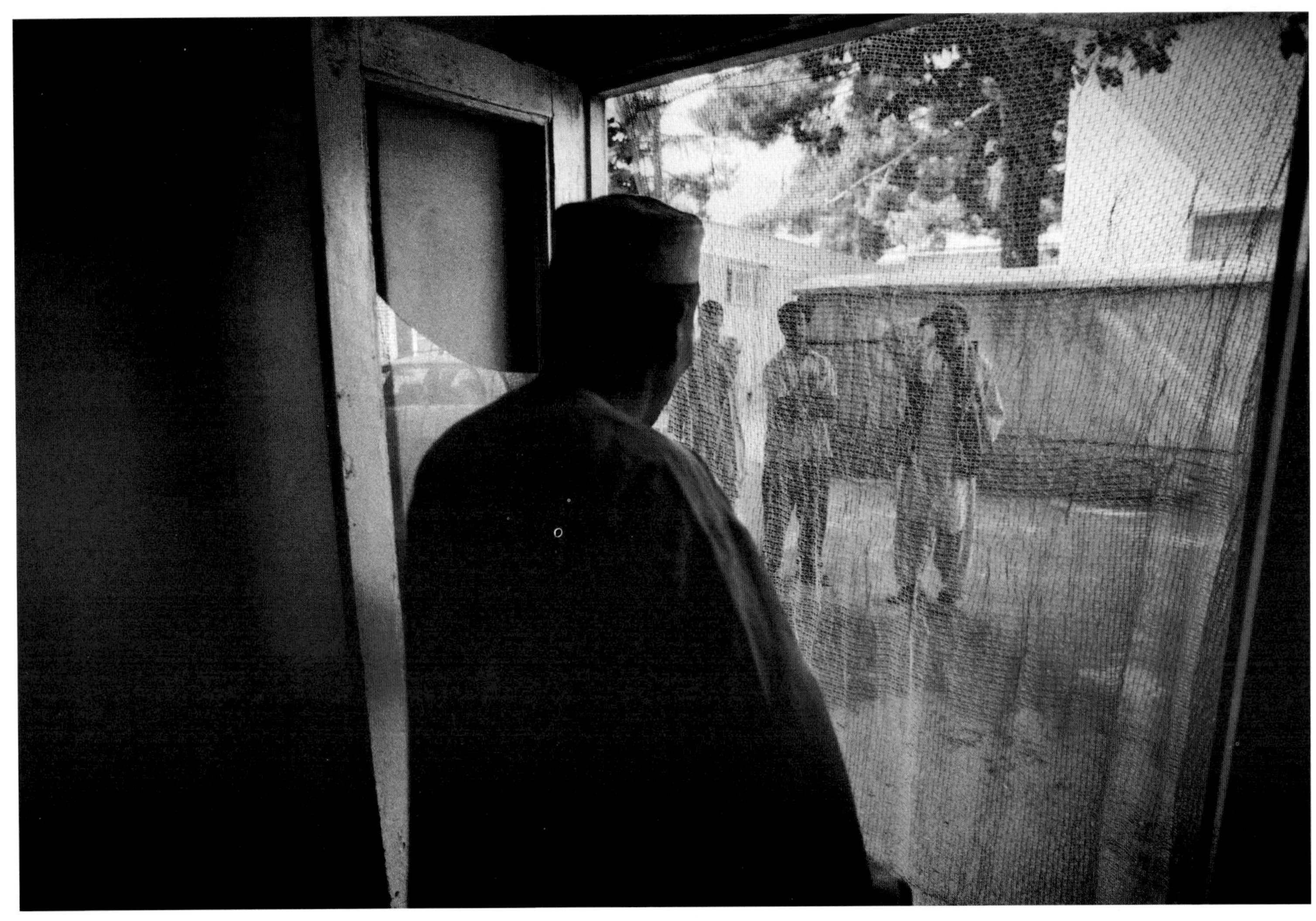

At the hospital, Dr. Ahmed Khan goes out to tell some visitors how their loved one is faring.
On this occasion he has only the worst news to give. "It's something one finally gets accustomed to", he told me.

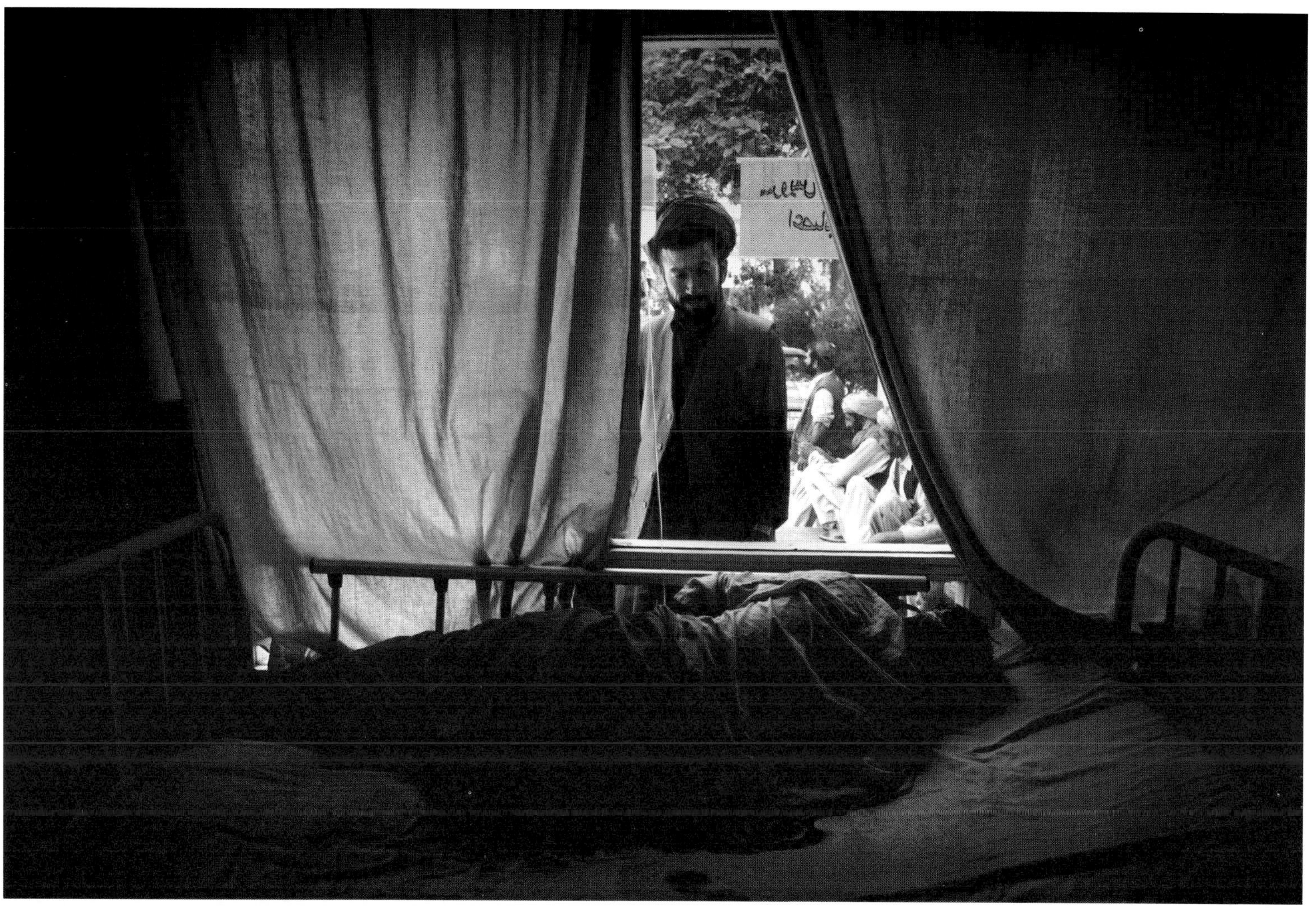

In Ali Abad hospital I took in this scene of a man with an air of resignation, gazing at his relative lying in bed flecked with blood.

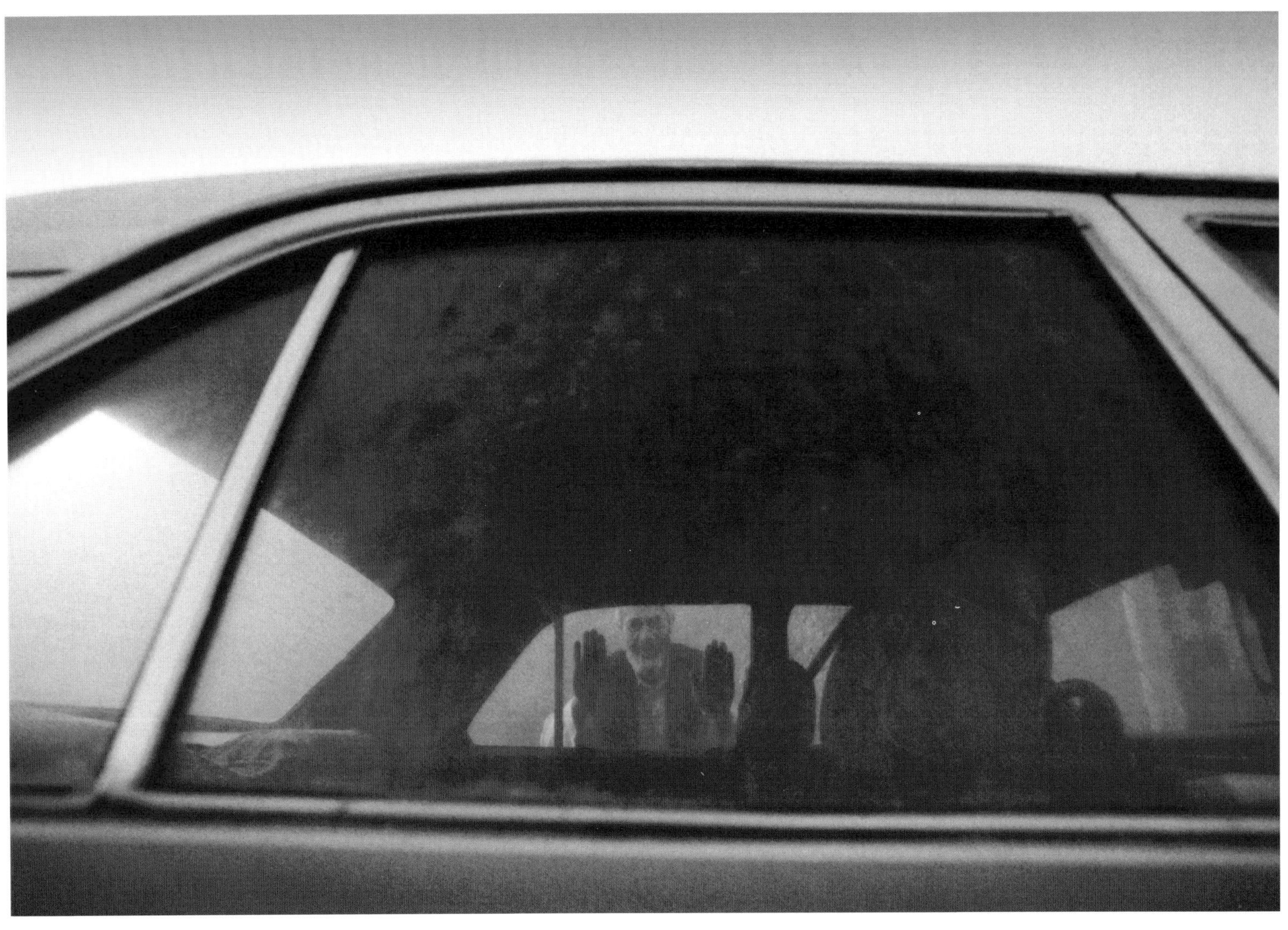

Hamid Ismail welcomed me into his home for the nights I stayed in the Panjshir valley, with a welcome like another member of the family. The Afghan people take it as a moral duty to harbor strangers and be good hosts, and that is exactly what he did.

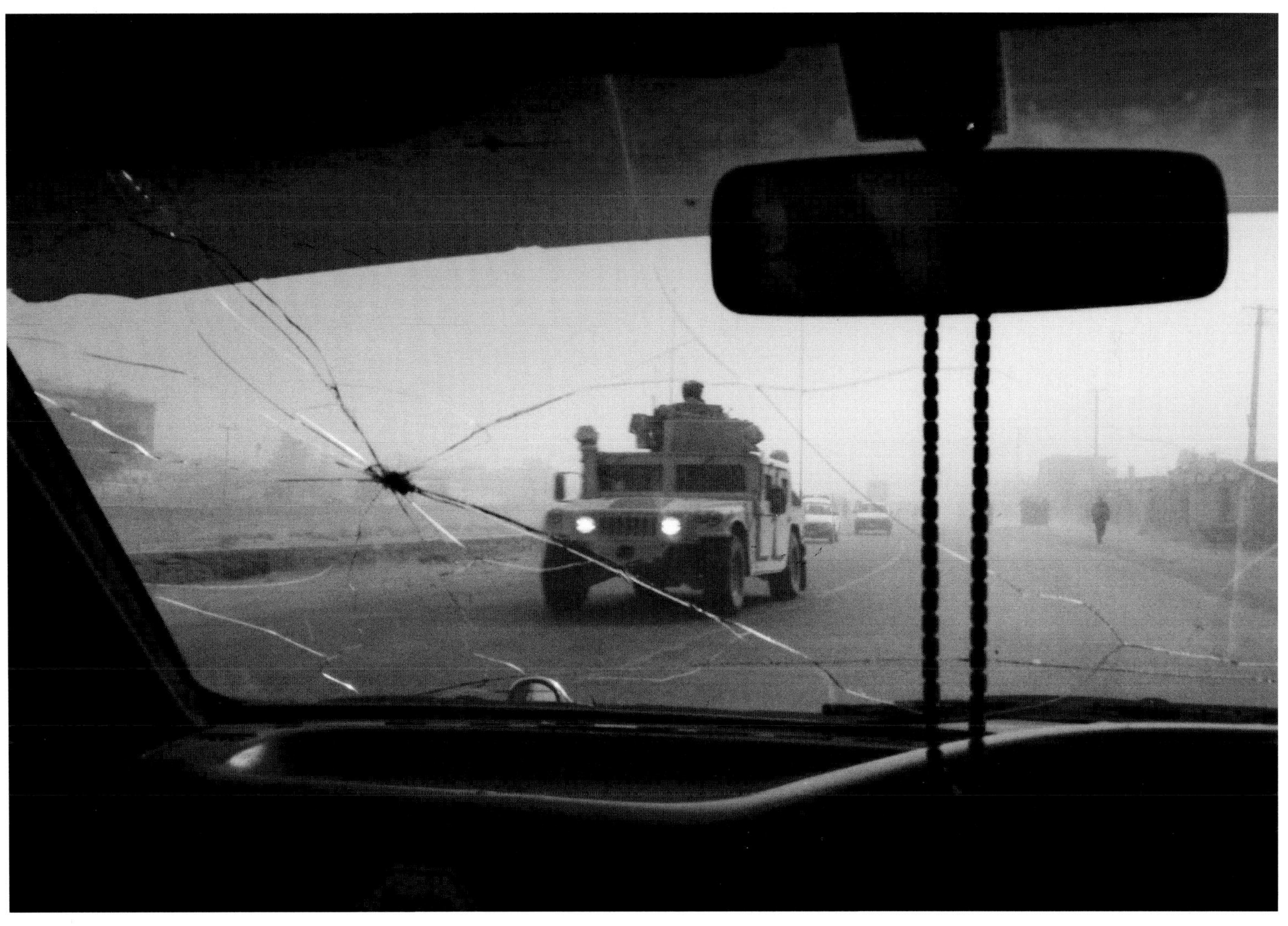

In the streets of Kabul I came across dozens of units of the ISAF, the International Security Assistance Force, who were patrolling the area. Prayer beads hang from the rear-view mirror of the car: a bizarre contrast anywhere, except in Afghanistan.

One day in Flower street, in the Sharenow quarter of Kabul, I saw how an American tank ran over a bicycle in the street, as the soldiers laughed with their derisive and arrogant air. They didn't feel like stopping. The aged owner of the bike was left without any means of transportation.
This attitude is typical of the U.S. troops in Afghanistan.

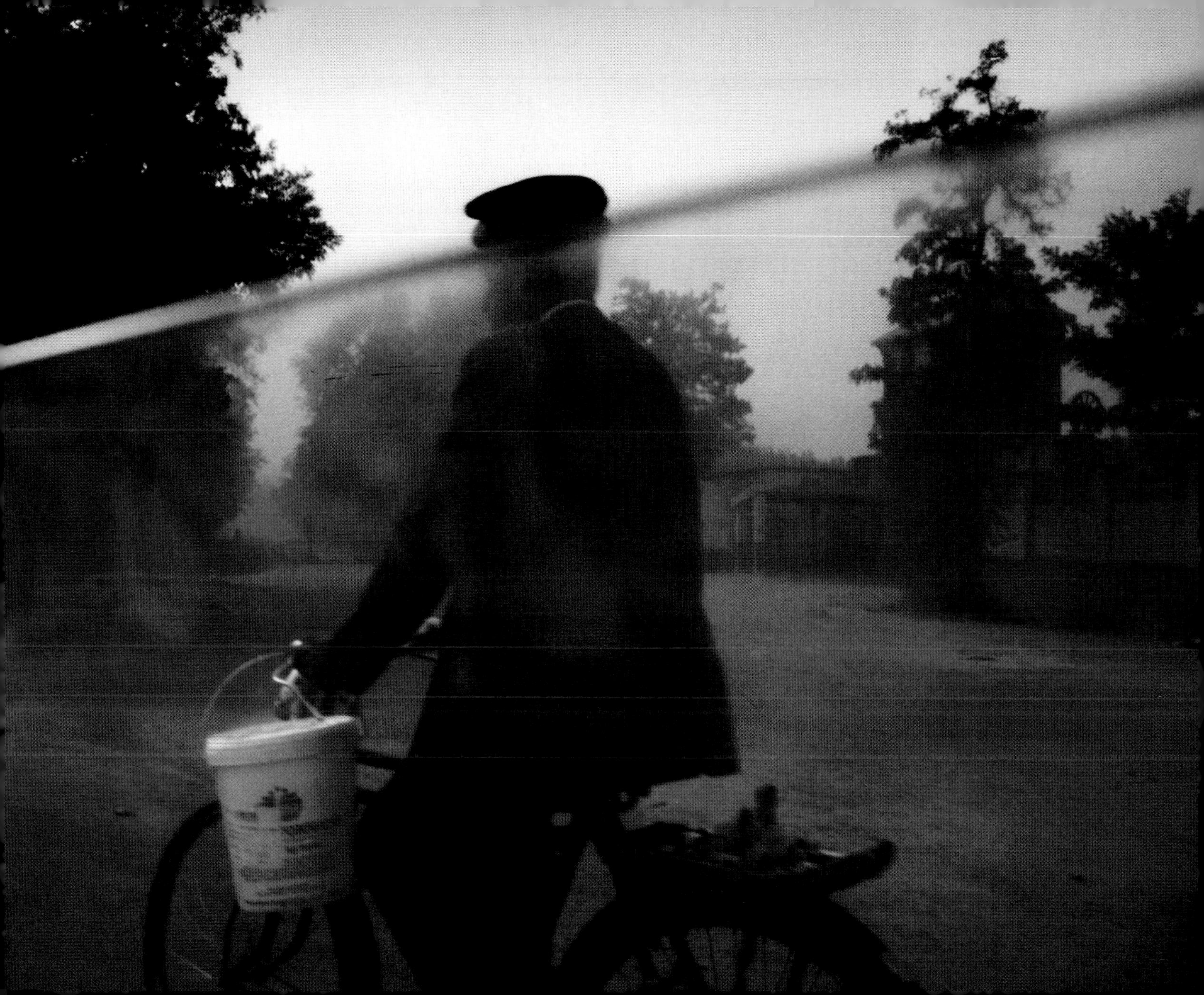

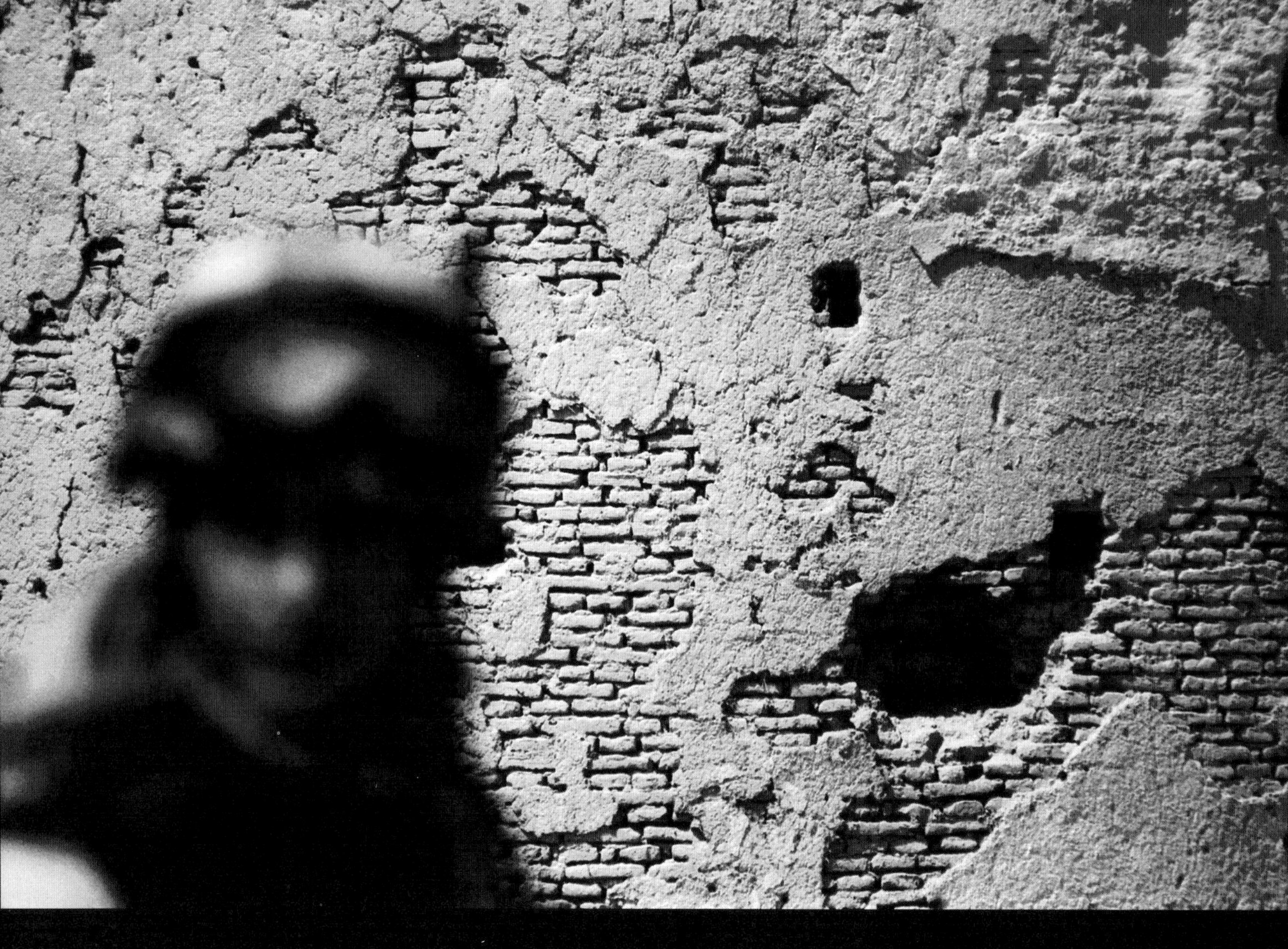

Outside Kabul I caught this glimpse of an Italian soldier of the ISAF against the scars of war in the walls of a ruined building. Afghanistan has been torn by thirty years of war between different camps, which have never made peace because of their desire for power over a devastated land. Now it is the West's turn

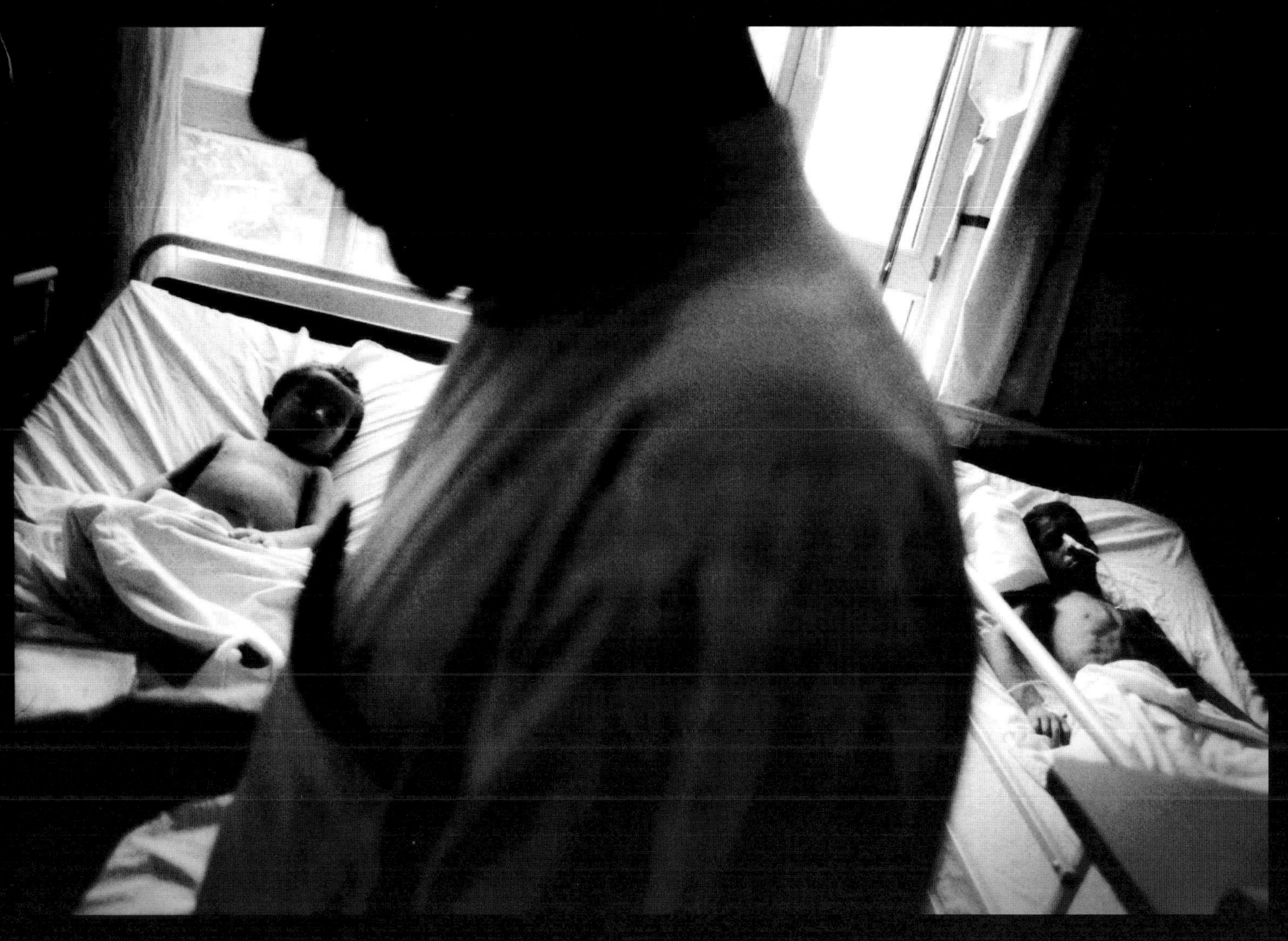

A doctor attending to two children at Indira Gandhi hospital.
With a salary of only $50 per month, the doctors make the most of the meagre resources they have. According to Gino Strada, a famous surgeon with the Emergency NGO, five children are killed by traffic accidents in Kabul every day.

EMPTY VASTNESS

Jon Sistiaga

He was called Fakudrin, he was prisoner number 25, and from the empty vastness of his glassy eyes, he looked at me and wondered what a foreigner like me was doing visiting a Taliban like him. I searched for some wisdom in that small man, who just before speaking to me droned in a monotone from a mud-splashed Koran. I tried to discover if he had the answer to the reason why Afghanistan had survived for centuries through an endless succession of wars; and why since the times of British dominion has this place been known as the killing fields of Asia. Were they so violent? Were they so incapable of creating a society not based on tribal laws and a blood-soaked code of honour?

Fakudrin, without getting up from his prayer mat, hardly whispering, answered that he was a good man, that tired of useless wars amongst brothers, he had decided to join the Taliban to take part in the "last" war. One that would bring stability to his land. He didn't know what was beyond the immense mountains which surrounded the small village where he had lived, fought and lost his last battle. He had never left his valley. He had no other option nor opinion.

That was in the winter of 2001. Alen's photographs, taken four years later, show me the same empty vastness that I saw in the eyes and the soul of that Afghan prisoner. That same inhospitable and desolate landscape which are the greatness and the misery of an unlucky country. Not many nice things are said about Afghanistan. They are tough people, proud and with severe hearts, like all those bare mountains and stone deserts which resemble the moon.

Before my first trip to Afghanistan I re-read Kipling. I memorized those verses which made me shudder before I entered the country: "When you're wounded and left on Afghanistan's plains, And the women come out to cut up what remains, Jest roll to your rifle and blow out your brains, An' go to your Gawd like a soldier."
Alen has put together a collection of images which also make me shudder, that capture the soul of a miserable country. Of a place where the open spaces are so immense and imposing, and the faces of their men are so blunt, that it is difficult not to want more, to come back—in spite of Kipling.

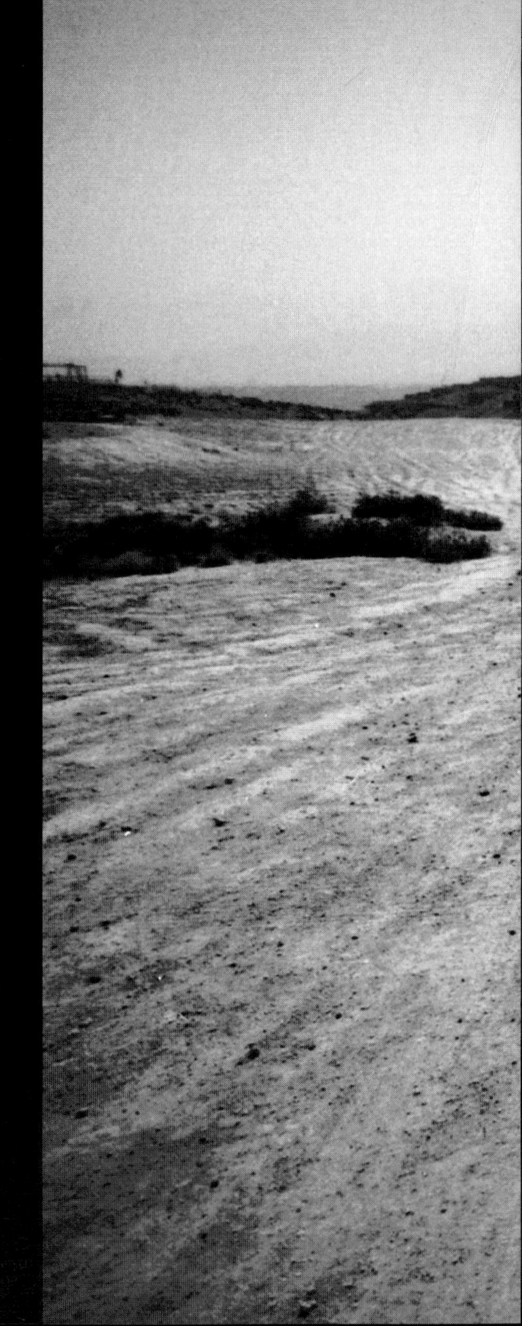

can
usty
ain.

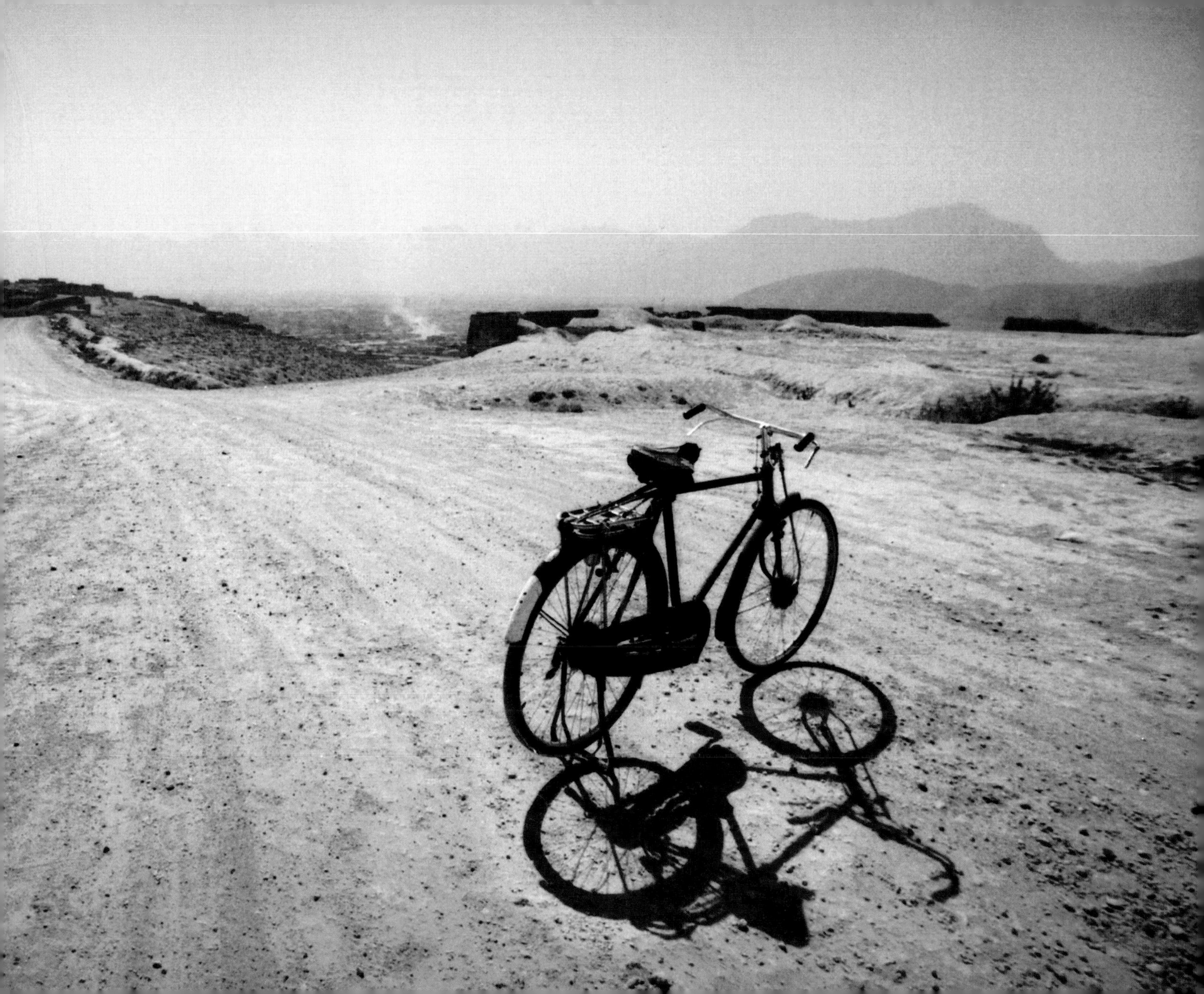

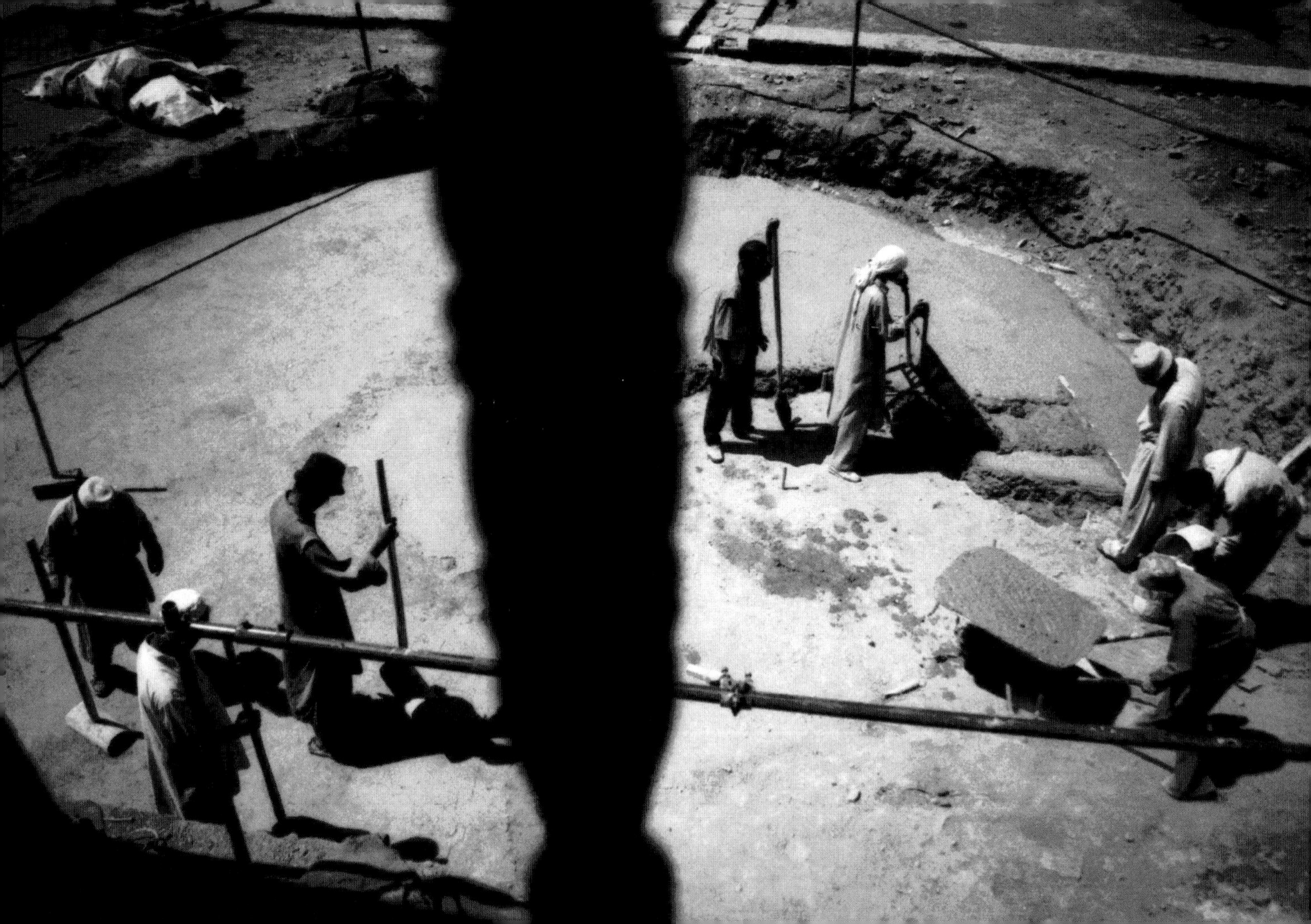

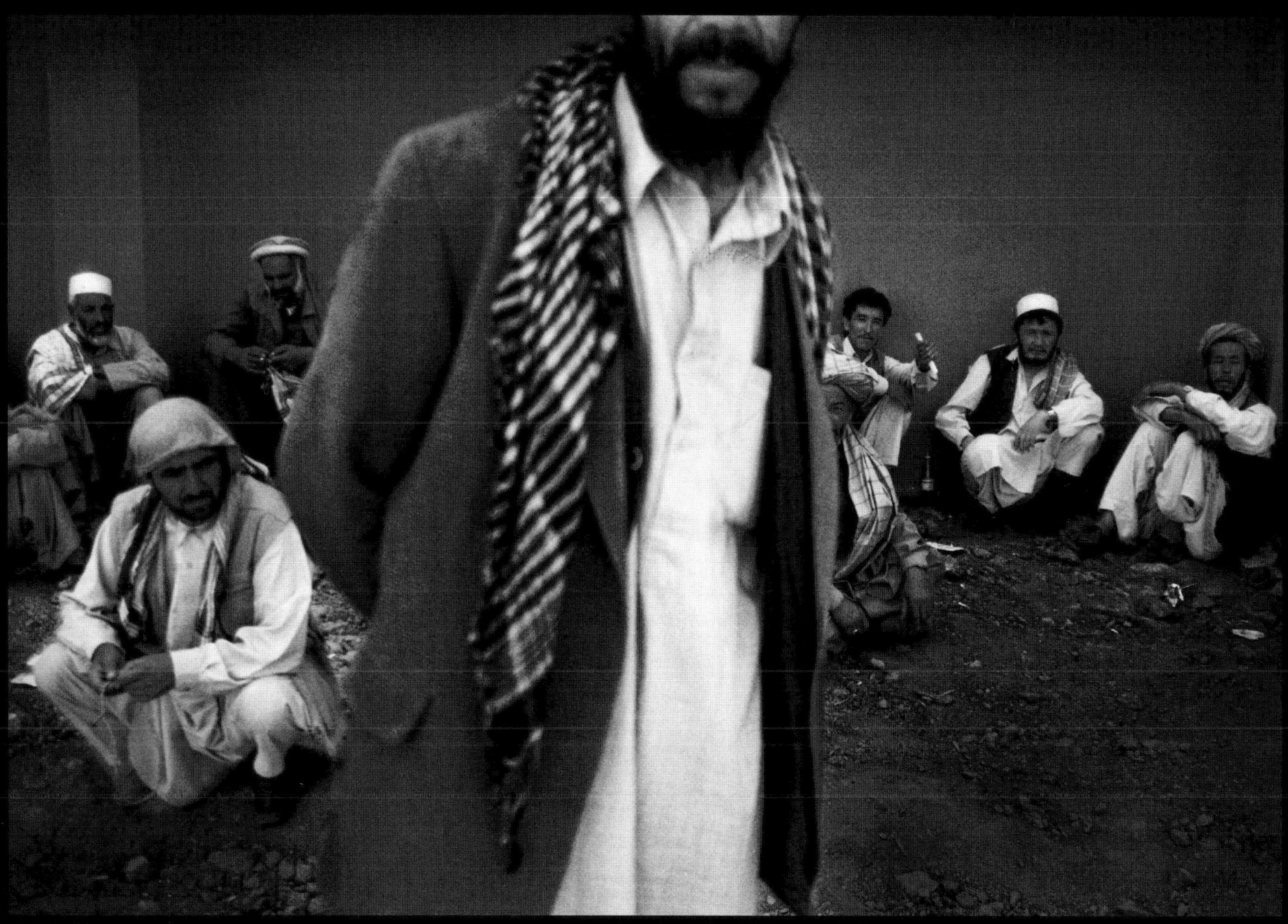

Countless lines of men crowd the entrance to the Kabul football stadium in memory of the death of Ahmed Shah Massoud, assassinated on 9/9/2001, two days before the destruction of the Twin Towers. Women are not allowed entry, of course.

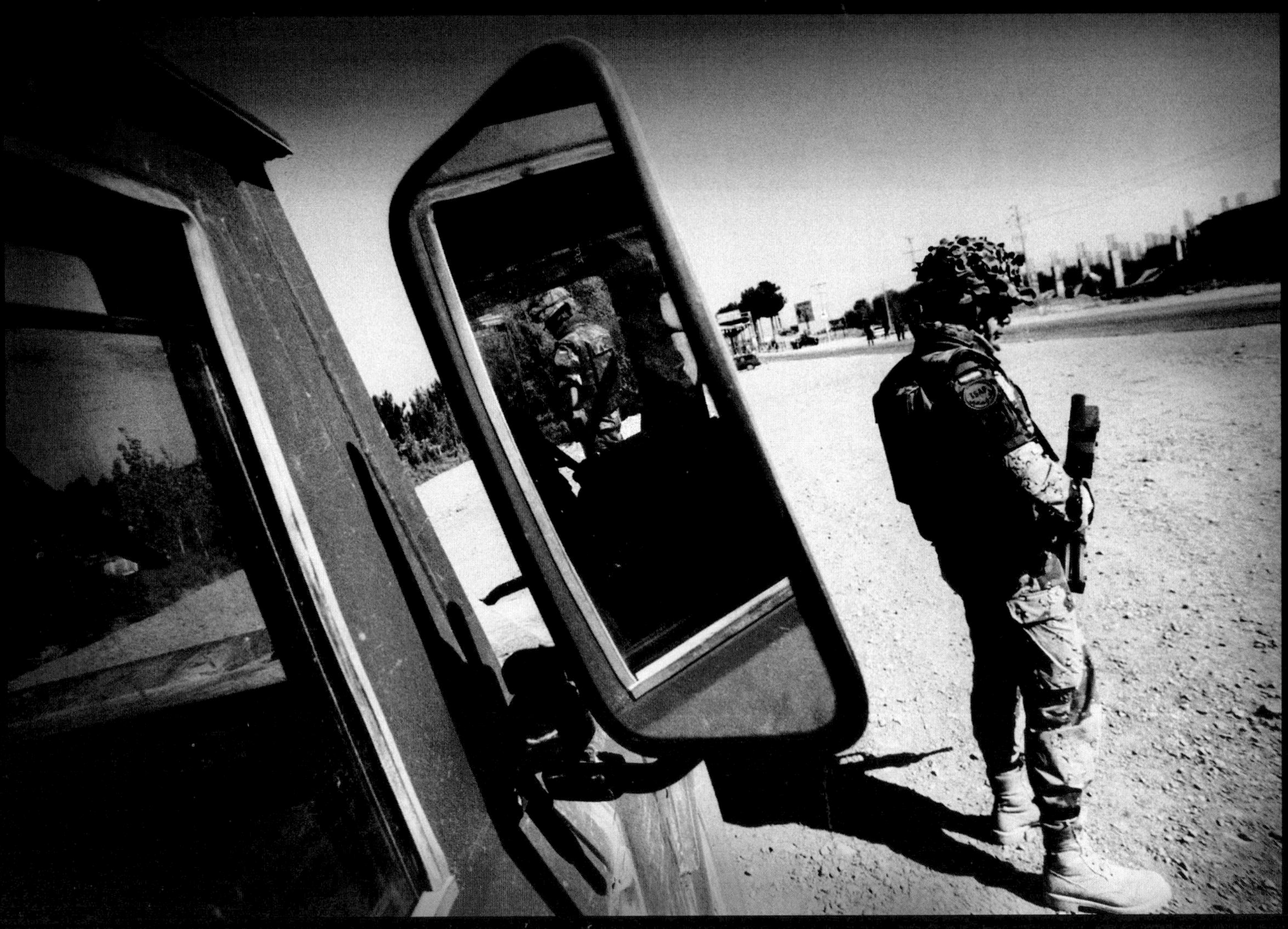

ISAF forces... and their countless "peace missions."
Because the Afghans wish for peace above all else, they want the foreign armies to leave their country at once.

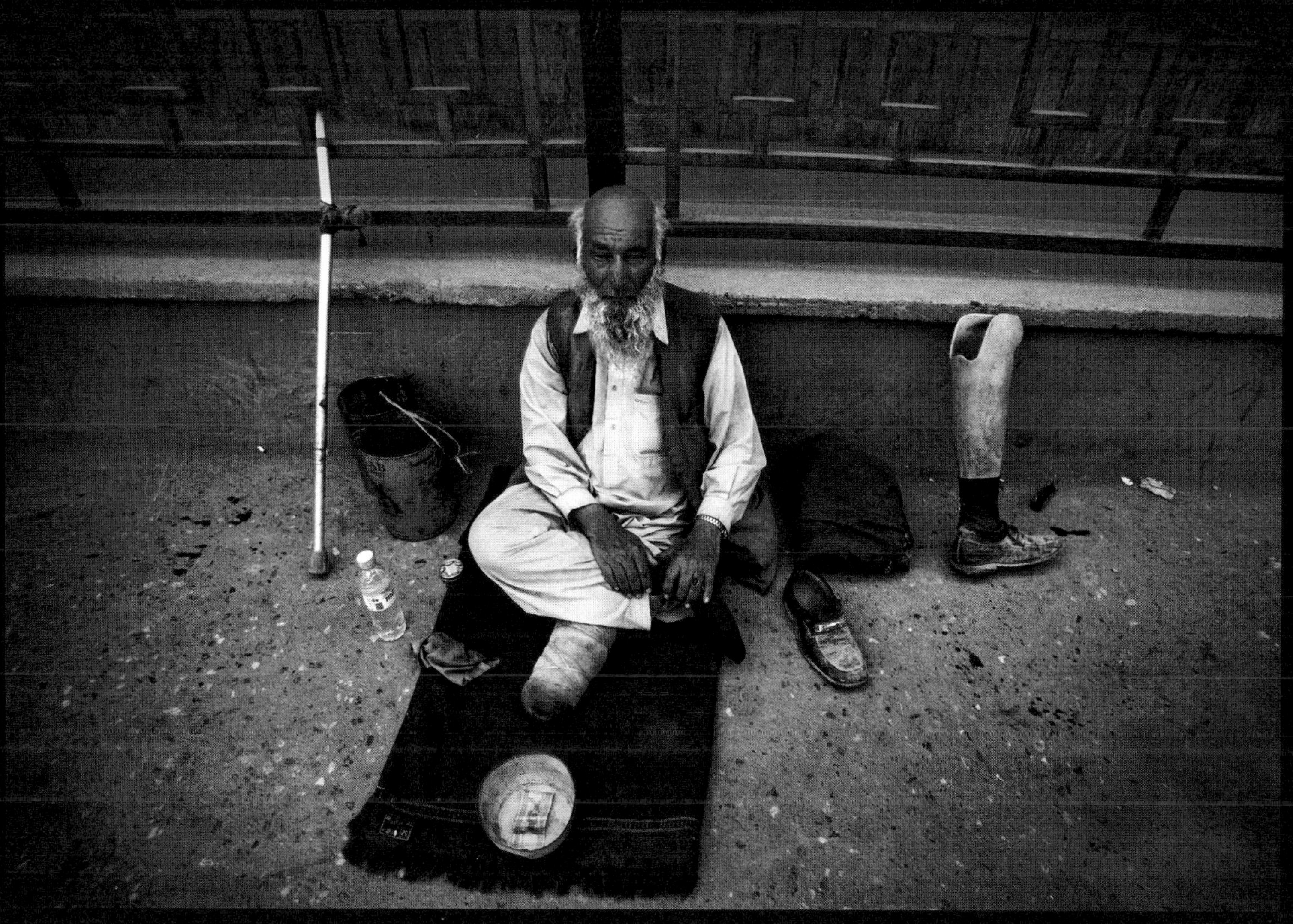

Hundreds of the maimed like Ibrahim live in the streets of every city, without the slightest assistance except from common citizens who do all they can for the victims of atrocity. The Afghans are very loyal to their own and try to help those in need, as far as their means allow.

ABANDONED

Gillian Anderson

No matter how many words can be strung together about the unconscionable behavior of false saviors, what I see in the shadow and light, in these crisp, haunting, sad sad documents, is ABANDONMENT, falling from the bone. Shame on all of us who colluded and continue to in our uselessness as brothers and sisters of the human race.

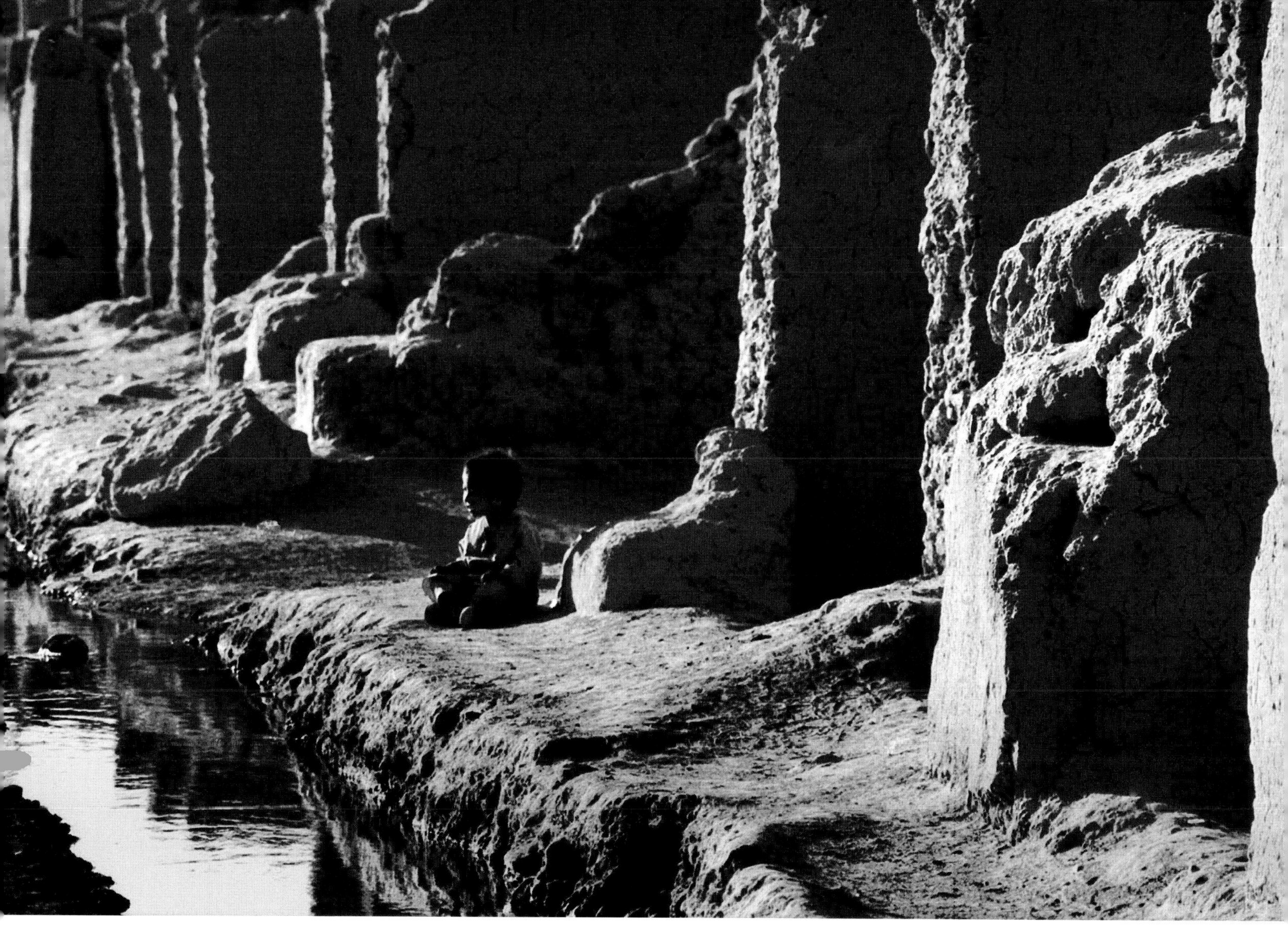

A child playing near ruined houses that serve as dwellings for a family in Bamiyan.
In many places there is no sewer system, which gives rise to many infections and illnesses.

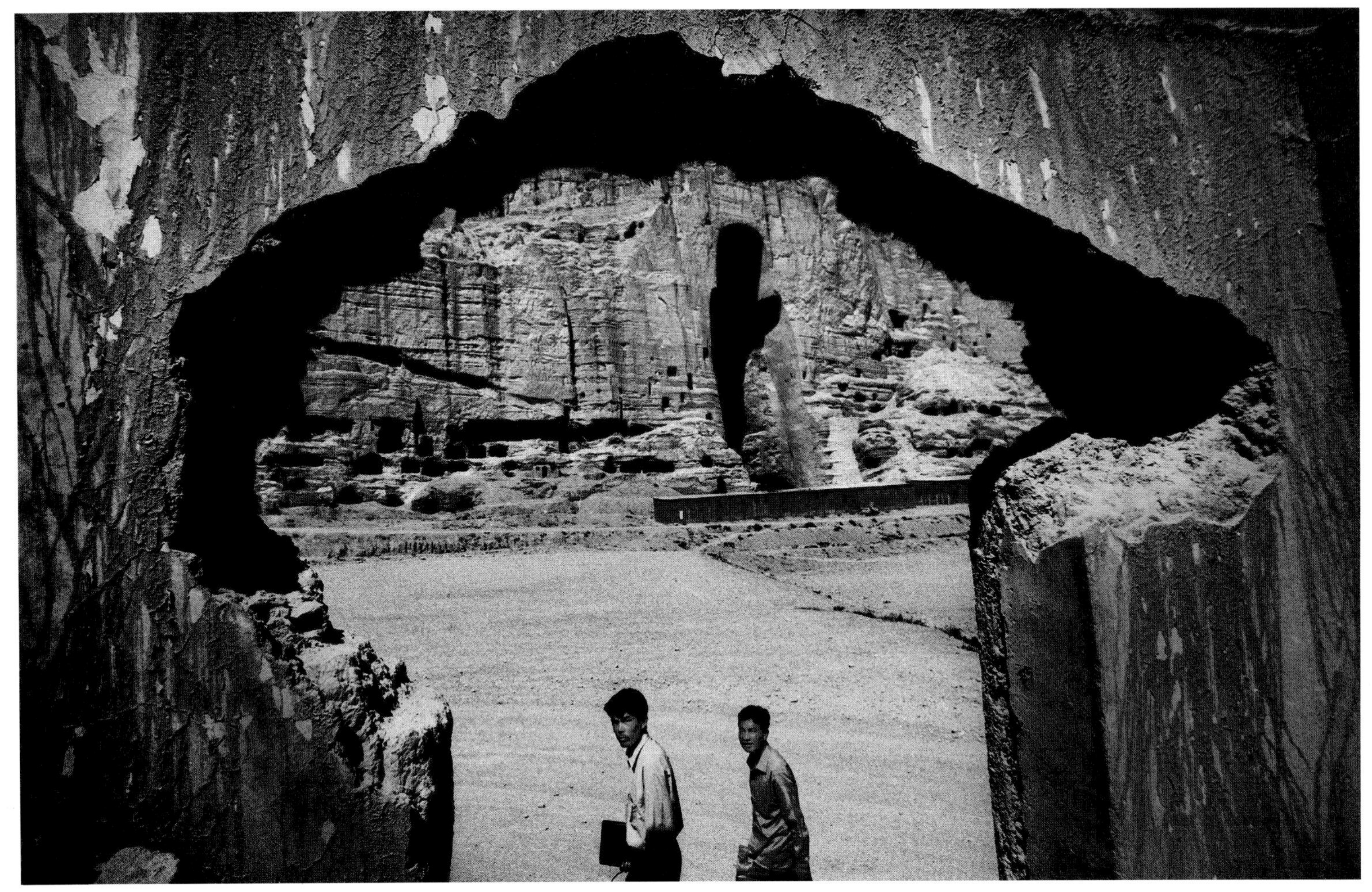

Nothing but ghostly hollows are left of what once were magnificent symbols along the Silk Road: the Buddhas of Bamiyan.

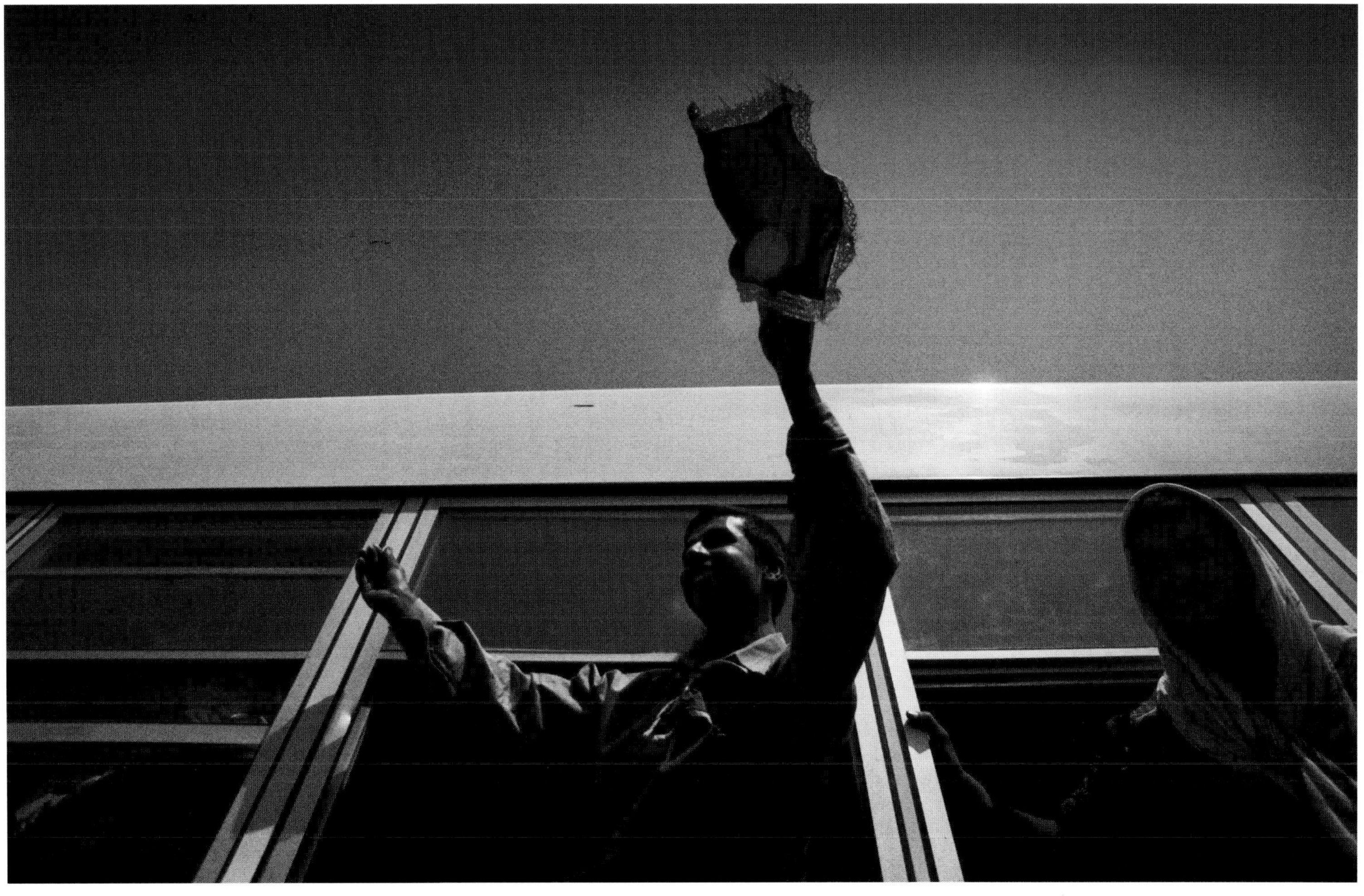

On September 9th, dozens of buses from all over converge on Kabul to commemorate the anniversary of Ahmed Shah Massoud's death. The ceremonies take place in the football stadium, which was used by the Taliban for public executions in former years, when football and most other sports were forbidden.

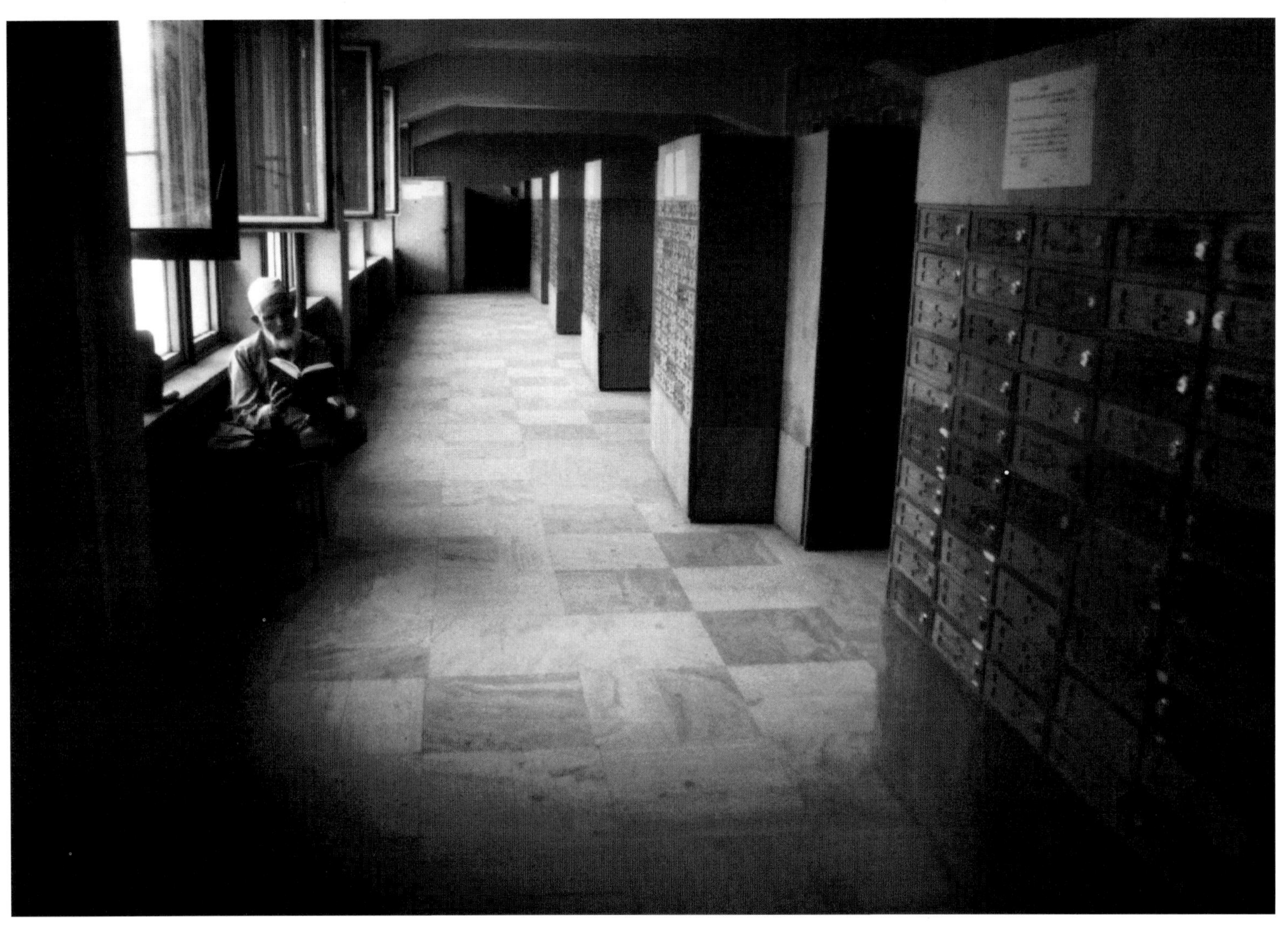

An image that contrasts with the situation that reigns in the country.
Seeing this man in the post office, I was struck by the tranquil atmosphere that bathed the place as he read a book.

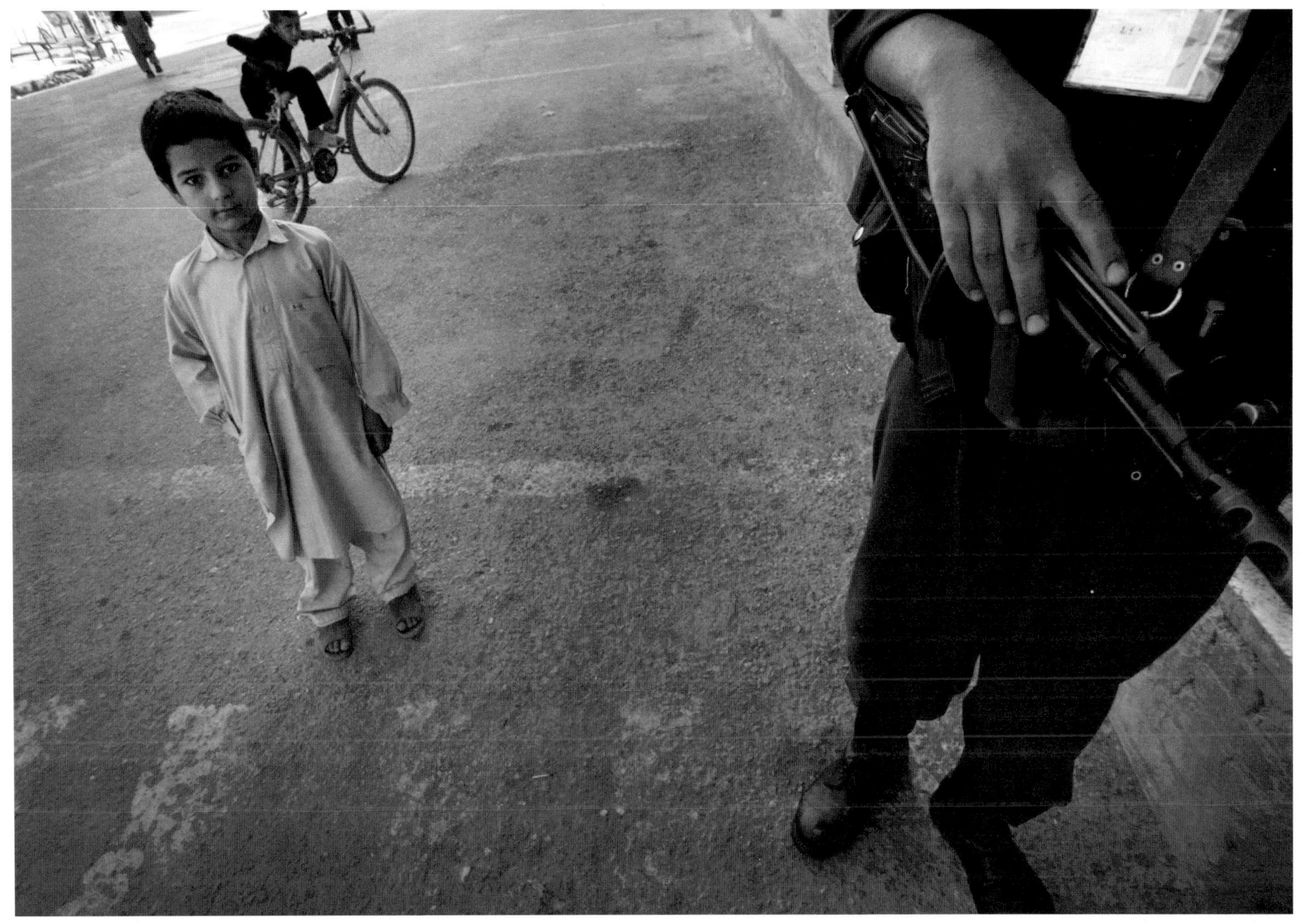

A common sight in Afghanistan, where children grow up seeing men bearing arms every day.

YOU'RE NOT A *MAN!*

Ezzat Goushegir

Ahmad M, the interpreter looked at Jim Gordon and said, "No pictures please".

Jim Gordon paused. He put the camera away, then gently said: "You must be in danger."

Ahmad M, the interpreter:
Yes…you can call me Ahmad M in your report. I was Jamshid's interpreter for the whole four days…Mr Jamshid was from Yakubi village…Yakubi village? Yes, it's… about 45 minutes away from the American military bases.
Yes, it was December 5, a few hours after the rocket attack on the military base, that the security guards captured him…the attack happened in the morning and they captured him after sunset…
just a few hours...
Jamshid's only possession was a used Toyota. His family bought it for him so he could work as a taxi driver. It was dusk when the guards at the base stopped his taxi at the checkpoint.
He was driving back towards Yakubi with three passengers.

"I didn't do it!" He repeated several times. Yes…and I translated "I didn't do it!" several times.
He spoke Pashto…with a certain dialect.

My language? I speak Dari and also Pashto.
No, I wasn't there when they arrested them. They found a broken walkie-talkie

in Karim's bag in the trunk. Karim was one of his passengers, who said that he had bought it cheap at the flea market. He bought it as a gift for his son.
Karim's job? …actually…
a baker in Yakubi.
He said he went to Kabul to buy pastries and clothes for his children for Eid ul-Fitr…the Muslim Holiday.
They confiscated the broken walkie-talkie and an electric stabilizer.

Jamshid's wife?
I know she is his second cousin and they married four years ago. No, I did not speak to her. She is around 19 and they have a 3 year-old daughter. Yes, I visited his mother, Bibi K.

Bibi K. at the door of her stone farmhouse:
Jamshid is my youngest son. We all gathered money and bought him a taxi... We? I mean his grandfather, his brothers, and myself…I sold my golden bracelet… over a month ago…
I asked him to give his three sisters a ride from their nearby villages, bring them to our house for the celebration of our Eid. Instead he went to make some money for gas and pastries. He said he will bring his sisters home before sunset. But he never came back.

Did you look at the sky that night? The moon never came out… never! And the next day we didn't have an Eid! Why? Tell him in the last night of Ramadan, The new moon should appear in the sky…

Stabilizer? What is it? I don't know what it is! Electric wire?
Sir! We do not have electricity!

That night I had a dream. In my dream giant locusts attacked our wheat farm. They had green eyes. Our land became barren in a blink of eye, and my son Jamshid cried out loudly: God…God… God… and I woke up!

Sergeant Selena M, the interrogator:
He constantly screamed: "God…God… God…" for twenty-four hours! For Specialist Joshua C and…-- for everyone I should say -- it was a kind of funny.
His voice…yes…his voice was like

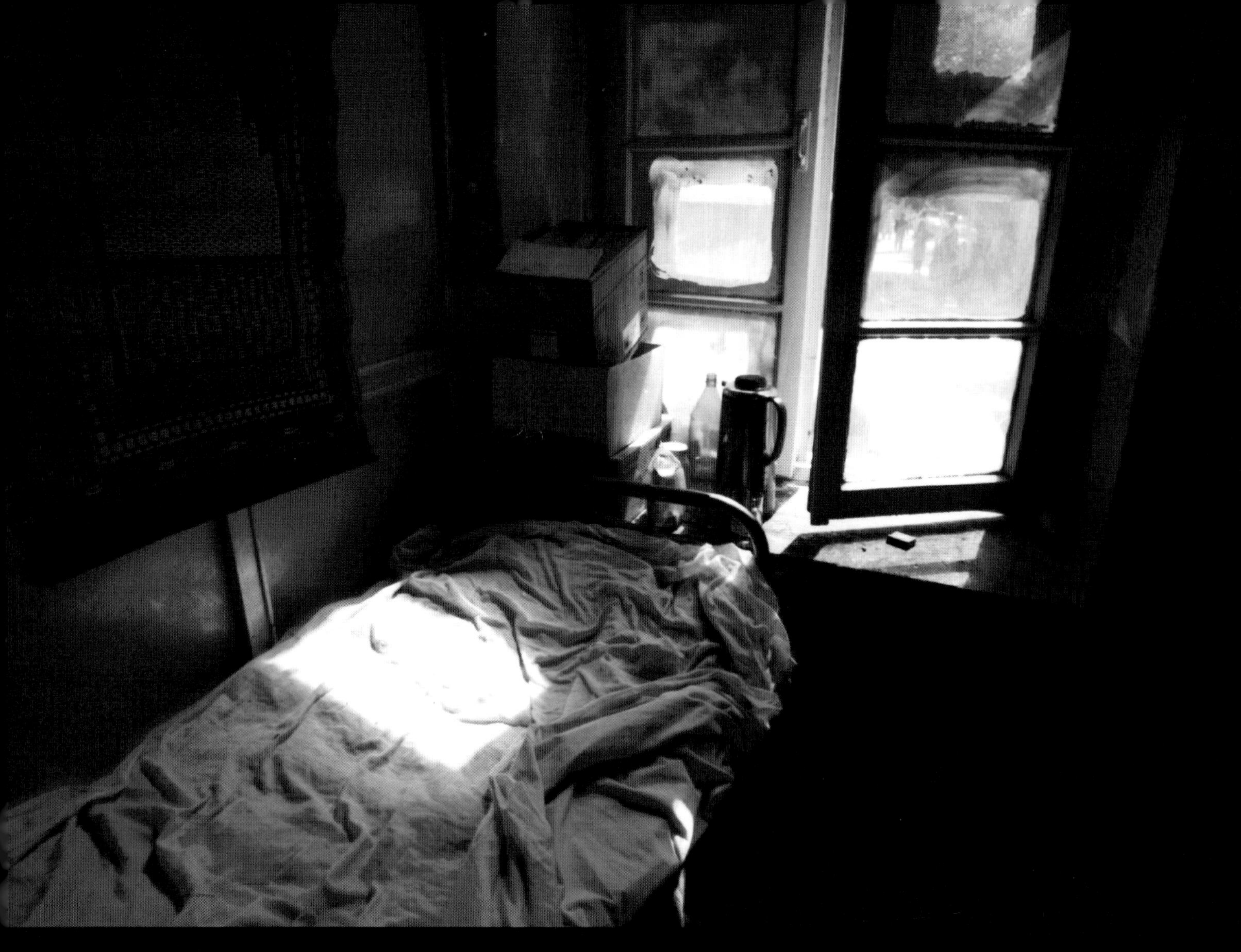

In absentia.

a….like a female clown who imitates the voice of a crow…even now when I remember his voice, it makes me burst into…sorry….Yes, at the military detention center at Bagram, about 40 miles north of Kabul…
What? Black cloth hood? Yes, his head was covered in a black hood, and he was shackled from the ceiling… for four days, I guess!
Water?
Yes, Specialist Joshua C was sent to his cell to give him some water, but instead Jamshid spat in his face and started kicking…yes, he was chained…Specialist Joshua C got so angry and responded back repeatedly with strikes to his legs… I would think it was over 80 to 90 strikes….Probably 100…

It became a kind of a running joke… everyone kept going to his cell to kick his legs just to hear him scream out God… God….
They also wanted to give him over 3,000 kicks for the number of those who lost their lives on 9/11….
Sorry?
Yes, I saw the bruise…his orange prison suit fell down and I saw the bruise….
My military boots? Yes, I wore them, of course! All the time. You mean if I… kicked him? No… I mean… you know we were told these enemies are not prisoners of war, they're terrorists!
…….
The size of the bruise?

Ahmad M, the interpreter:
The size? … bigger than a fist. One on his right leg and one on his left.
He screamed over and over: "Release me and take me down, I can't breathe."
His Pashto dialect was very strong…it was hard for me to understand what he was saying. The guards got annoyed.

In the interrogation room, he was unable to walk, to stand or sit…or hold his cuffed hands…he could not bend his legs when sitting on the plastic chair. He fainted on the floor.

His mouth was dry, his lips cracked. Specialist Joshua C asked him, "Why did you launch rockets to hit the American base?"

quarter, I met these children playing in blithe ignorance of everything that has
st brutally punished part of Kabul has neither electricity nor sewers (the people
having to do their necessities in the nearest ruined house.)
dential areas under the control of international organizations, or the new banks
and shopping mall in the center which have been built recently.

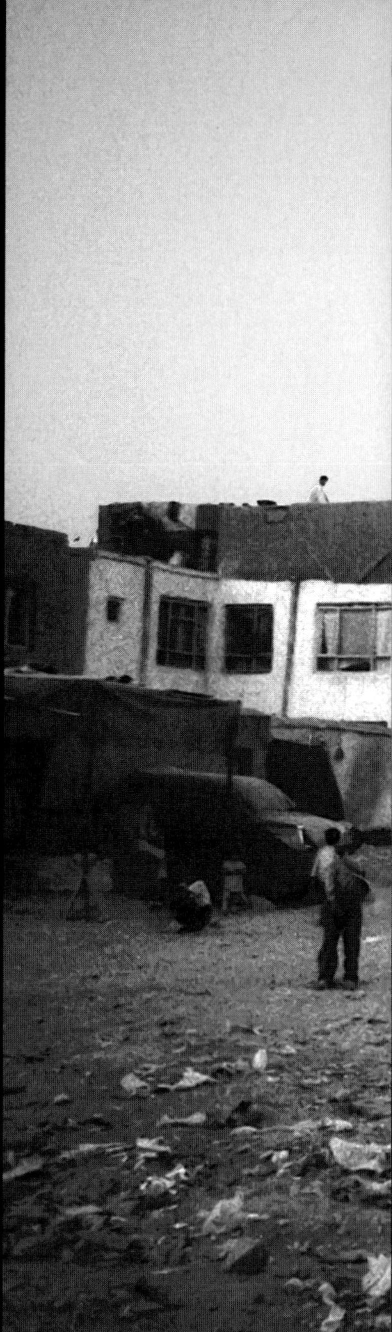

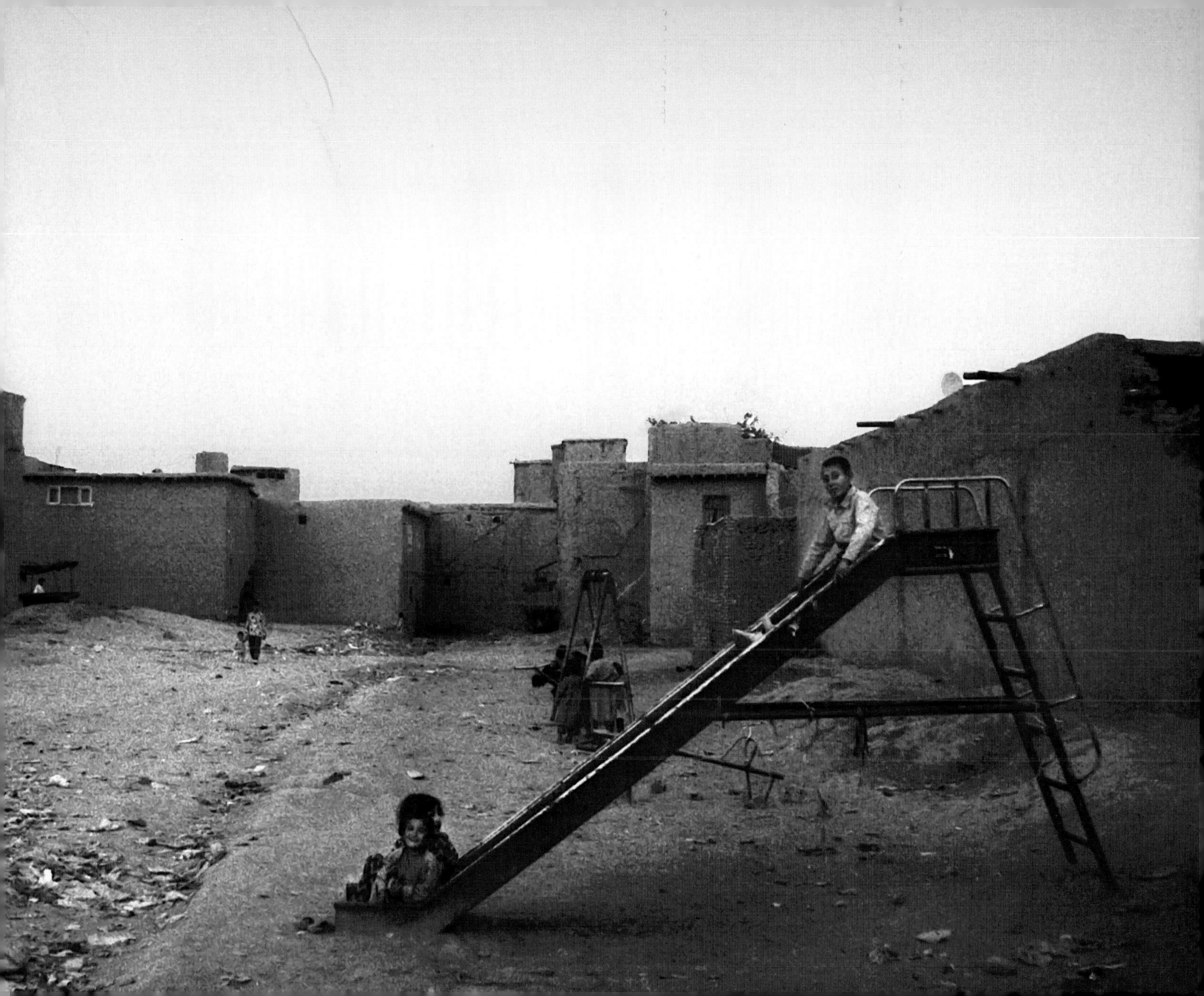

He said: “I’m thirsty.”
Specialist Joshua C picked a large plastic bottle of water and punched a hole in it. Jamshid’s eyes were fixed on the bottle. Then he tried to take it, but couldn’t hold it. The bottle fell on his orange prison suit. The hole opened bigger and water poured all over him. He moved his fingers slowly to reach the bottle, but his hands were numb, I guess.
Specialist Joshua C grabbed the bottle back and began splashing water forcefully on his face, and shouted, “Drink it bastard, come on, drink it!”

Jamshid’s mouth was dry like a fish out of water! A drop of water dripped from his long black lashes on his lips. It moistened his tongue.

Specialist Joshua C, the interrogator:
Water?
We must make sure the prisoners stay hydrated!
No, we didn’t use dogs. We were well trained to perform our duties.

Sergeant Selena M, the interrogator:
No, no dogs. Specialist Joshua C had always said: “My nose can detect terrorists from miles away”.
When Jamshid did not answer questions, Specialist Joshua said to him: “If you do not cooperate, you’ll be shipped to a prison in the United States, where you’ll be treated like a woman, by the other men who are very angry with anyone involved in the 9/11 attacks.”

What did I see in his eyes? I can’t remember! But I remember the color of his eyes!
Hazelnut. Yes, hazelnut!

Ahmad M, the interpreter:
“You’re not a man, you’re a woman!” Sergeant Selena shouted at Jamshid three times.
Jamshid opened his eyes and I saw an unexplainable sharp ray flash in his eyes… and then it fizzled out. It died. She grabbed him by his beard, pulled him up and shoved him on the floor, stepped on his feet and kicked him in the groin… then his private parts….He had a small body, about 122 pounds.
Specialist Joshua C shouted: “F***ing bastard, where are the rest of you, son of

the bitch?!"
I didn't translate all the bad words!...I couldn't....My voice automatically got loud and violent at the same level as his....
Jamshid screamed.
His right leg was smashed, like a car had run over it. There was no break. With each strike, the two interrogators questioned him. I think after a while he couldn't hear the questions anymore. It went on for over 10 minutes. He was just screaming loudly, "Oh...God...God... God," and then suddenly he got silent.

Sergeant Selena and Specialist Joshua stopped too.

He was then instructed to be kept chained to the ceiling. In his cell I could barely hear the delirious words coming out of his lips...repeatedly: "My wife ...is dead!"
Then he was silent for a moment.
The last words I heard before I left his cell were: "God! Why are you silent?"

Sergeant Selena M, the interrogator:
Yes, I used to go to our little church with my aunt when I was a little girl. I used to look at Jesus Christ nailed to the cross, wondering what he would have thought in his last moments before he ascended to heaven.
He must have said: "My God...why have you forgotten me?
Why have you deserted me?"

Bibi K.:
Where is my son? Why no one is telling me where he is? My son? My son is a shy and simple man. He might think we have forgotten him!
He rarely went far from our farmhouse before he got his taxi.
Yes, he shares a room with his wife and has a little daughter.
The name of her daughter? Bibi Rashidah.
No, he never attended school. He has only a small portable radio that he would carry to the wheat fields where he used to work before becoming a taxi driver!

What is written on this piece of paper?

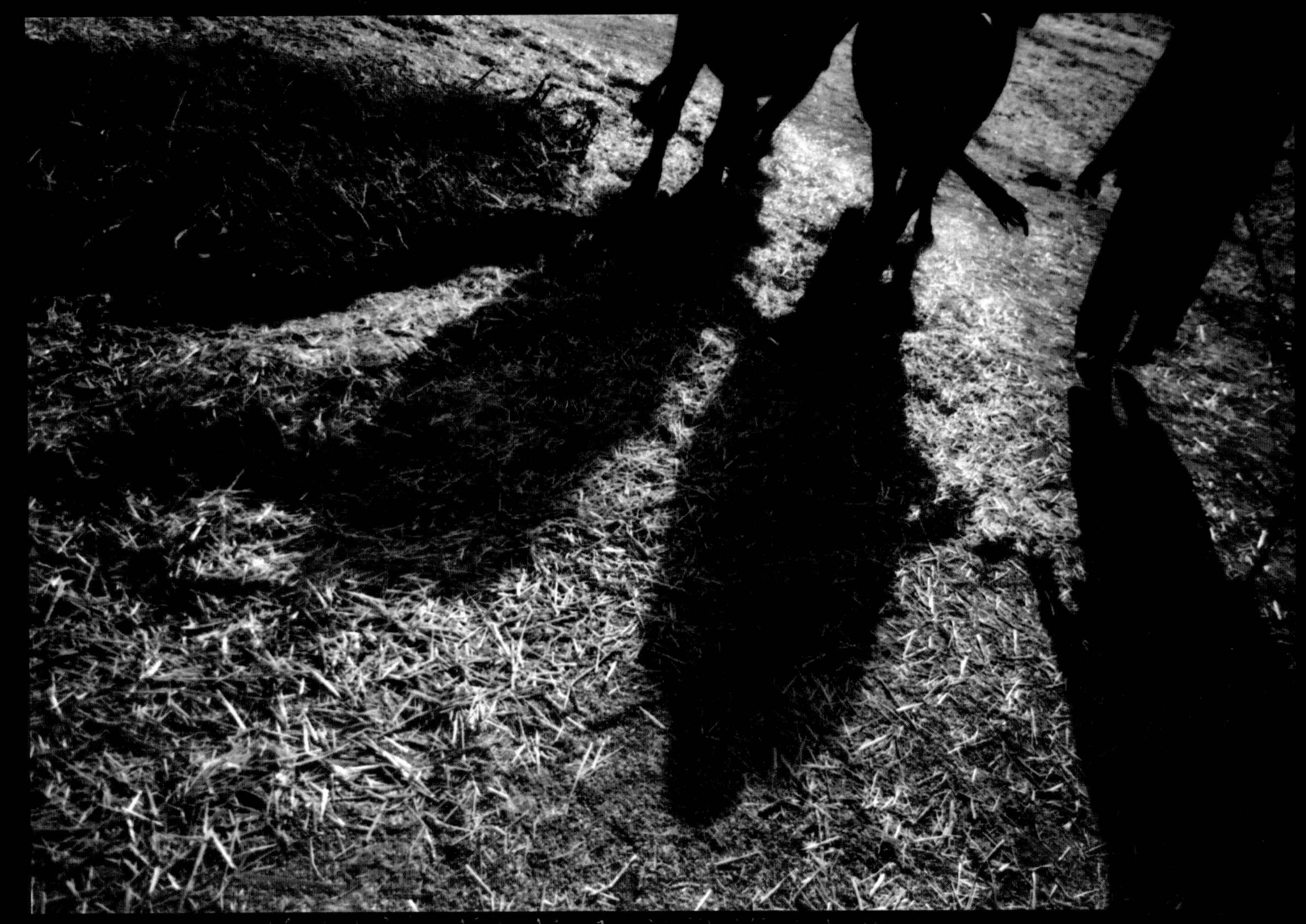

The shadows of an ancient method of labor in Jalalabad.
The farmers work the fields the traditional way, using their animals for the hardest tasks.

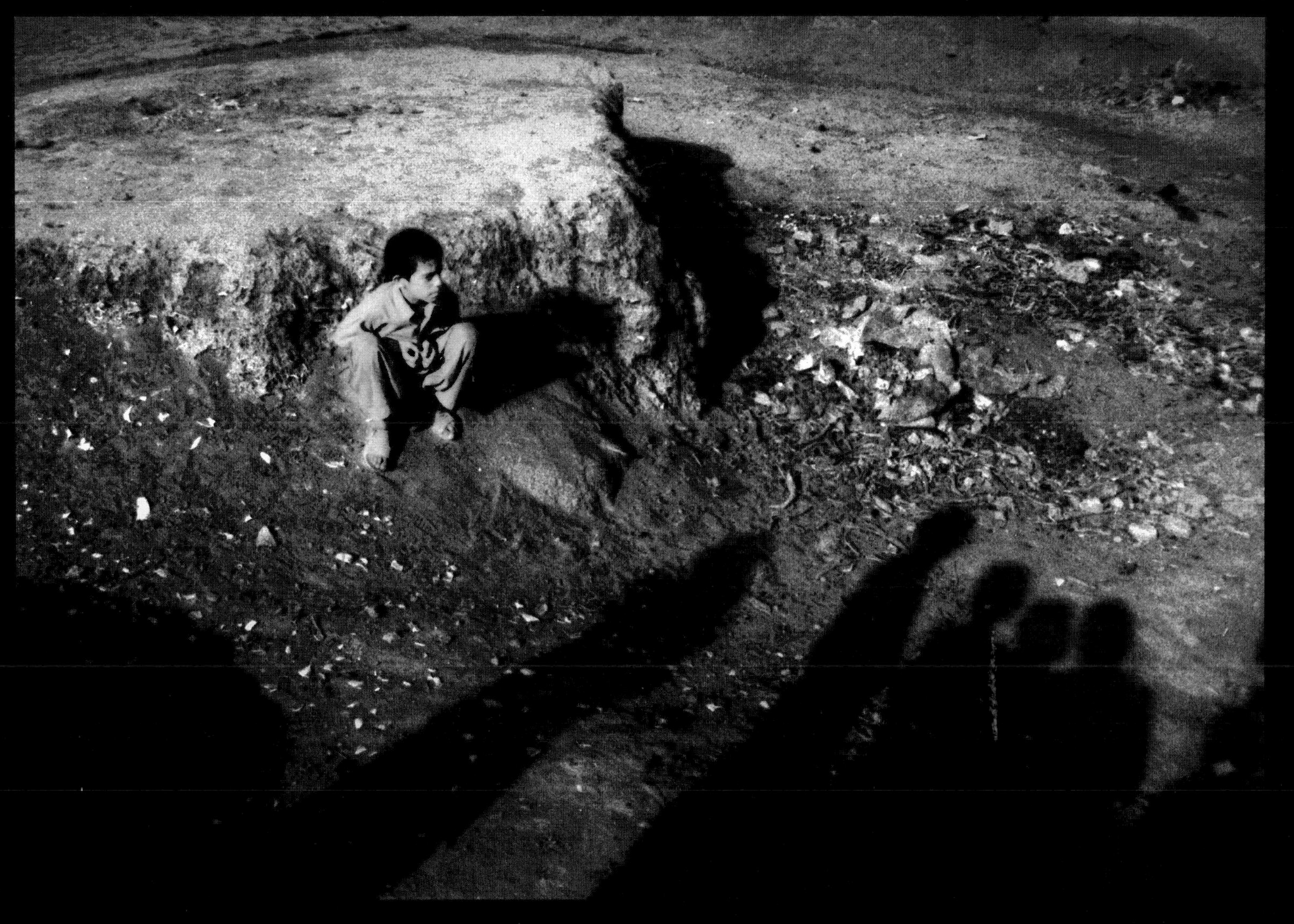

Shar-e kohna is the most completely devastated neighborhood in Kabul. Its dwellers live in a space framed by ruins, filth and misery. Out of the hundreds of NGO's that operate in the country, not one has come to lay a single brick here.

Ahmad M, the interpreter:
"It tells you where your son's body is!"
Sergeant W responded.
I couldn't translate his words.
"What is written on this piece of paper?"
Jamshid's mother asked again.
I looked at her, then Jamshid's wife, then each one of his family members and the crowd, the people of Yakubi village under the pale sun.
Sergeant W looked at me and asked,
"Why are you silent?"

Specialist Joshua C, the interrogator:
Food? Yes, we gave them food and water.
Yes, a black cloth hood was pulled over Jamshid's head.
Yes, he was shackled for 4 days.

Sergeant Selena M, the interrogator:
I'm sure… they provided food! No, I didn't see him eat.

Ahmad M, the interpreter:
No, I didn't!

On the 4th day he started screaming again at around noon. They asked me to shut him up. I went to his cell and said, "Look, please, if you want to be released from the shackles, you need to be quiet."
He mumbled: "I need a doctor. I need a shot. I don't feel good. My legs are hurting."
I said, "I'll ask them to bring you a doctor."
He said, "If I'm shackled for one more hour, I'll be dead."
I said, "You'll be alright!"
After a moment of silence he said, "God, why have you deserted me?"
In his voice there was a horrible doubt.
I don't know…
I could see the silence of God!

Half of an hour later he was dead!

Bibi K.:
What is written on this piece of paper?

Ahmad M, the interpreter:
"It tells you where your son is!" Sergeant W repeated.
I couldn't translate his words.
"What is written on this piece of paper?"
Jamshid's mother asked again.
I looked at her, then Jamshid's wife, then

each one of his family members and the crowd, the people of Yakubi village under the pale sun.
Sergeant W looked at me and asked, "Why are you silent?"

Sergeant Selena. M, the interrogator:
Yes, I'm charged with assault. The whole situation is unfair! It's all going to come out when everything is said and done.

Specialist Joshua C, the interrogator:
I didn't lie! I didn't…

Ahmad. M , the interpreter:
Most of them in the military Camp were convinced that Jamshid was innocent.
……………………
Yes, I was paid well!
……………………
My father? He was executed by the Taliban Regime in 1997.
No, I learned English from the radio… from English-speaking stations. Then I took classes….

Yes, I was paid well!

Karim, one of the 3 passengers sent to Guantanamo prison:
After 18 months of being in Guantanamo prison, they sent us back home with a letter saying we were no threat to the American forces.
Jamshid's mother and relatives begged us to explain what had happened to him.
I told them he had a bed. I said Americans were very nice to him because he had a heart condition.

Ahmad. M , the interpreter:
Yes, I was paid very well!

No, no, Mr. Gordon. Not any more!

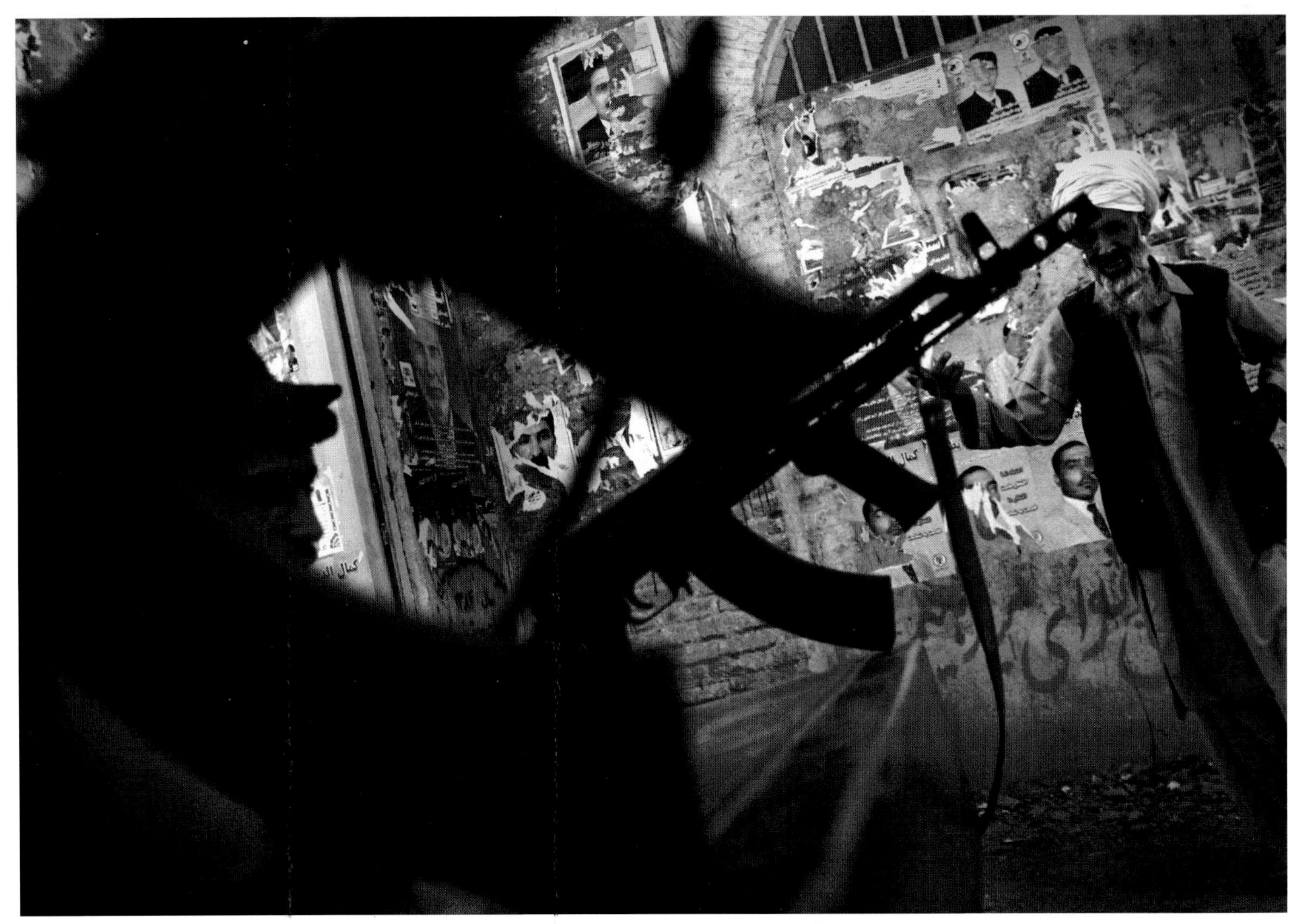

This man was berating some soldiers who were pointing at civilians with their Kalashnikovs.
They had a heated discussion, but in the end, nothing happened.

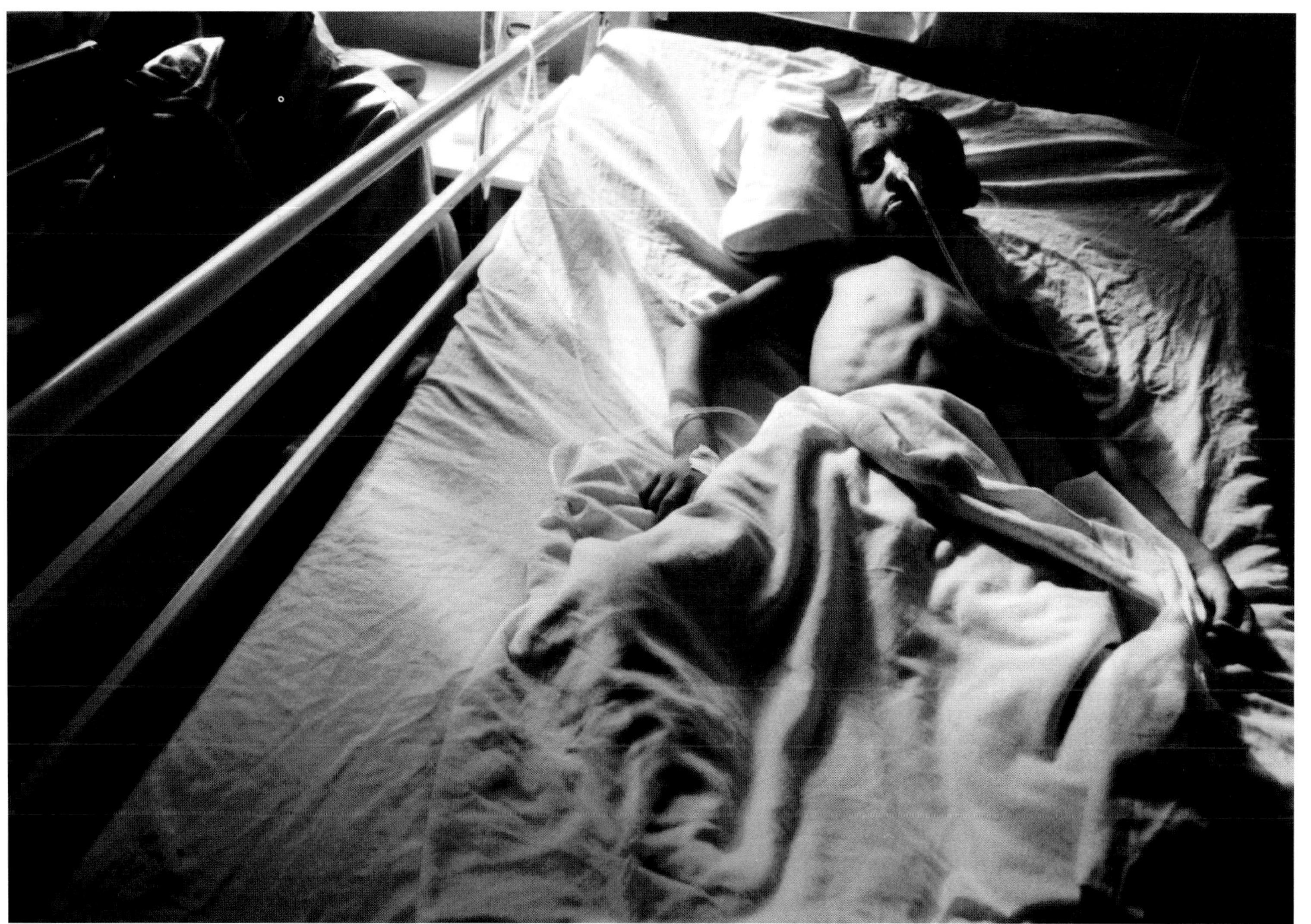

At Indira Gandhi Hospital.

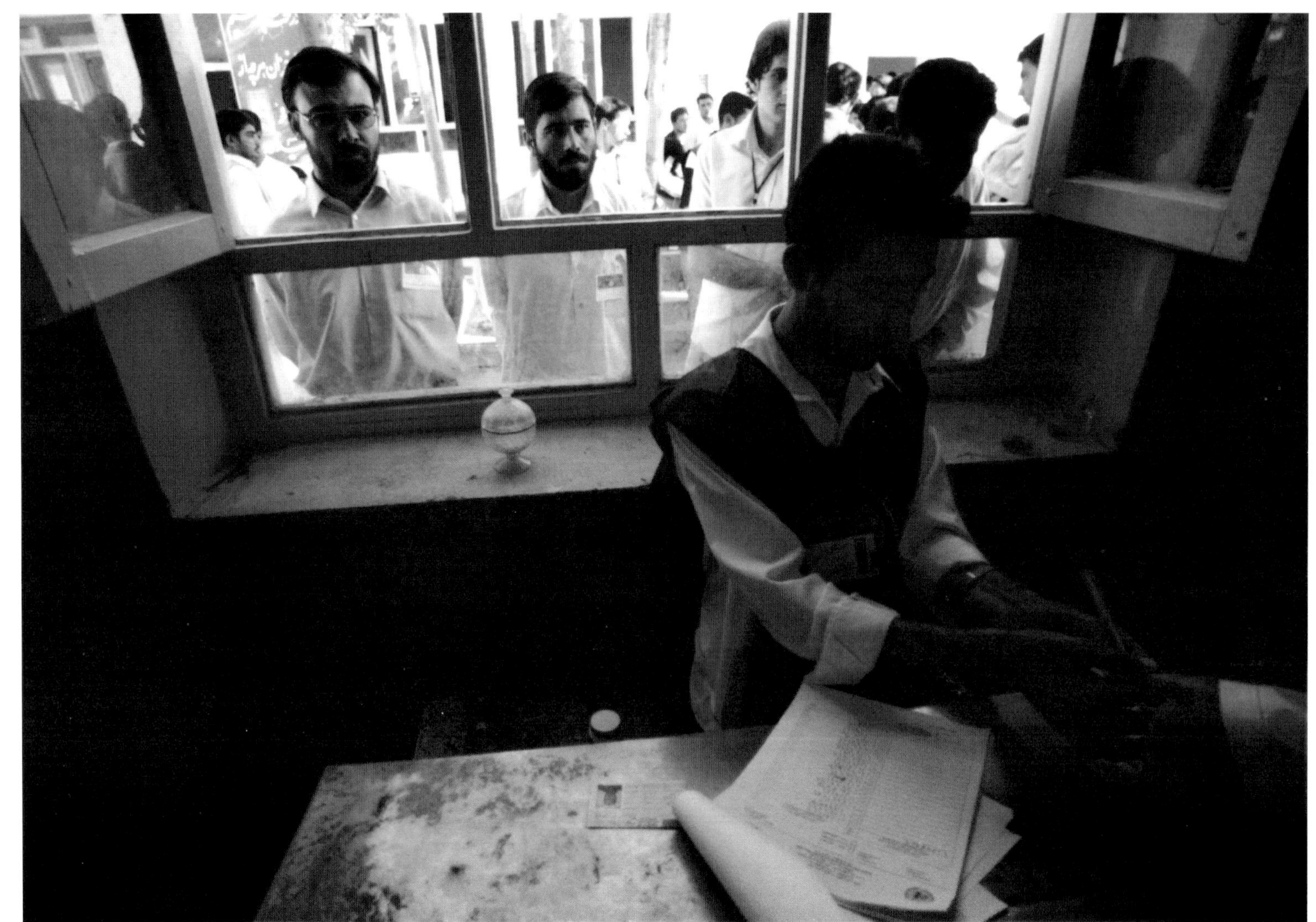

Election day in Herat.

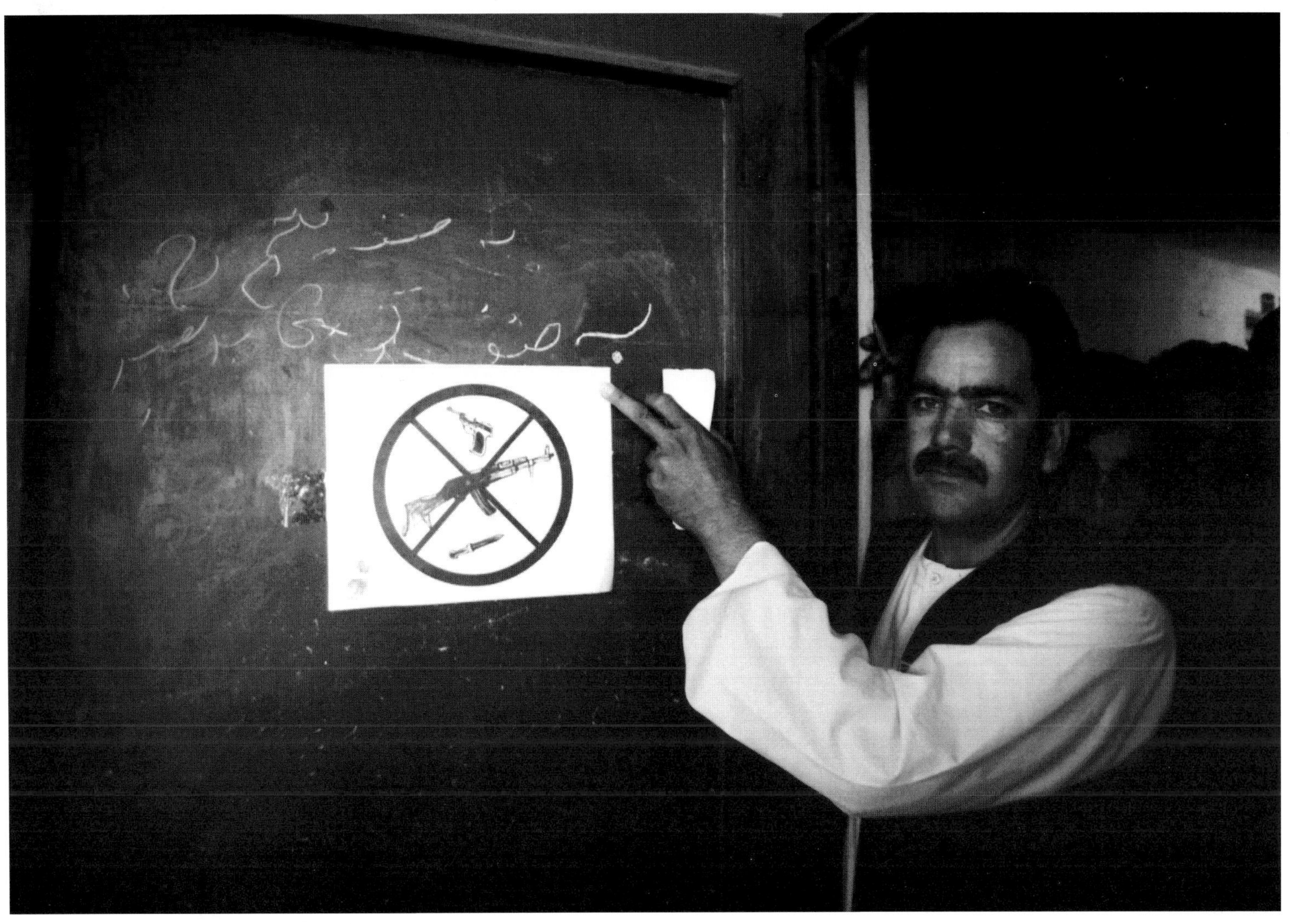

Election day found me in Herat. In a school that was serving as a polling place, I noticed this sign warning that it is prohibited to enter bearing knives, pistols or Kalashnikovs. Before voters were allowed entry, they were exhaustively searched for weapons.

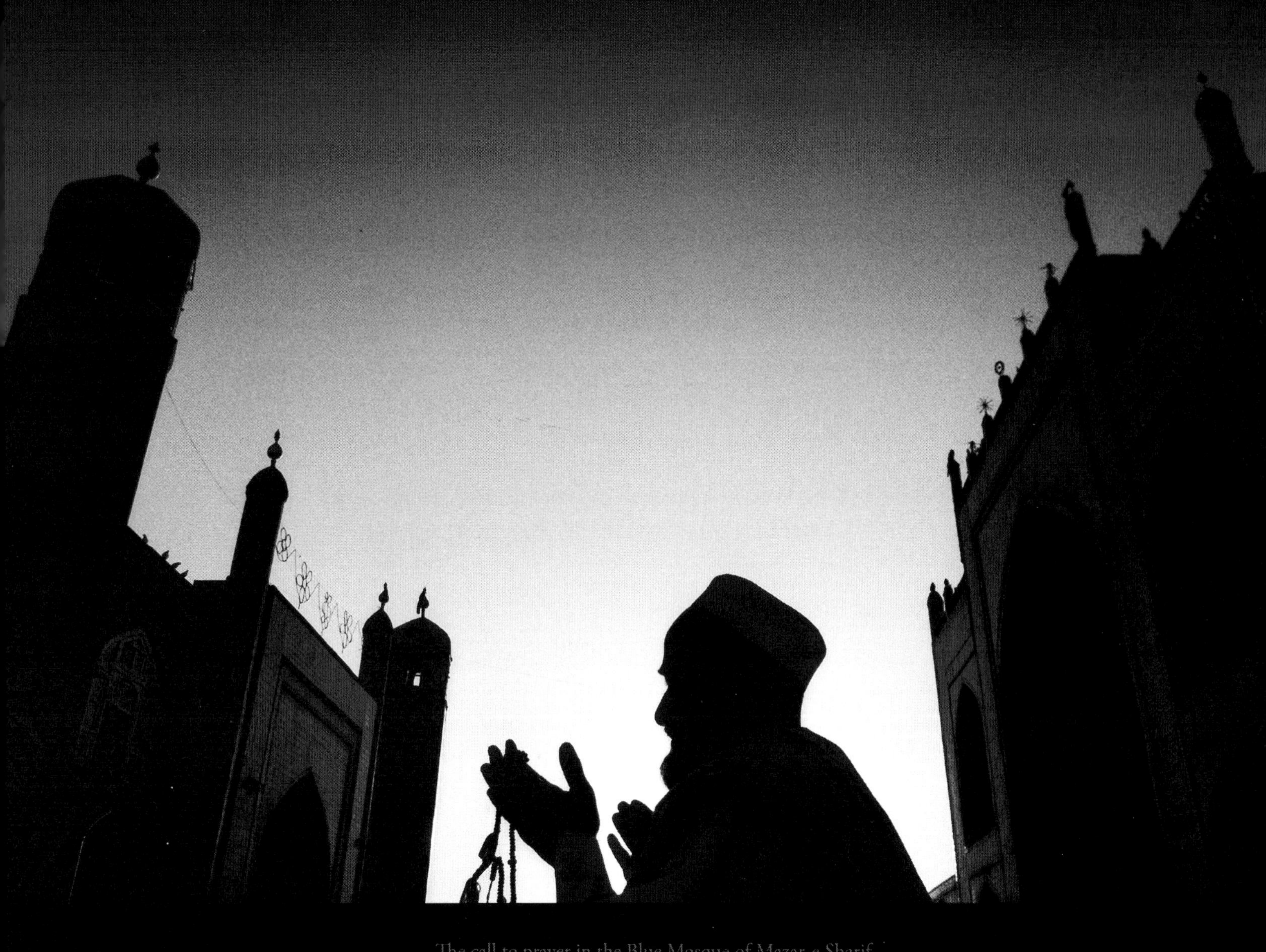

The call to prayer in the Blue Mosque of Mazar-e Sharif.

HANDS

Susan Kelly De-Witt

Kabul, 1996

"They punished the rebels
by cutting off their hands…"

What can you do
with a mountain of bloody
hands?

You can't wash them.
You can't ever use them
for caressing again
or for planting.

They'll never hold a pencil
or trace soft black lead
over paper in intricate glyphs.

How many pounds
did the rebel hands weigh
and how many men did it take
to cart the load away?

Did they
carry them off

in willow baskets?
in rubber buckets?
in plastic garbage bags?
soft, so callused, so sticky?

Did they bury them
in the hot, dry earth,
digging a hole large enough
for a small army
to crouch in first?

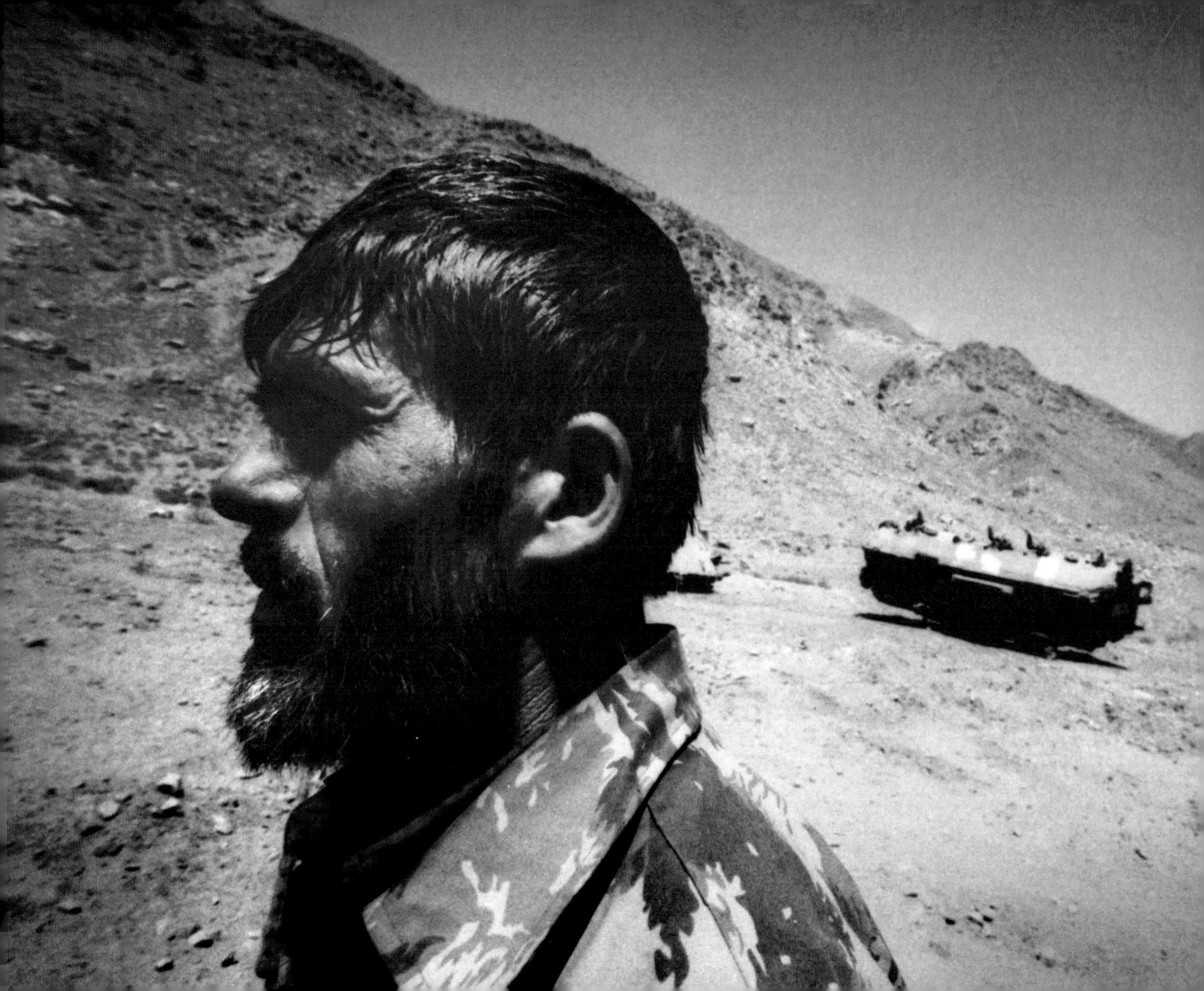

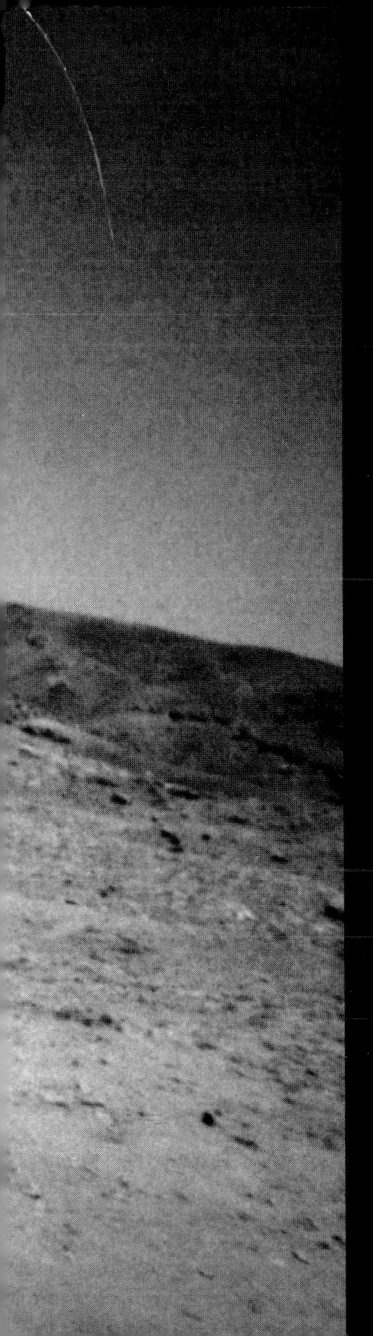

A soldier on patrol in the Panjshir Valley, where remains of Soviet tanks may be seen, testimonials to their offensives against Ahmed Shah Massoud, the "Lion of Panjshir."
The soldier tells me to be careful where I walk, because the entire region is infested with anti-personnel mines.

Next page
Soviet skeletons pepper the landscape as far as the eye can see. Indelible testimonies of the battles that took place in Panjshir. I was entering into these lands where cruel battles raged to gain power, yet neither the Soviets nor the Taliban ever managed to enter. It was dangerous to leave the road, as the entire area is full of mines.

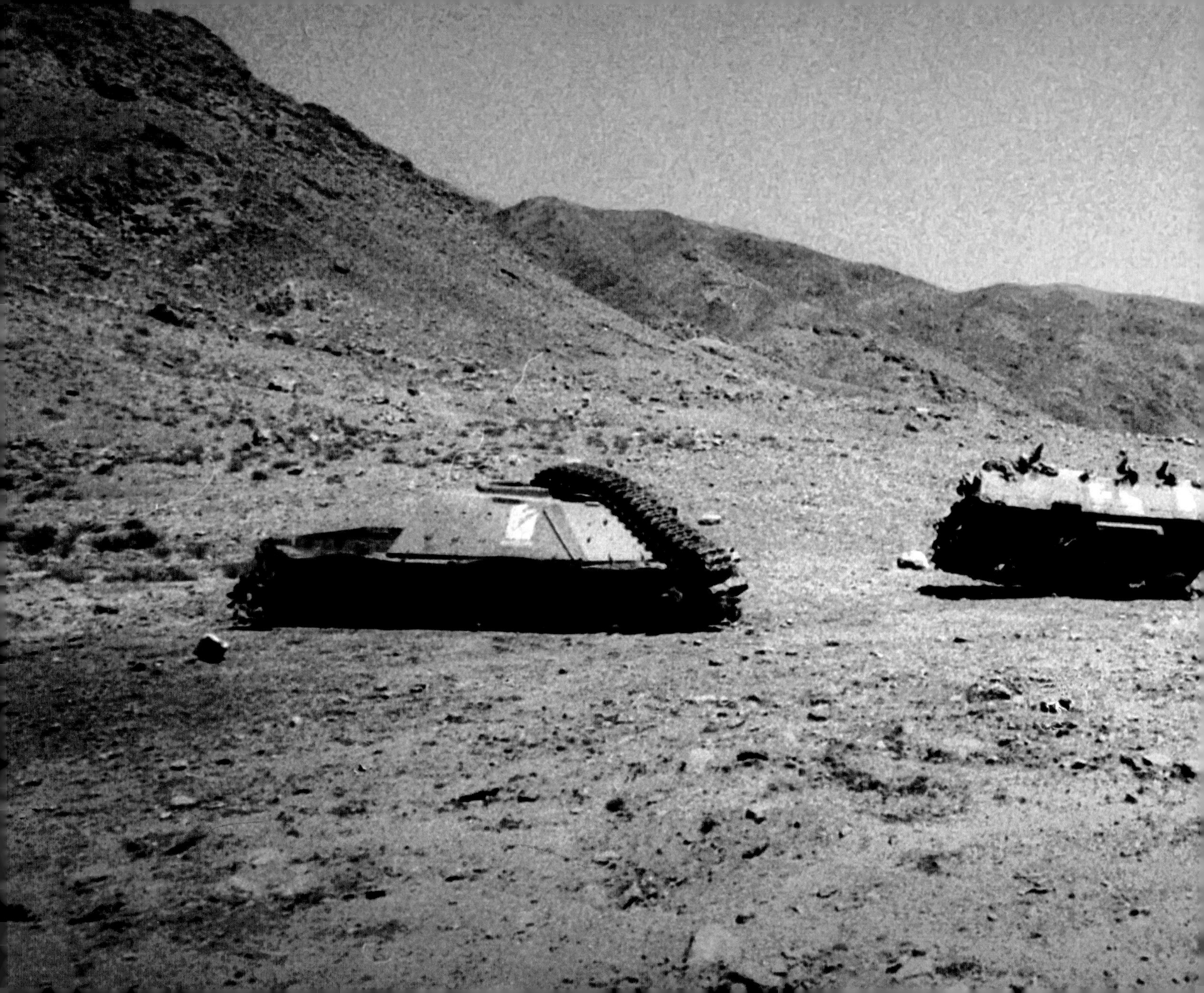

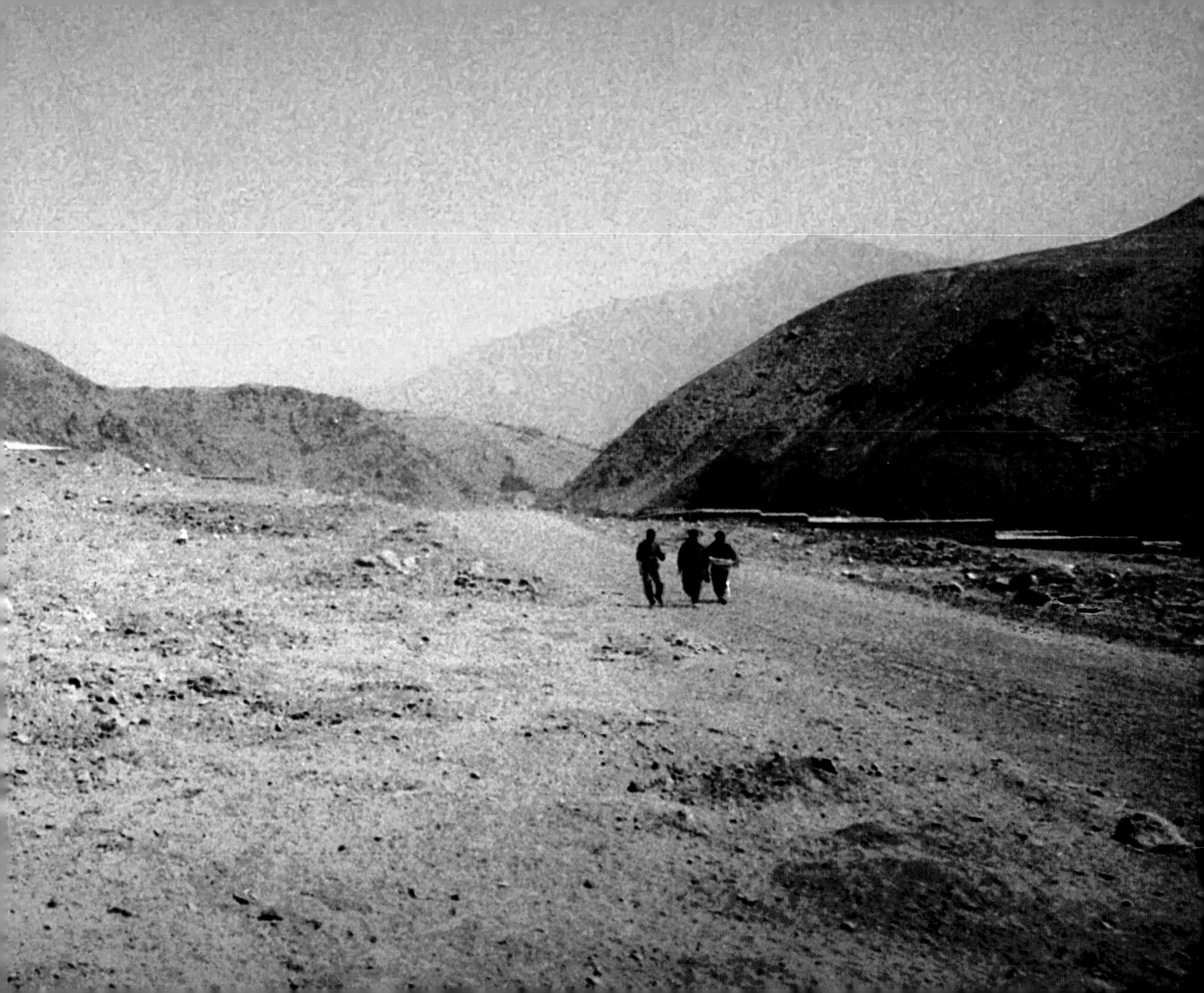

WHO?

Toti Martínez de Lezea

Who will explain to that boy, whose legs were ripped off by a land mine, the reason why he will never be able to run after a ball, ride a bike or, simply, feel the grass below his feet?

Who will tell that woman hidden under a burka that she has the same rights as a man, that she was born his equal, but that the freedom she glimpsed for a few instants was just a lie?

Who will convince that boy, brought up among rubble and fed with hatred, that the only use of weapons is to kindle the fire of war and fill the pockets of those who sell them?

Who will convince that grandfather—who has lost his grandson and children in a bombing, and remains astounded, staring into space—that God loves him?

Who will sit next to that wounded person, and will tell him that the sky is an immense dome covered in stars under which all people have a right to life?

Who will have the words to explain to the suffering Afghan people that they are a flock of sheep amongst a pack of hungry wolves?

Who, in the end, will tell them that nobody cares about the death, misery, pain and desperation that they put them through day after day?

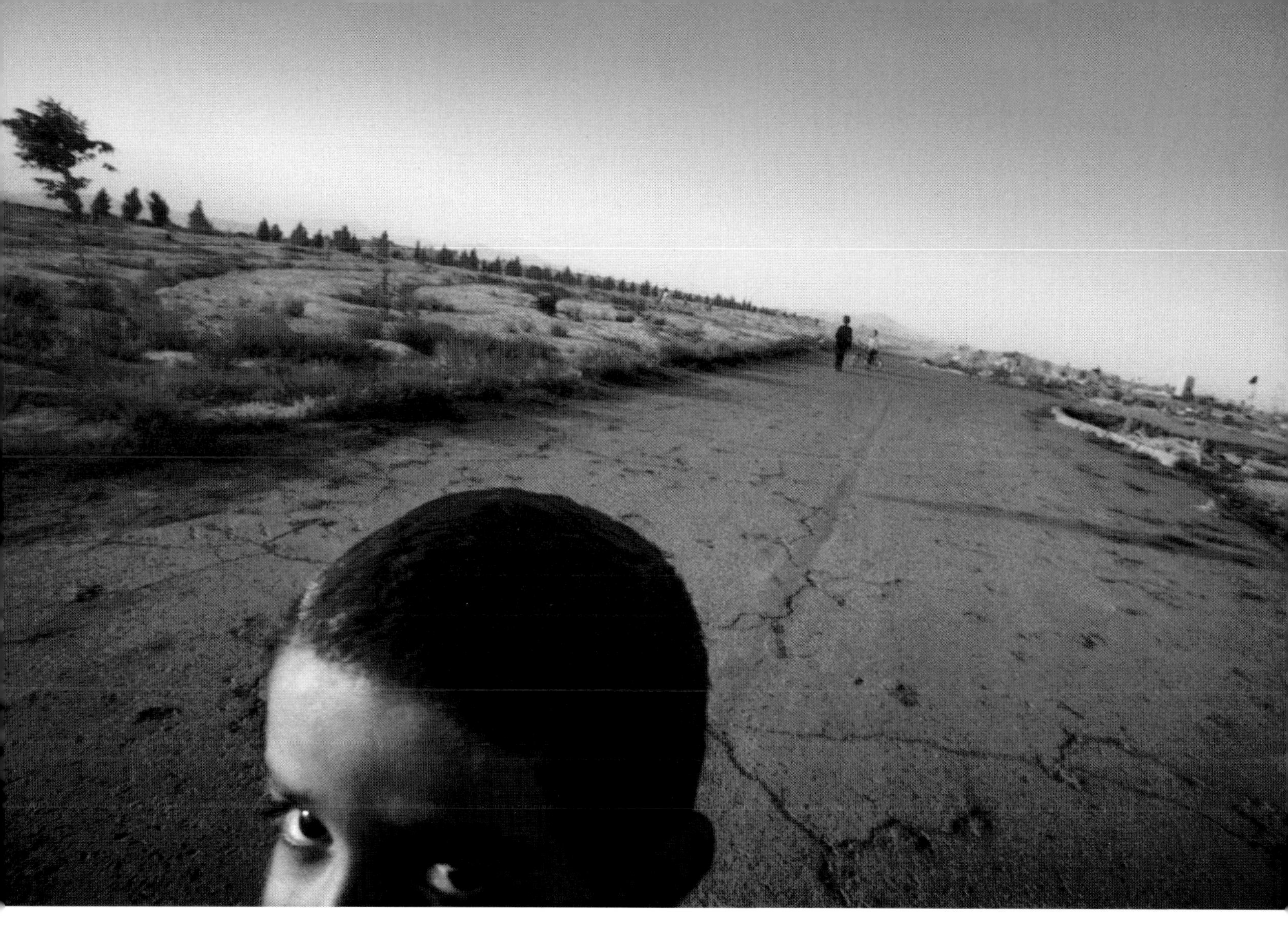

A child on the outskirts of Kabul. His eyes spoke to me of the poverty and sadness of a generation that has known only war.

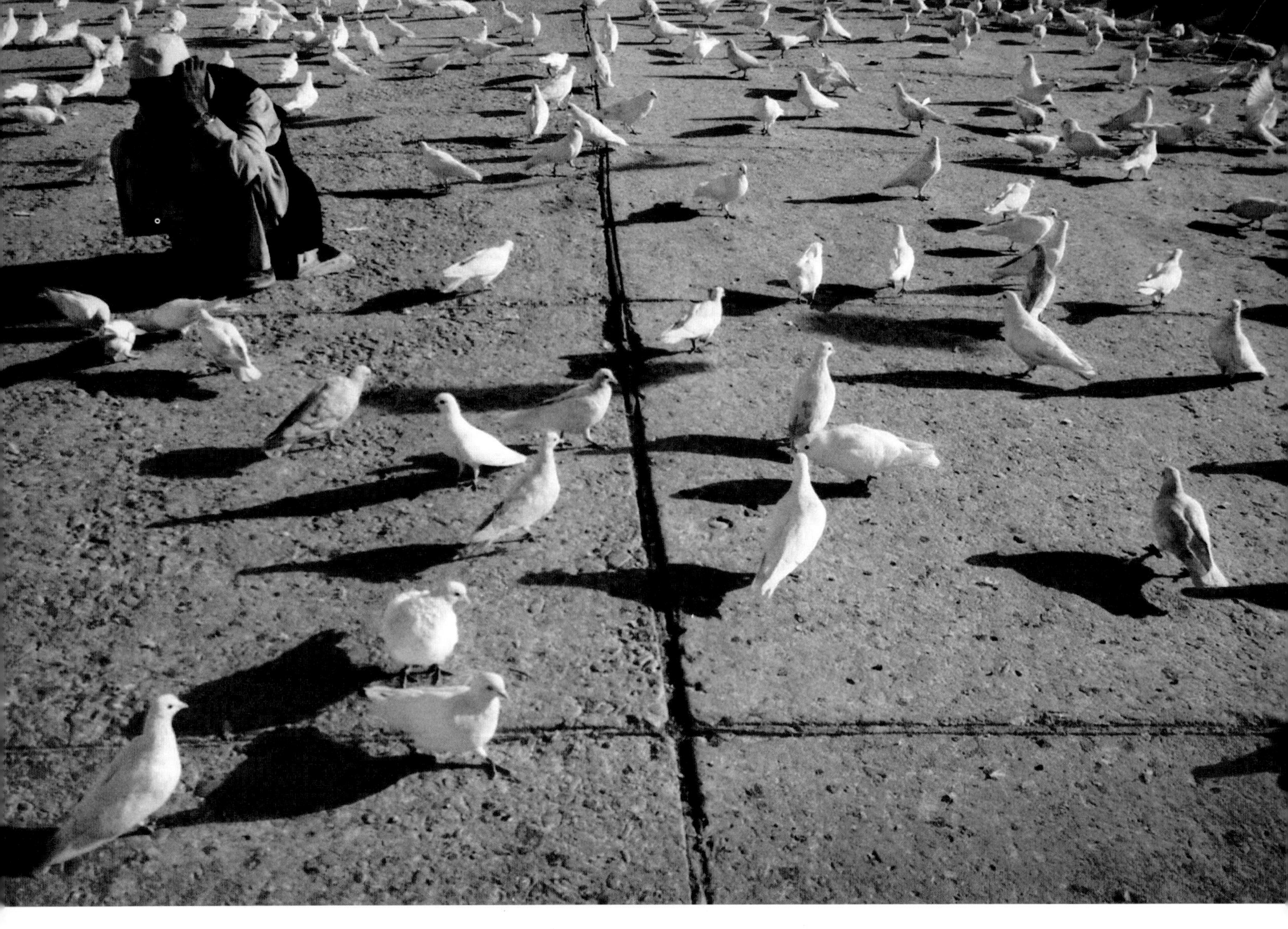

I was drawn to this tableau of a man crouching on the ground, surrounded by white doves, the international symbol of peace – which never arrives to this land; the situation only goes from bad to worse.

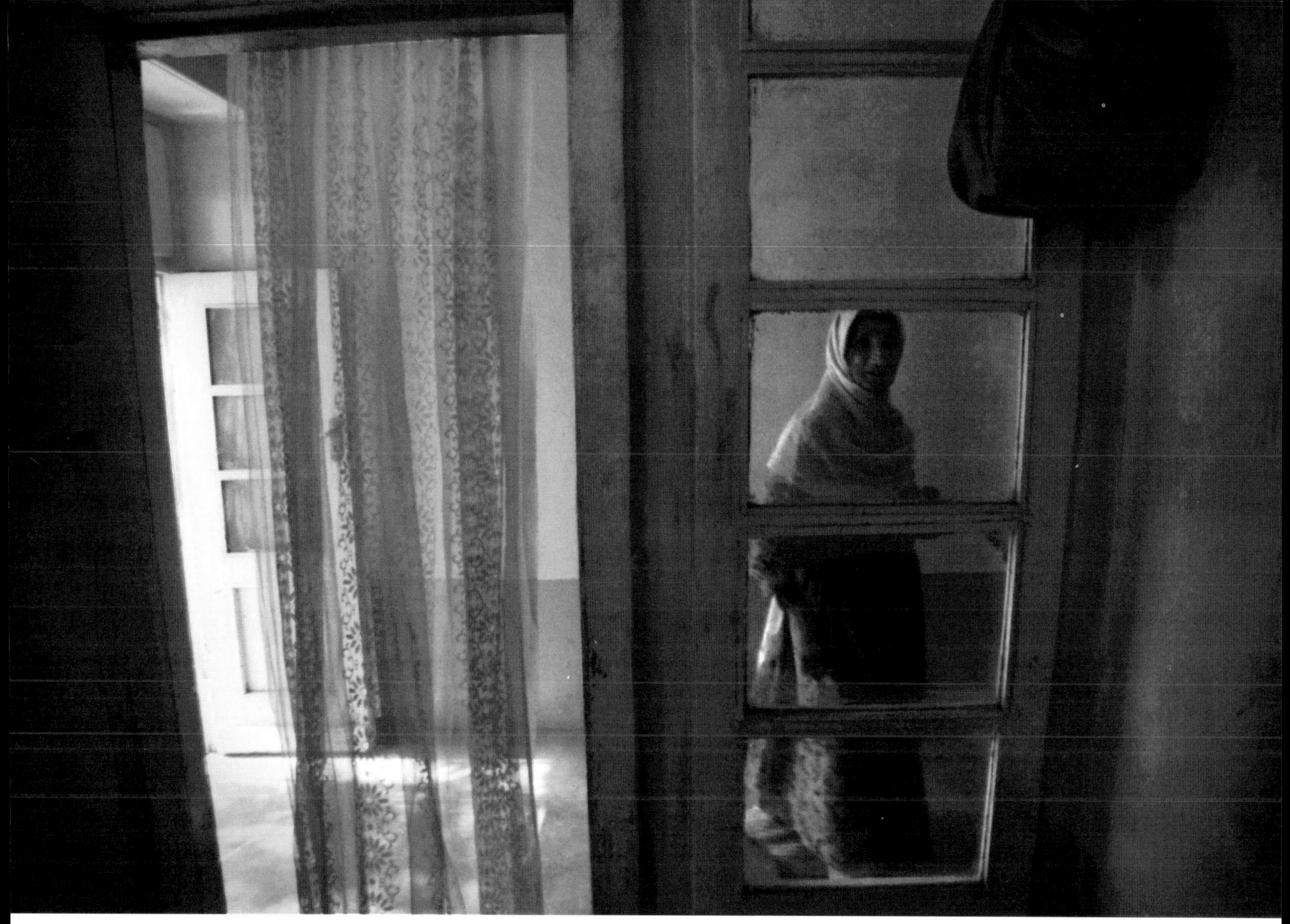

A corner in Ali Abad hospital in Kabul. The women don't wear burkas within its walls, and are more open with strangers there. They can even have a conversation with foreigners, something unthinkable on the outside.

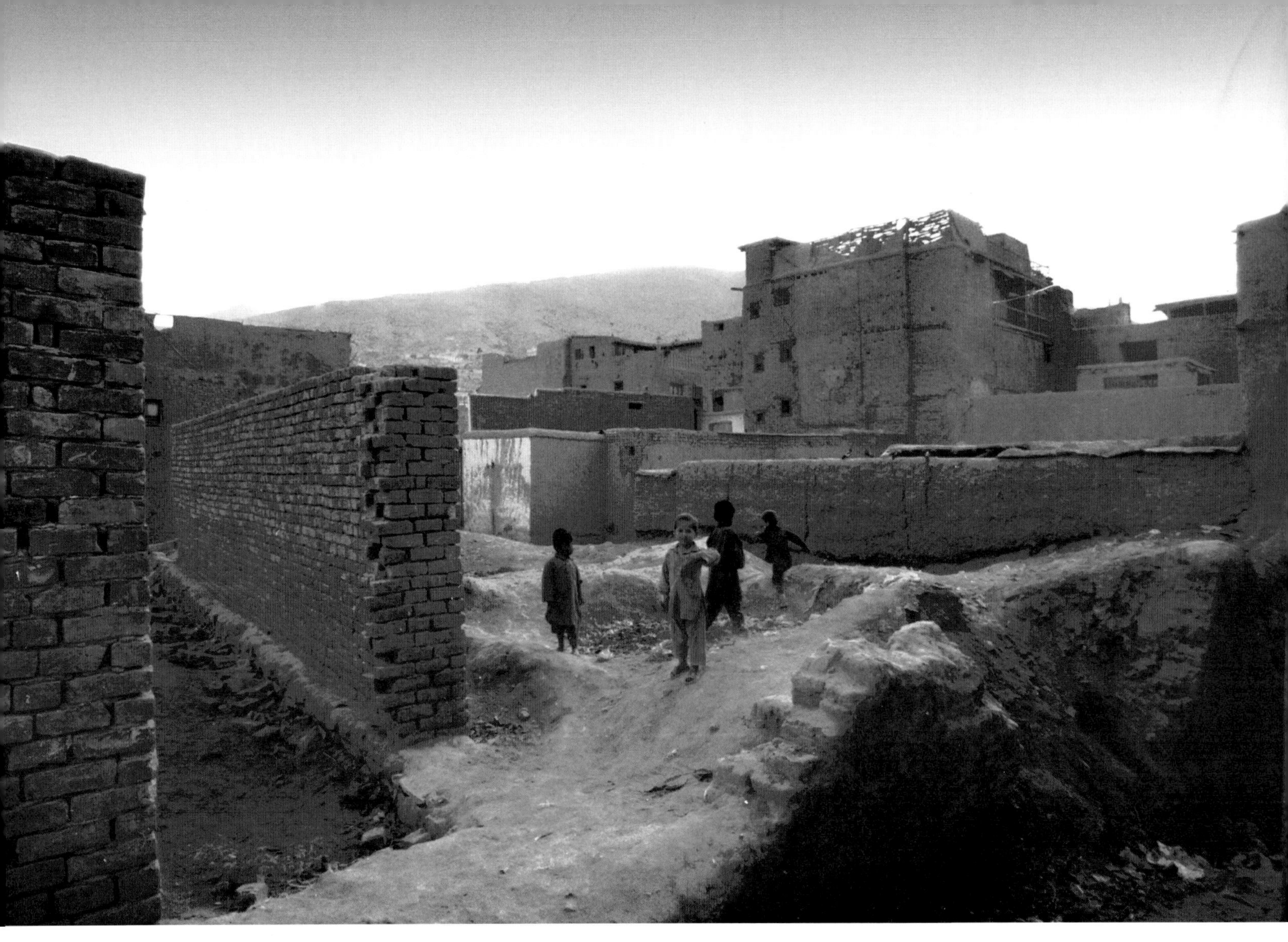

Boys playing in the neighborhood of Shar-e kohna, surrounded by ruins and refuse.
I had no papers with me, as my passport was at the Interior ministry for a visa extension, so a policeman wanted to take me in to the station, but he ended up inviting me home to have lunch with his family instead.

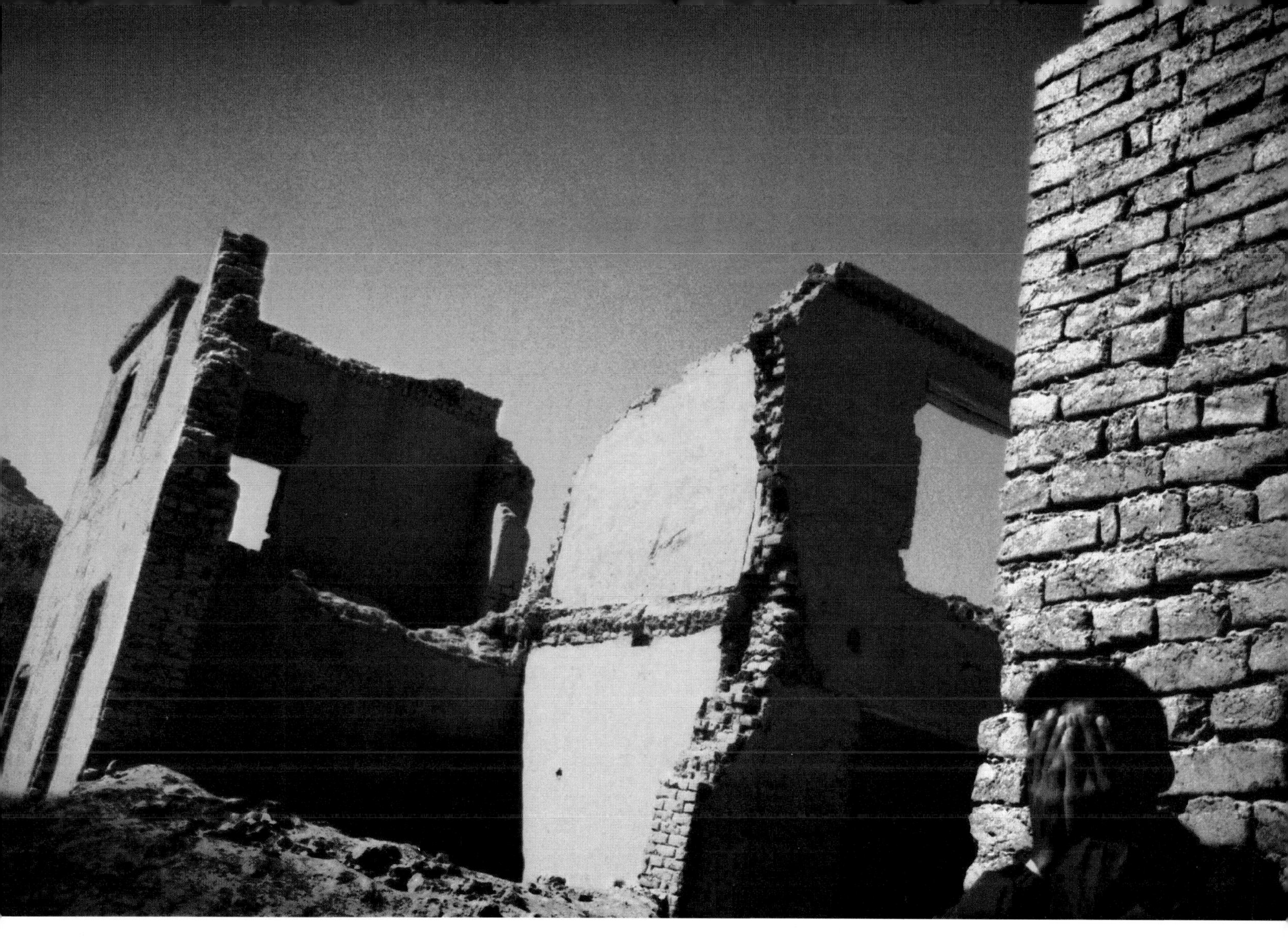

I make Ahmed Abdullah's acquaintance on a walk outside Bamiyan. As we are talking, we stop before a place which he tells me was his home, now completely destroyed by enemy bombs. Telling me his story, he begins to weep at the misfortune of losing all he had.

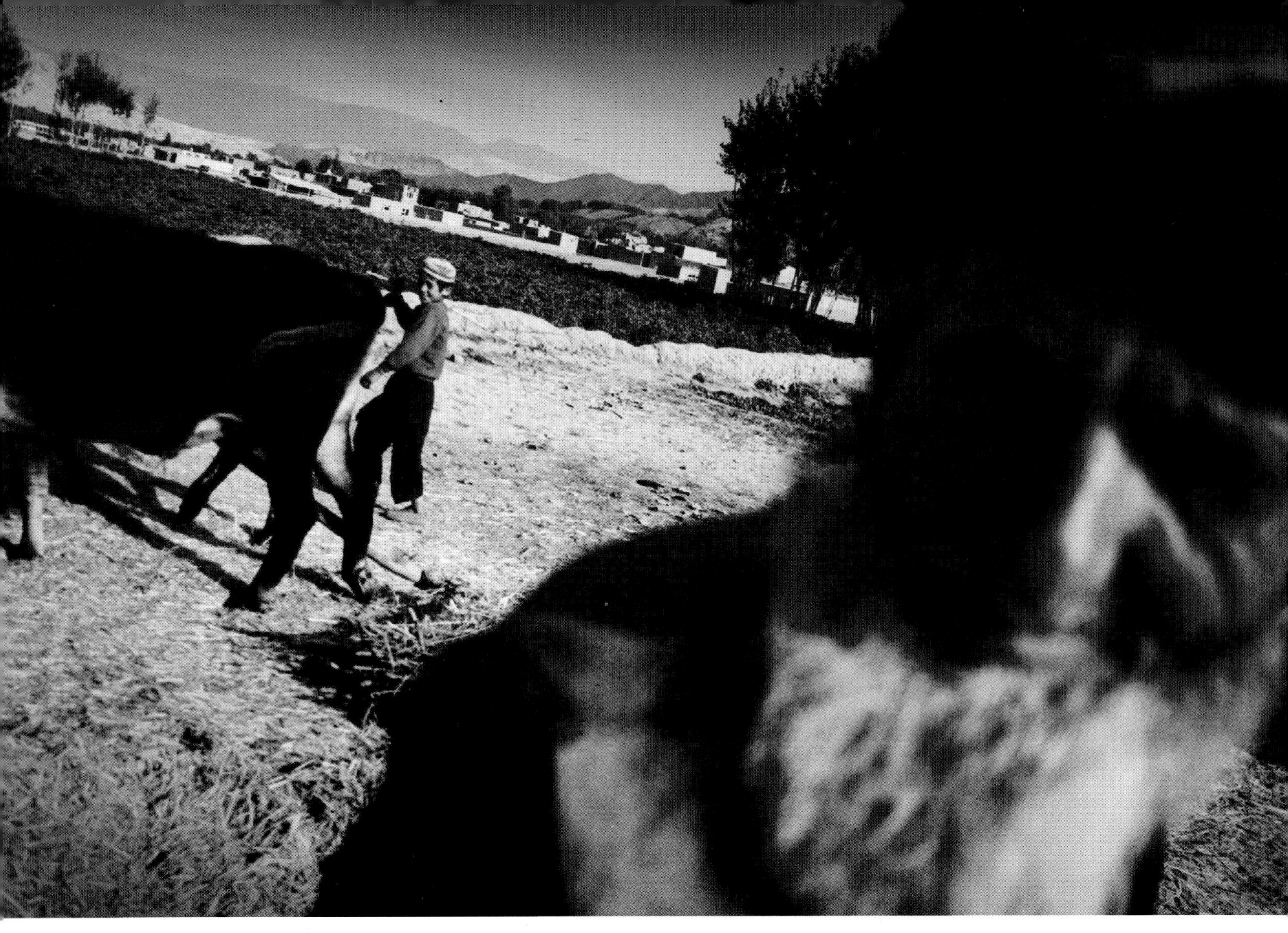

A rural scene. The peasants work the land the old-fashioned way, using oxen to plow and carry loads.
People can't afford tractors nowadays in Afghanistan.

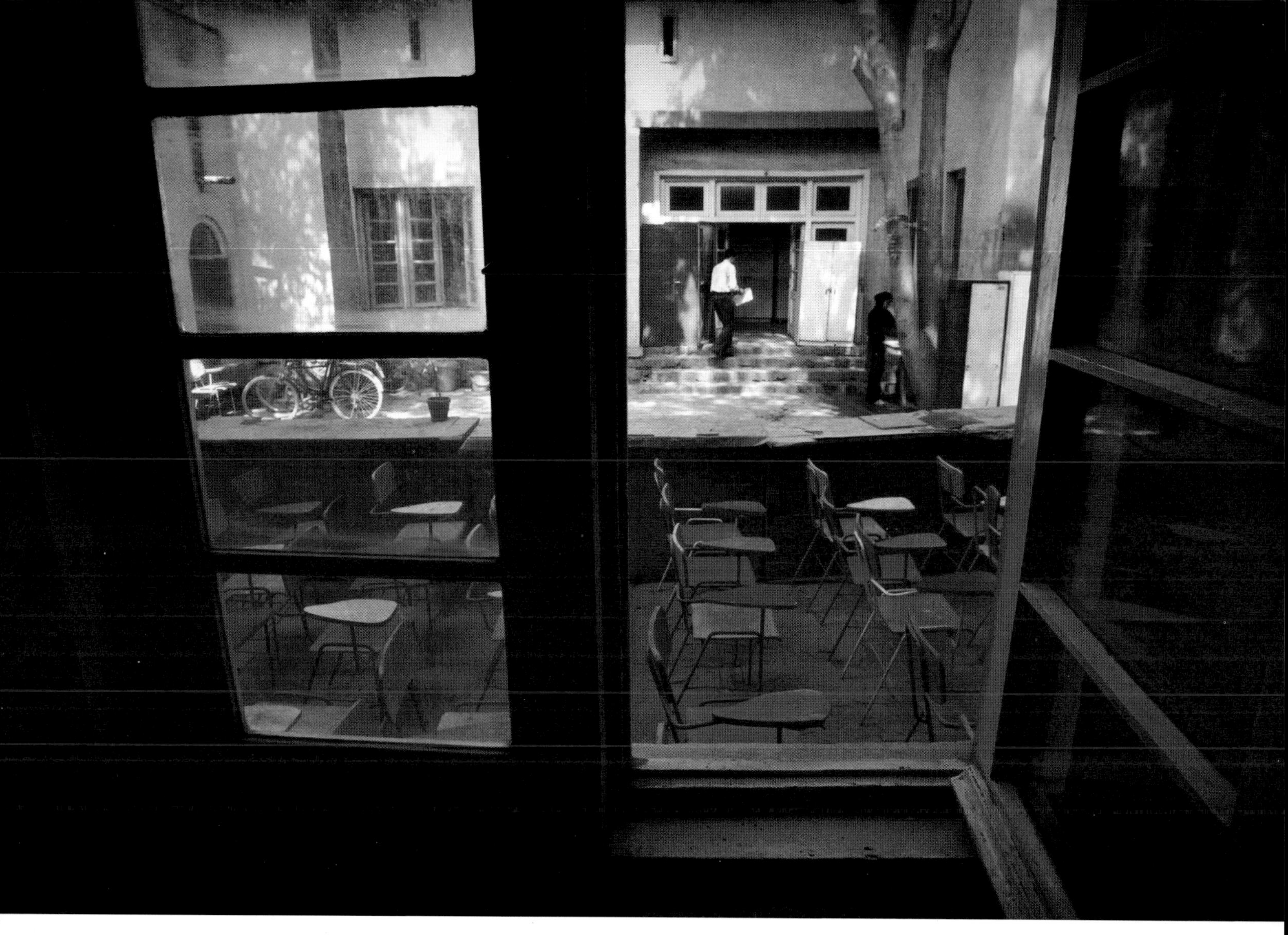

Writing desks in the open-air classroom of a school.

MYSTERY

Alan Rachins

It's a bit of a mystery why I was asked to write this, and why anyone should think what I have to say might help shine a spotlight on Afghanistan and its people. I don't consider myself a passionate "advocate" as much as one who struggles to be an informed observer. Although I admire those who devote themselves to a particular cause in the hope of relieving suffering, and making the world a better place, I write from the point of view of someone who is so involved with the demands of his own life—who like Sisyphus, pushing the boulder daily up the mountain, can only take in so much of what is going on elsewhere in the world, beyond the task at hand.

I am often confused by world events. One can't help hearing, seeing, and reading the various bulletins from the news, frequently finding, days later, the new contradictory bulletin. What are we to believe? The latest area of confusion is what is happening in Afghanistan. The Taliban seem to be becoming more powerful. Recently, they were invited to the table to discuss the possibility of sharing power. The Taliban were the original target of the U.S. invasion of Afghanistan, both for sponsoring terror by aiding Osama bin-Laden, and for their oppressive and inhumane regime. Yet America's Washington representatives segued from Afghanistan to Iraq, leaving the original objective (whatever that was) incomplete, and the country abandoned. Now the Taliban's power rises again. People in power often make confusing decisions and often are accused of lying. The White House defends their decisions citing what they call " irrefutable facts". The opposite side contradicts them citing their own set of facts. All this leaves me with a feeling of doubt, uncertainty, and distrust. I have participated in protests, standing near the person with the microphone, who seems to be so absolutely sure of his or her position. I usually wind up thinking that while the speaker seems powerfully persuasive, how can he be so absolutely sure of his position? How much of their position is well reasoned from the available facts, and how much is simply a way to grab the lion's share of righteous indignation and extend their ego into the world. In protest groups, as in Government, leaders vie with one another for the greater share of the power. So I have often asked myself, "Am I standing in a group protest to change some policy, or am I just a pawn in someone else's future ambition?" Doesn't a truly honest position leave some room for doubt, for new information, for humility?

Are power and truth incompatible?

Just as leaders grapple with one another for the microphone, the world's issues struggle to become the center of attention. In America, Iraq has obviously maintained center stage for the last few years, with many people thinking, "But what happened to Afghanistan?"

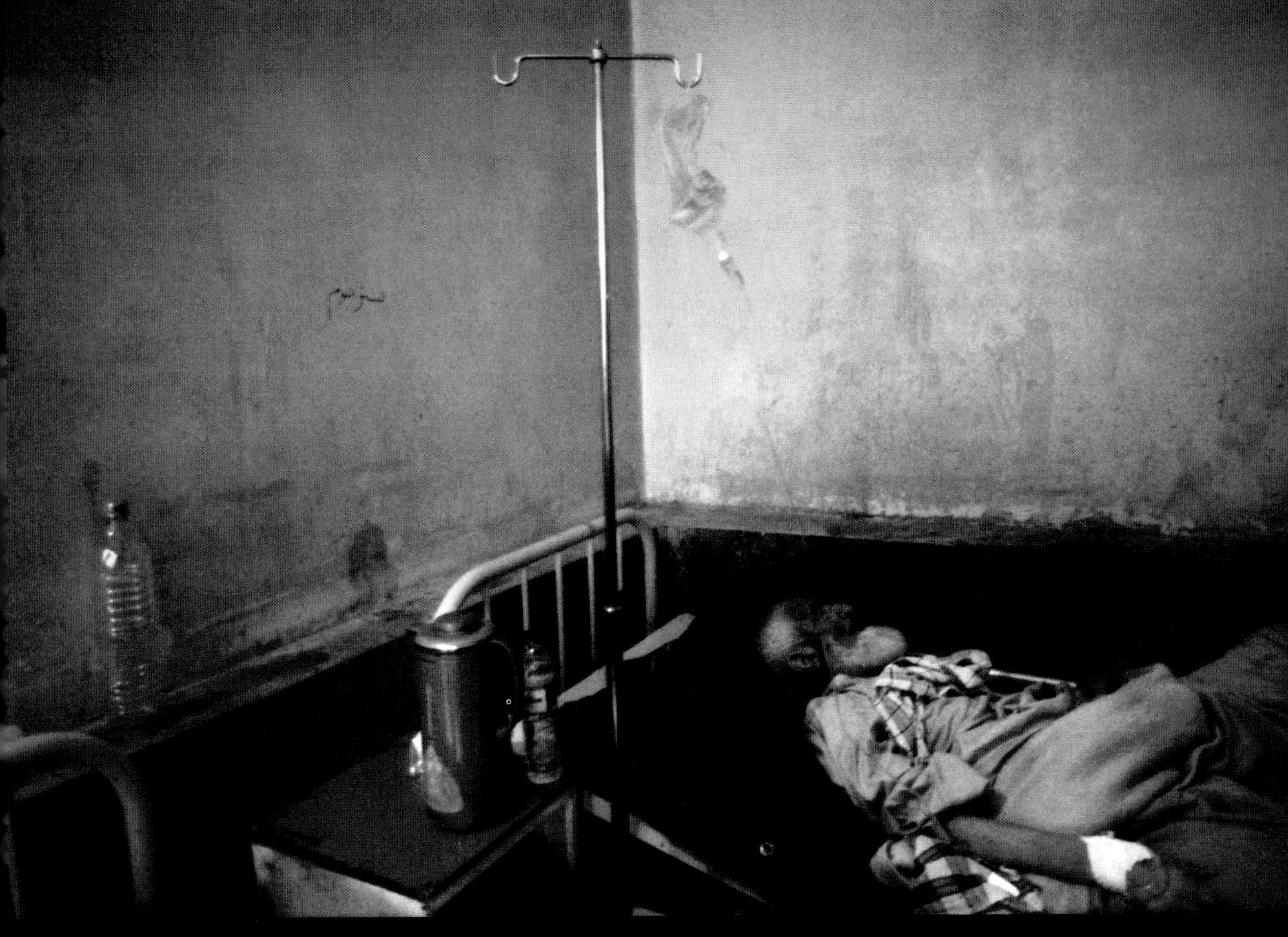

A patient in Ali Abad hospital.

At the moment Pakistan and its stability are at the forefront, and the question of Iran's nuclear program remains unanswered. Africa has a number of regions demanding attention. There are various local issues in our own country that claim attention as well: the unfinished business in New Orleans caused by Hurricane Katrina, the cost of oil, the current real estate depression, and so many others.

I don't know where my responsibilities to the world begin and end, or even how to conceive of something as vast and complex as responsibility to the world. With so many competing issues, domestic and foreign, photographs are reaching out, begging, screaming, moaning, whispering for our attention. Afghanistan. Don't forget Afghanistan.

And what is any country if not its people? In these photographs there are isolated hospital beds with young and old, soldiers with machine guns, men with amputated limbs, children playing in the ruins of buildings. Joy surfaces on occasion like drops of water in a desert. What has happened to this country? What has happened to these people? Are they better or worse since the U.S. intervention? Has the U.S. liberated them or collapsed their country and abandoned them in chaos? And, politics aside, what do their faces tell us? Do they speak of policies and politics, or do they speak the humbler, more basic, language of humanity, of humans struggling for the necessities of life, the very elements of existence.

Afghanistan, as these pictures show, is not just another bullet point of foreign policy, but another face of the human tragedy that is unfolding all over the world. The subtitle of this book is "A window on the tragedy." The first step toward change is always to shine a light on the issue. To illuminate. To look. To see. To recognize. Is it enough to just look? To give a nod in a direction and move on? I can't say that it is enough, but it is a beginning.

Forgive me if I compare what I see in these photographs to what I have seen in movies. Film has been a part of my imagination and my understanding of the world since I was very young. I experience both these realities via film, and often the images in movies are more real than the stark realities of such photographs, because the meanings in film are more black and white (even if the images are in color). While we struggle toward autonomy growing up, and as we try to convince our children that we are adults with answers until they catch on to us, we still have to find some kind of sanctuary. I think of Marlon Brando as Terry Malloy in "On the Waterfront", standing up to the evil son of a bitch who controlled the waterfront:

"You want to know something? Take the heater away and you're nothin'— take the good goods away, and the kickbacks and the shakedown cabbage away and the pistoleros—(indicating the others)—away and you're a great big hunk of nothing—(takes a deep breath as if relieved) Your guts is all in your wallet and your trigger finger! And I'm glad what I done today, see? You give it to Joey, you give it to Nolan, you give it to Charley who was one of your own. You thought you was God Almighty instead of a cheap—conniving—good-for-nothing bum! So I'm glad what I done — you hear me? —glad."

Budd Schulberg wrote those words. In movies, bad guys often get their comeuppance. In real life, there are complications upon complications, and often stories without endings. These images of Afghanistan speak not only to a particular crisis in a particular time and place, they speak to what for many of us exists, buried under the trappings of the modern world. Without all these tools of sophistication and power, what are we? Take all our goods away and what are we left with? Beneath technology and media and ideology, an eternal struggle unfolds, and it is common to humanity. In some places it is laid bare; in others it is concealed by modernity. But it is ever-present. The human tragedy that these photographs document is not only abroad, it is at home.

So we engage with our own personal lives, and with the problems of our country, and we try to stay aware of the problems in the world and in some way reach out to them. Certainly the problems of the world reach out to us. Photographs that are bleak, sad, austere, mysterious, and haunting look at us, even if we don't want to look at them. An empty hospital bed turned upside down. A man staring into the camera with one eye. There are overturned tanks. Young men saluting with their faces like frozen masks. There's a young boy, 5 or 6 years old, with two artificial legs. A man sleeps outside on the ground. These photos demand a place in one's awareness: to be pondered, contemplated, felt, shared. Sometimes I do just that. More often than not, I am too involved in my own daily thoughts and concerns to confront this alternate— but equally real— reality before me. I wonder about our leaders. Are they leading? If not, what are they doing? How do they get their information? How open are the policy debates they engage in, to determine the allocation of so many financial and human resources? Are they surrounded by yes-men? Do they have a deep understanding of the people in other regions of the world? Are they motivated by self-interest or the striving to do what is right? We have a Presidential election coming up. A powerful vote could send a message and could make a difference.

It's humbling to attempt to introduce this book of photographs. Afghanistan is far away, and yet its issues and its people are present. How to respond, to this and so many issues in the world, and still pursue the small yet central problems of our own lives? I wrestle with these conflicts. We sleep, we dream, we act, we expand, we engage, we contract, we retreat. But the images look on.

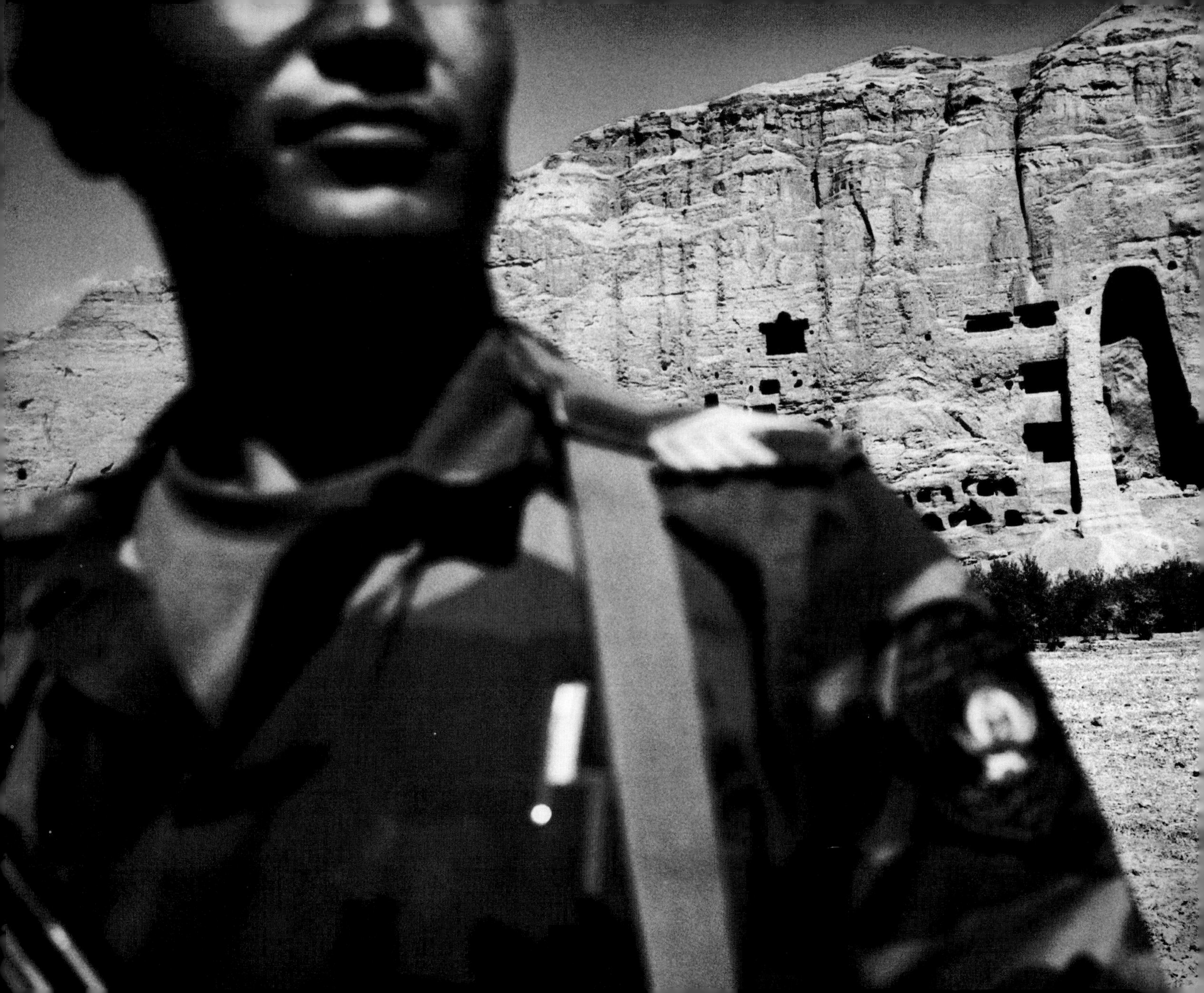

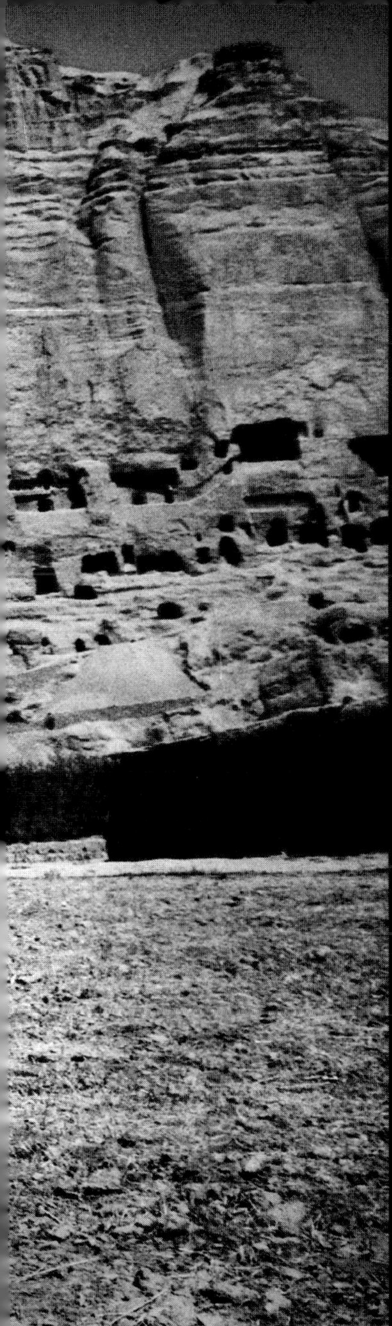

The Taliban destroyed the Buddhas of Bamiyan with explosives and tank cannon fire in March of 2001, claiming that the Western governments wanted to dedicate thousands of Euros to renovate the statues, instead of money for the needy population. While people living only a few hundred yards away are lacking gas, electricity (the temperature in winter drops into the minus twenties), water, or means to feed themselves, there are new projects to illuminate the Buddhas (what is left of them) with laser beams, and to reconstruct them from the remaining fragments that have remained. This will require far more money than the original renovation project.

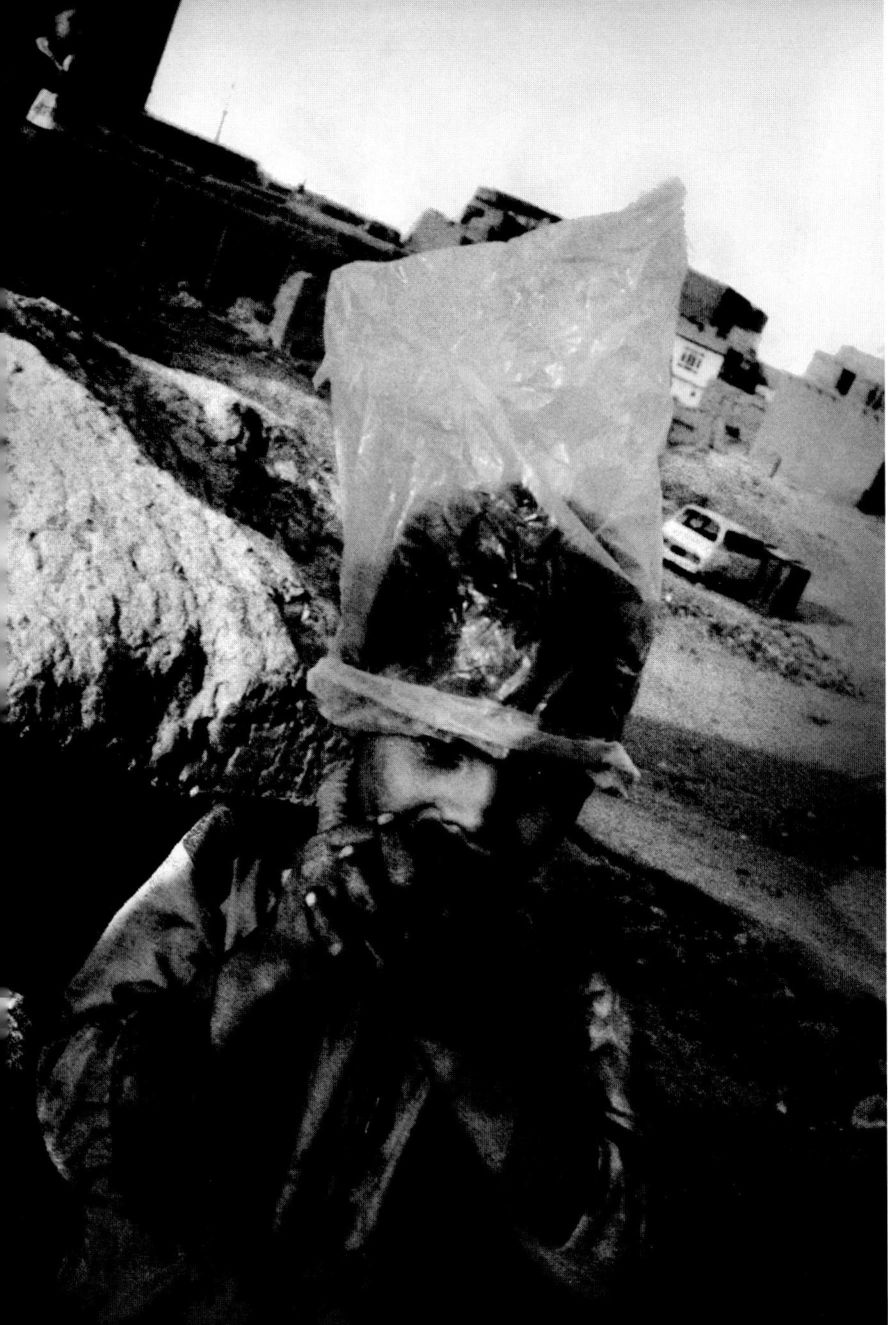

Sharif has lived in the street since he was very small. An orphan, he survives the best he can, sleeping in the streets, with what he gets from people who help. In Afghanistan there is an intense sense of community, and everyone pitches in to contribute what help they can.

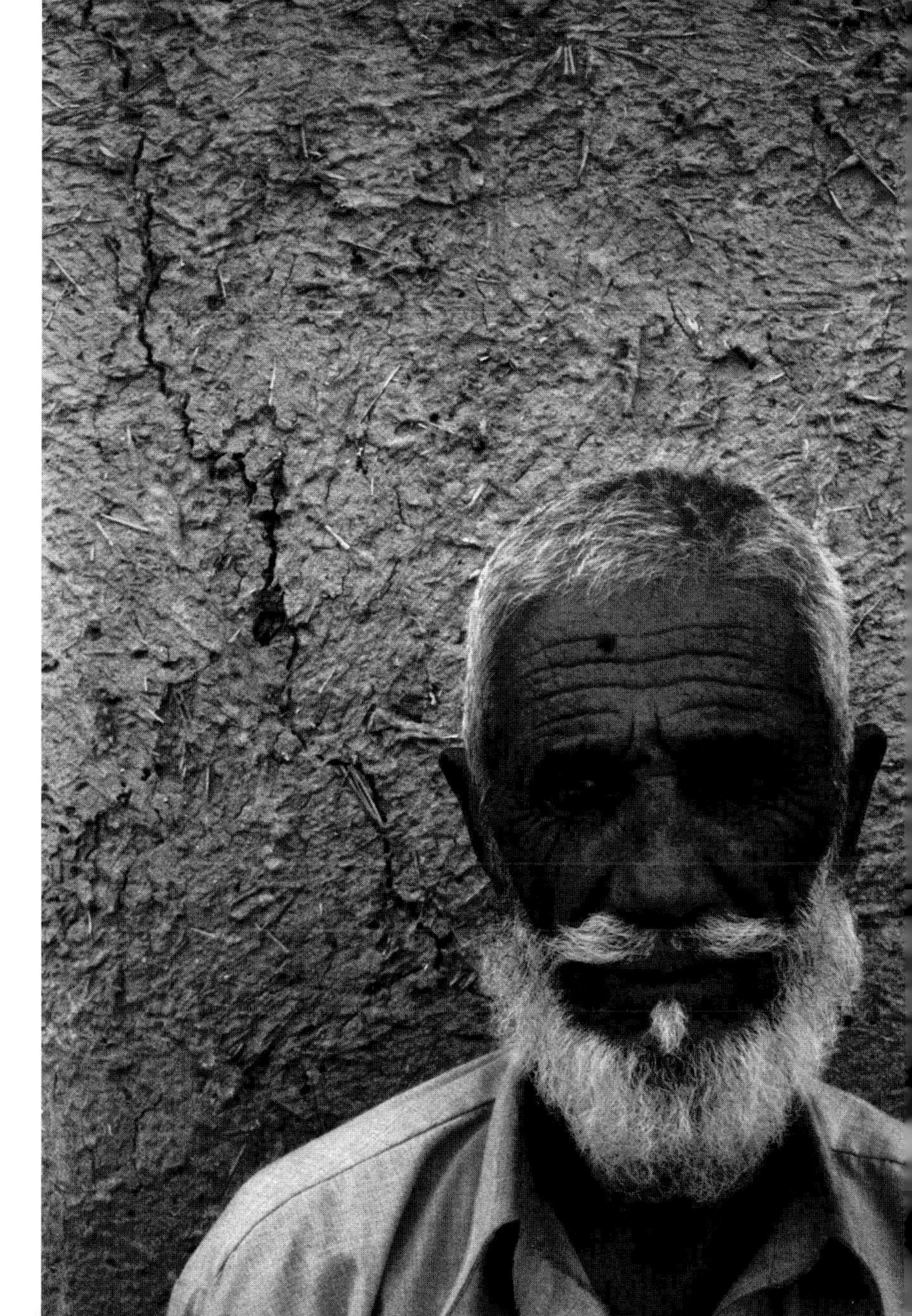

A grizzled old man before the mud walls of his home.

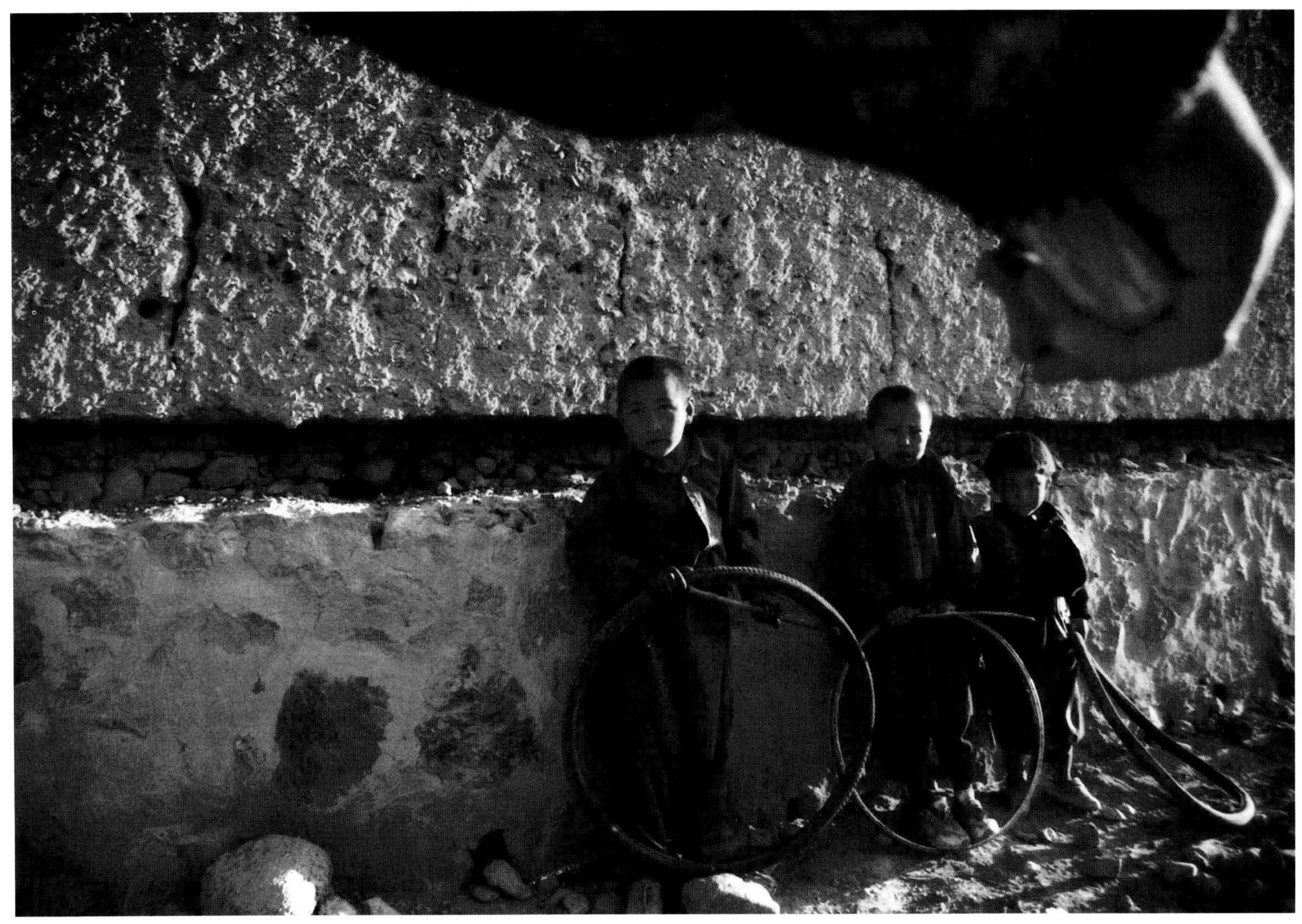

Some Hazara boys playing with bicycle tires in Yakawlang, near Band-e Amir Lake, in Hazarajat province.

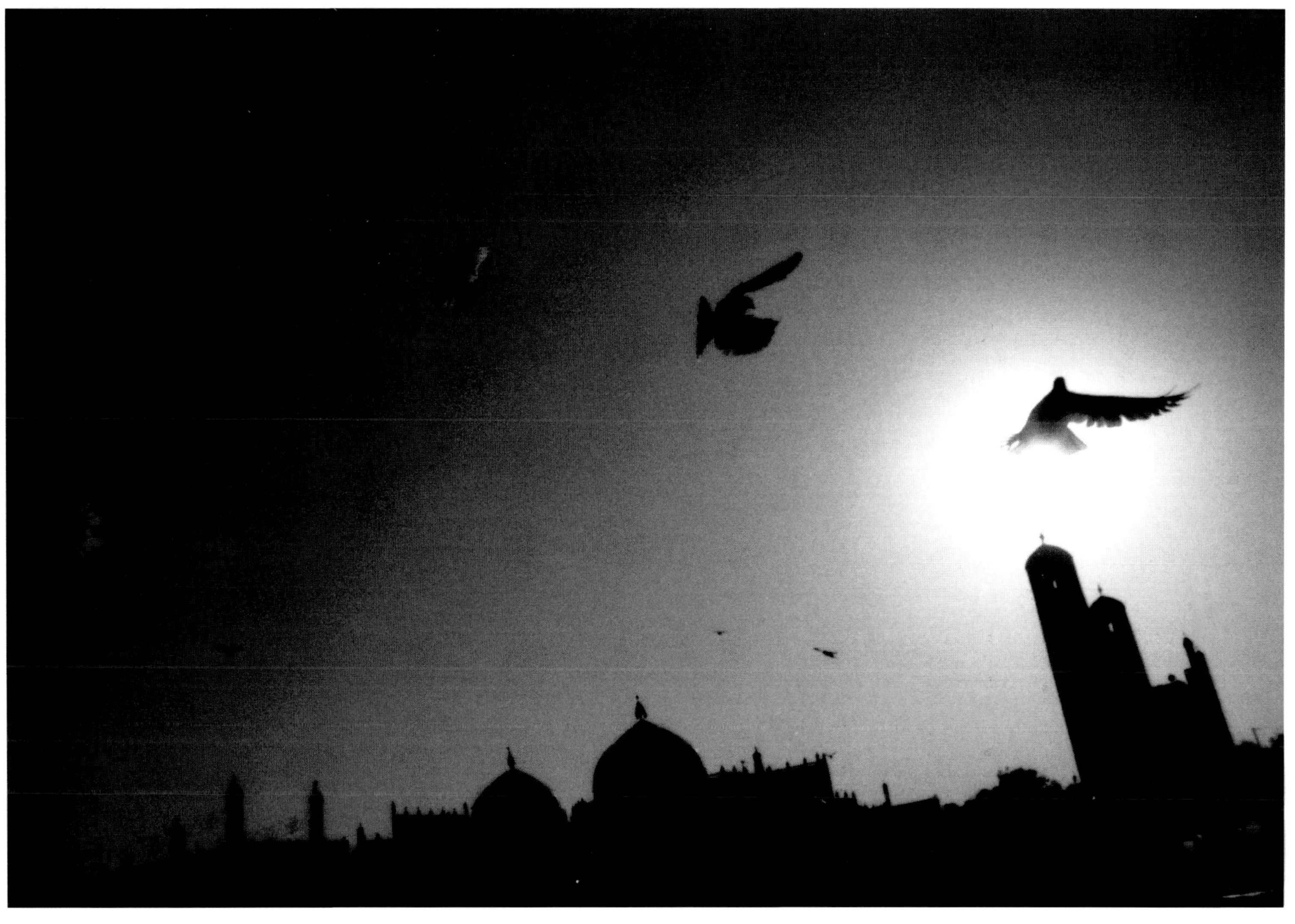

Some white doves circling above the Blue Mosque of Mazar-e Sharif in late evening.
The symbolism of the white doves adds a curious twist to the picture in this land under the lash of war.

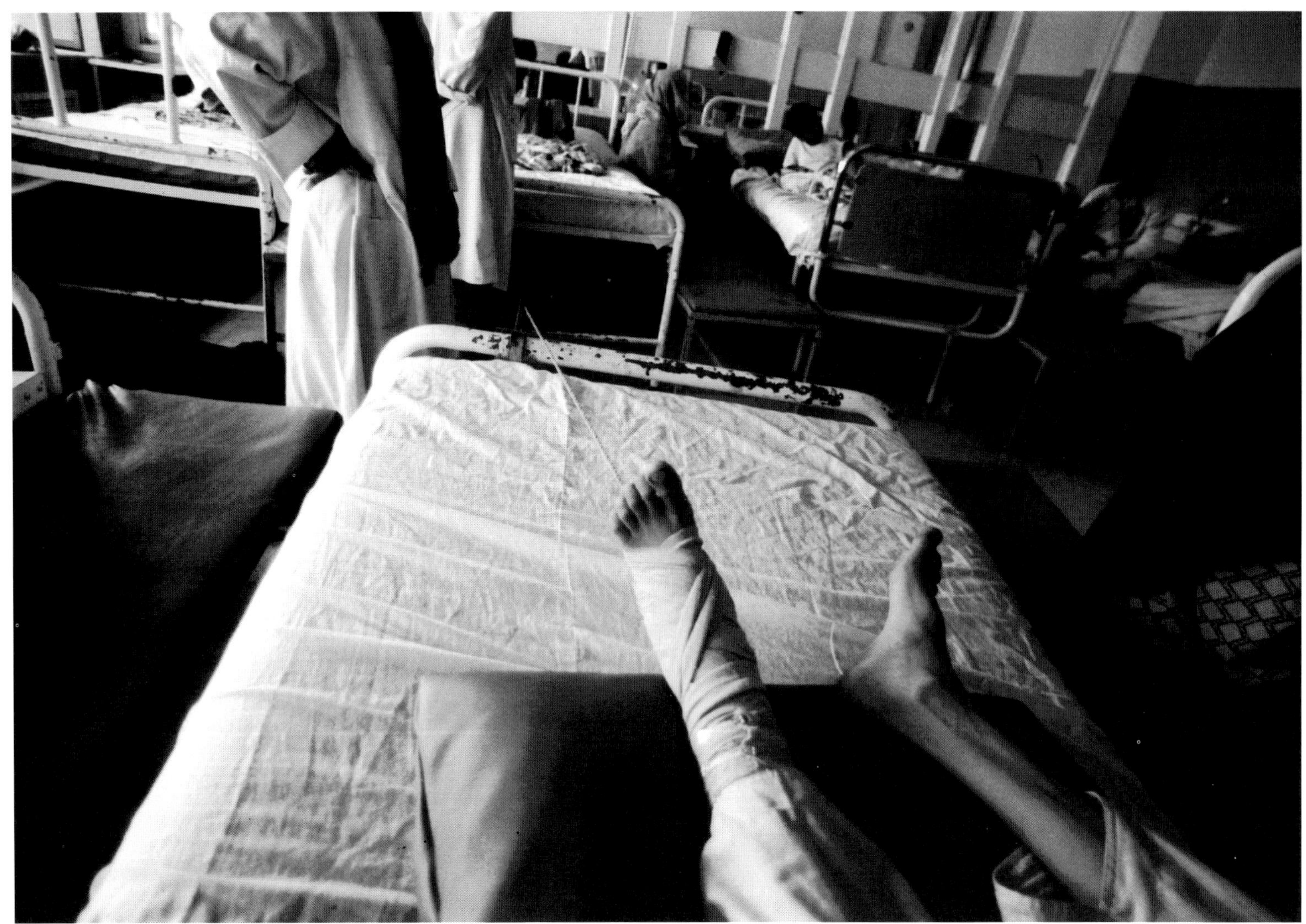

War Victims Hospital, run by the Emergency NGO.

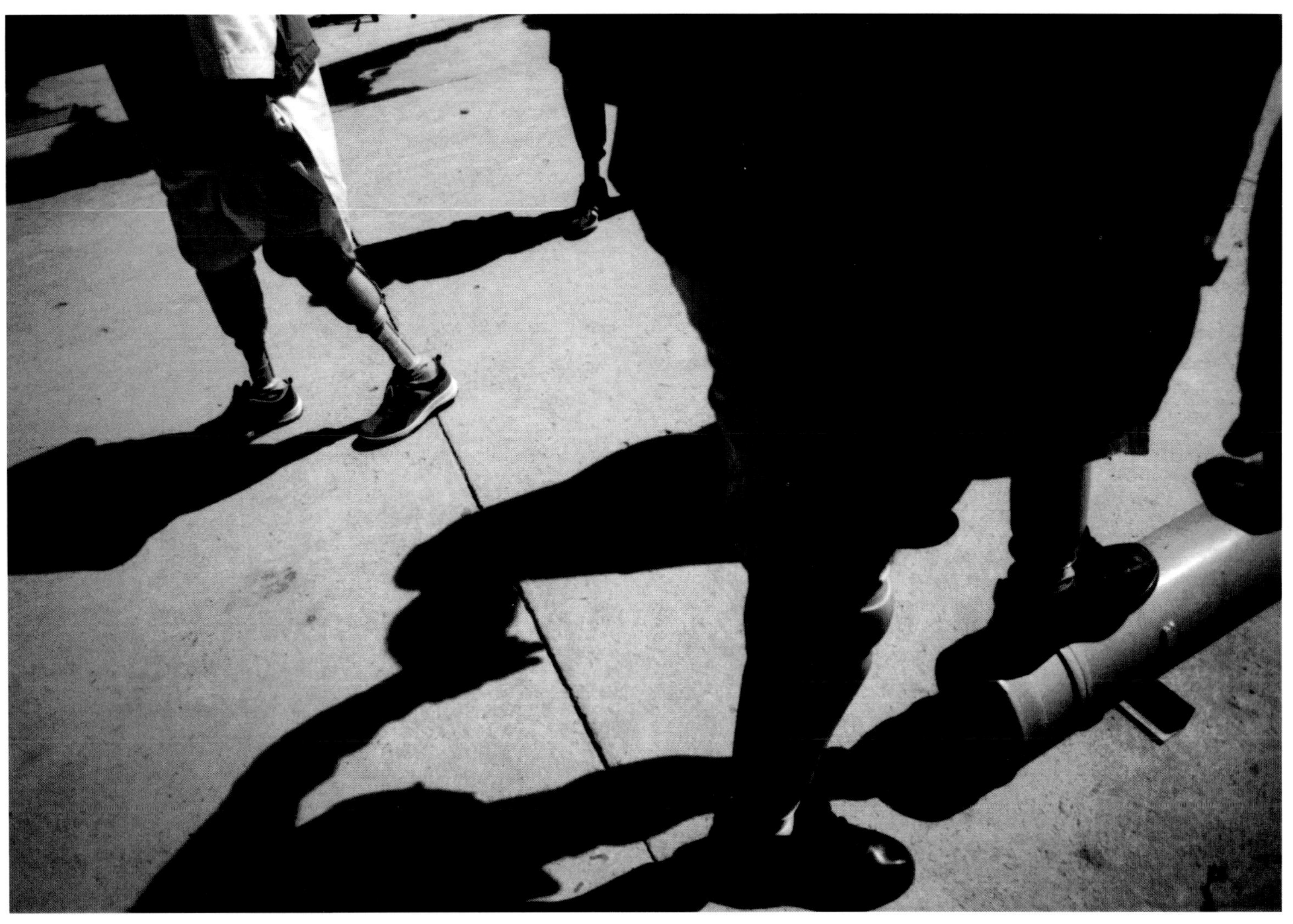

Some men who lost limbs to land-mines, doing physical rehabilitation exercises on artificial legs in the Orthopedic Center hospital.

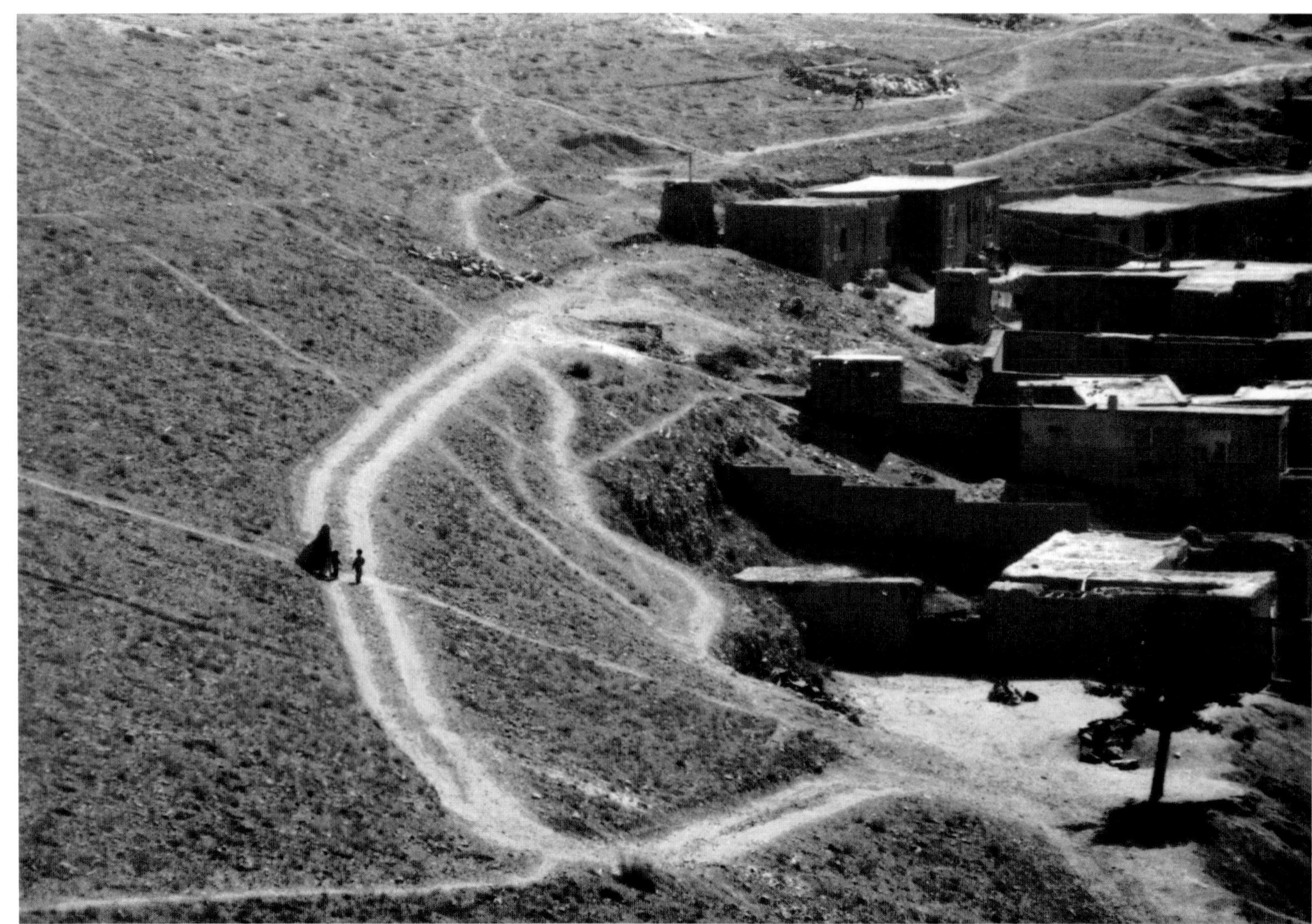

On the outskirts of Kabul.

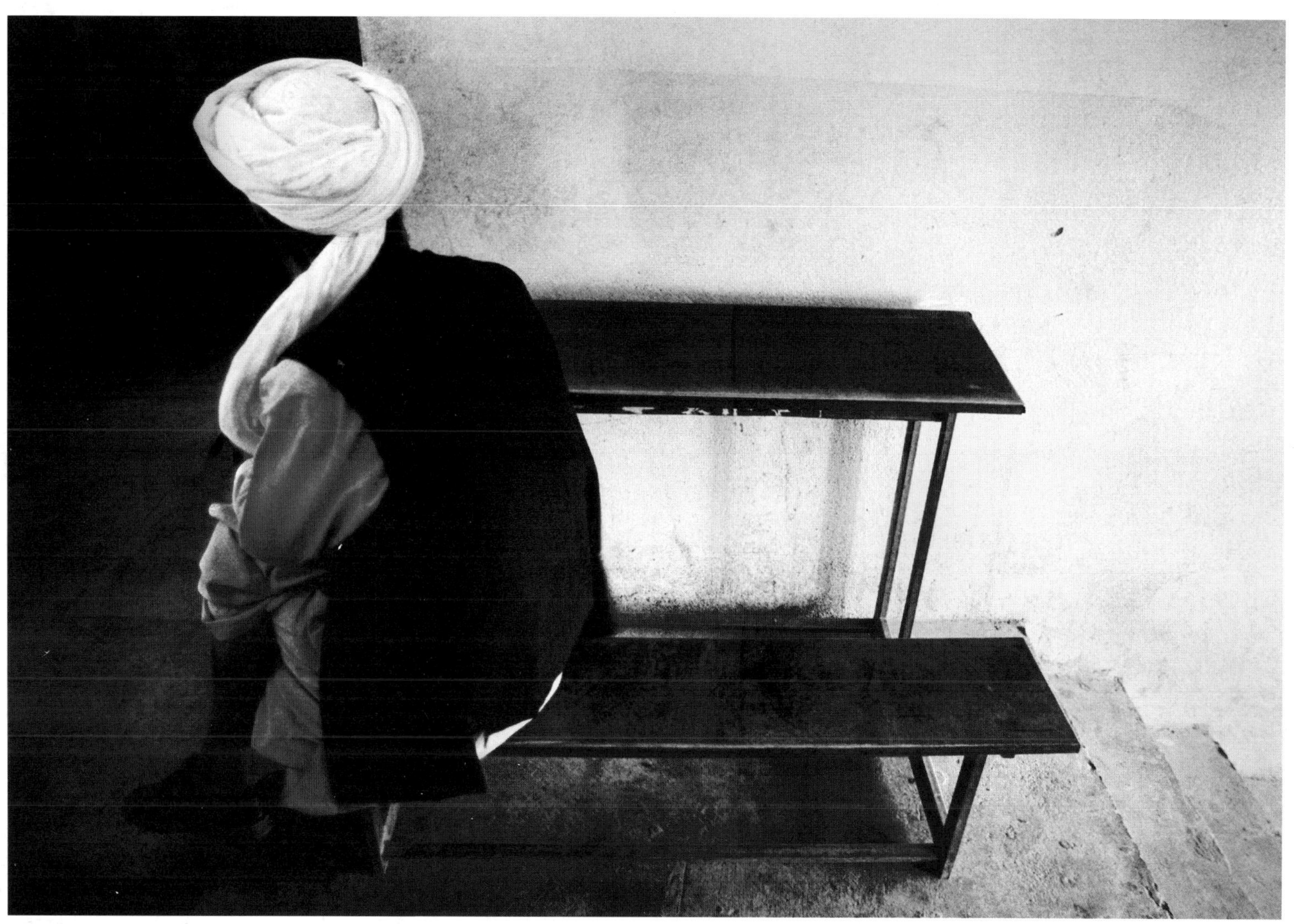

In a school in Kunduz.

CONQUISTADORES

Bernardo Atxaga

How strange is the game of associations. The first thing that comes to mind, on seeing the photos of Afghanistan taken by Alen Silva, is a passage from the memoirs of a Spanish soldier who, in the early XVIth century, penetrated the territory of modern day Florida, and discovered the truth. The Indians were not as many theologians had claimed; they were not creatures which, lacking a human soul, behaved like animals and could therefore be treated as such. This soldier, Alba Nuñez Cabeza de Vaca, one day saw from the undergrowth a native village: a mother cradling her baby; young girls larking and laughing; an old man teaching some youths. He also saw, above all, how they suffered in misfortune: "These people, more than any others in the world, love their children and treat them best; when a child dies his passing is mourned by parents, relatives and the whole community alike…" With the noble logic of one who is capable of overcoming prejudice, Cabeza de Vaca deduced that those men, though "Irrational and crude like beasts", that is to say uncivilised, were, however, fully human. They ought not to be mistreated or killed in the worst possible way, without compassion or fear of God, without even being conscious of wrongdoing; neither should they be enslaved.

On his return to Spain he published his impressions in the book "Naufragios y Comentarios", and it is to be supposed that some of his contemporaries would have agreed with him, while the great majority did not. The Indies were far away, and that great majority had little interest in the fate of unknown Indians. The theologians, who knew where their own interests lay – dictated by the Royal policy: a slave in the hand is worth two in the bush – would do everything in their power to foment and consolidate that indifference. Afghanistan is also very far away from us, and the numerous theologians – or equivalent – who write the books, daily create thousands of reasons for us to accept the present state of affairs. They work, all of them, in the immense surroundings of Washington, the place from which the chief representative of the economic powers speaks in the terms also used by the kings and emperors in the time of Cabeza de Vaca; terms also used, why not remember, when the bomber which carried the atomic bomb took off for Hiroshima and Nagasaki, and chaplain Downey addressed his crew with a passionate plea: "Almighty God, Father full of grace, we beg your mercy for those who are going to fly this night. Watch over and protect those who are going to venture into the darkness of your sky… Above all, Heavenly Father, bring peace to your world…" The language of the theologian again and again. And then Afghanistan. And later Iraq.

I look again at the photographs of Alen Silva. I see him there in Kabul, in the thick of it all, observing with his eyes and with his camera, witnessing. And in fact, they are like us. We see, thanks to him, the children without legs; the men who look directly at the camera and smile; the old man stretching out his arms to the child walking on the window sill, that he may not trip and fall. It becomes evident that our indifference is indifference towards a brother; towards the innumerable Abels who populate those distant lands, and not towards those Cains who, they tell us, hide among them. We might repeat, with this in mind, the words of Cabeza de Vaca, on realising how some Christians treated the Indians: "where we can see how deceptive are the thoughts of men, how we went in search of their freedom and, when we thought we had achieved it, the opposite occurred; they had agreed to go in peace and safety".

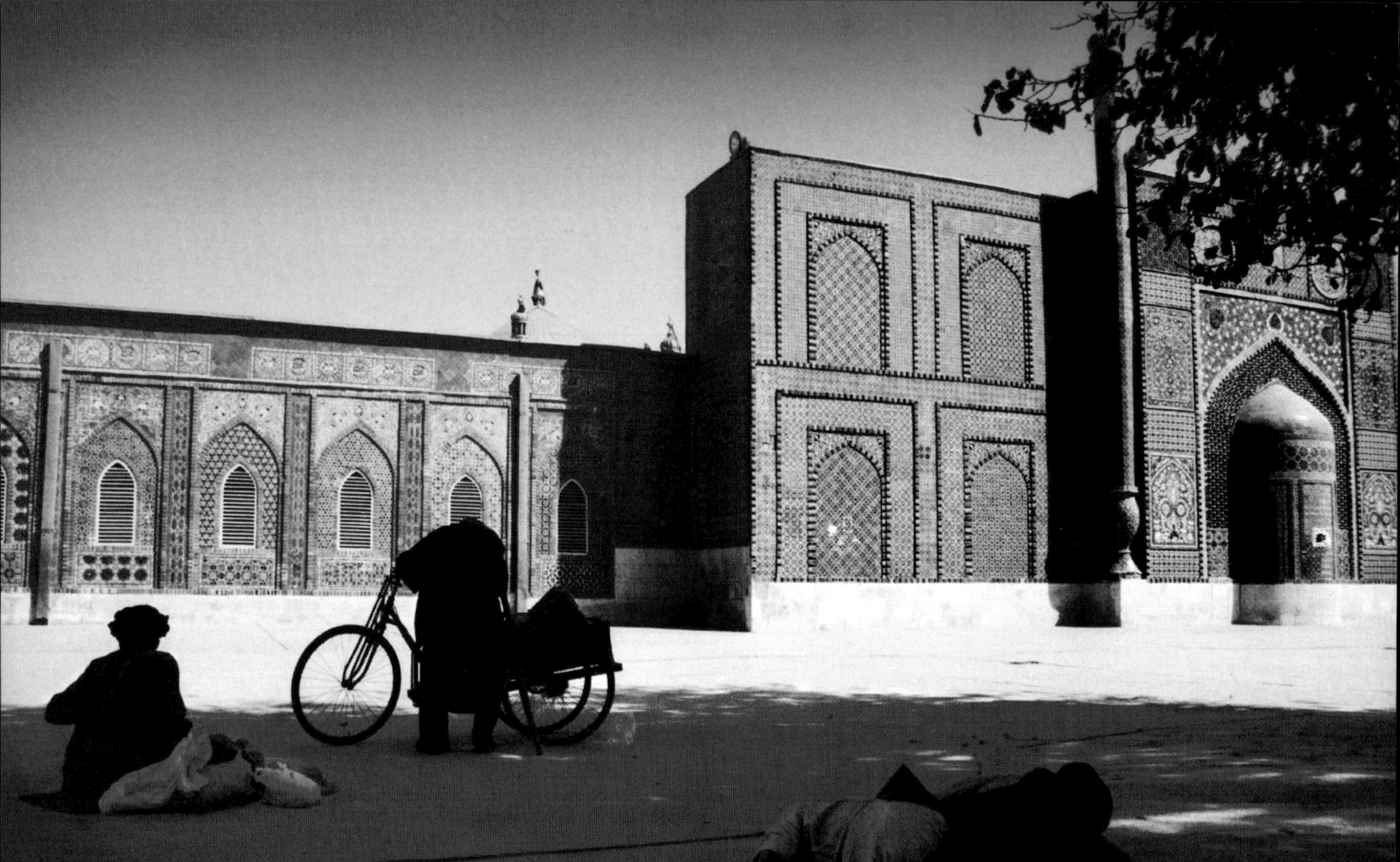

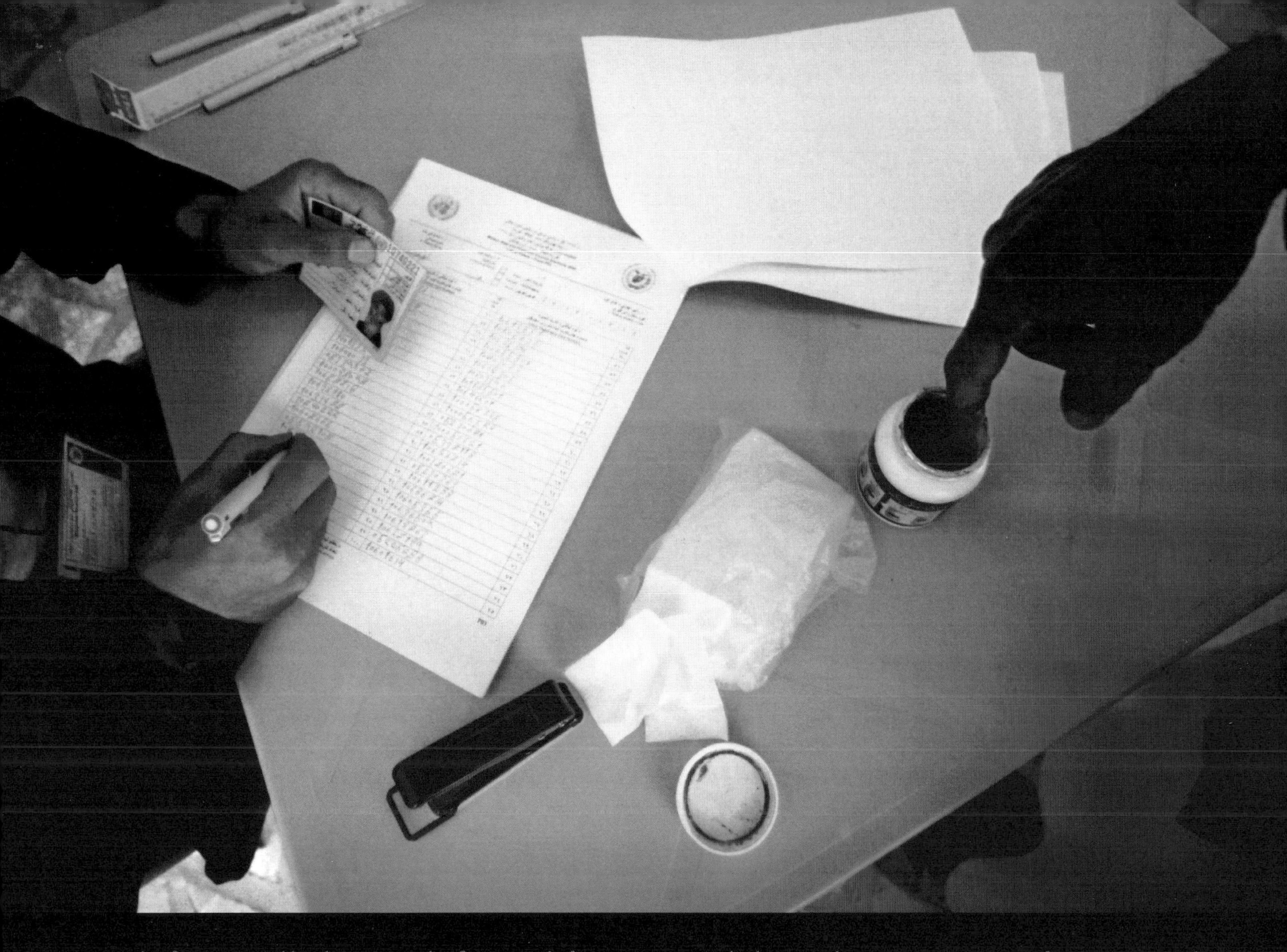

A man puts his finger in an inkbottle to register his fingerprint before voting. A special ink was used to try to prevent anyone from voting more than twice, as had happened in the previous election. The discoloration from the ink does not disappear for three or four days.

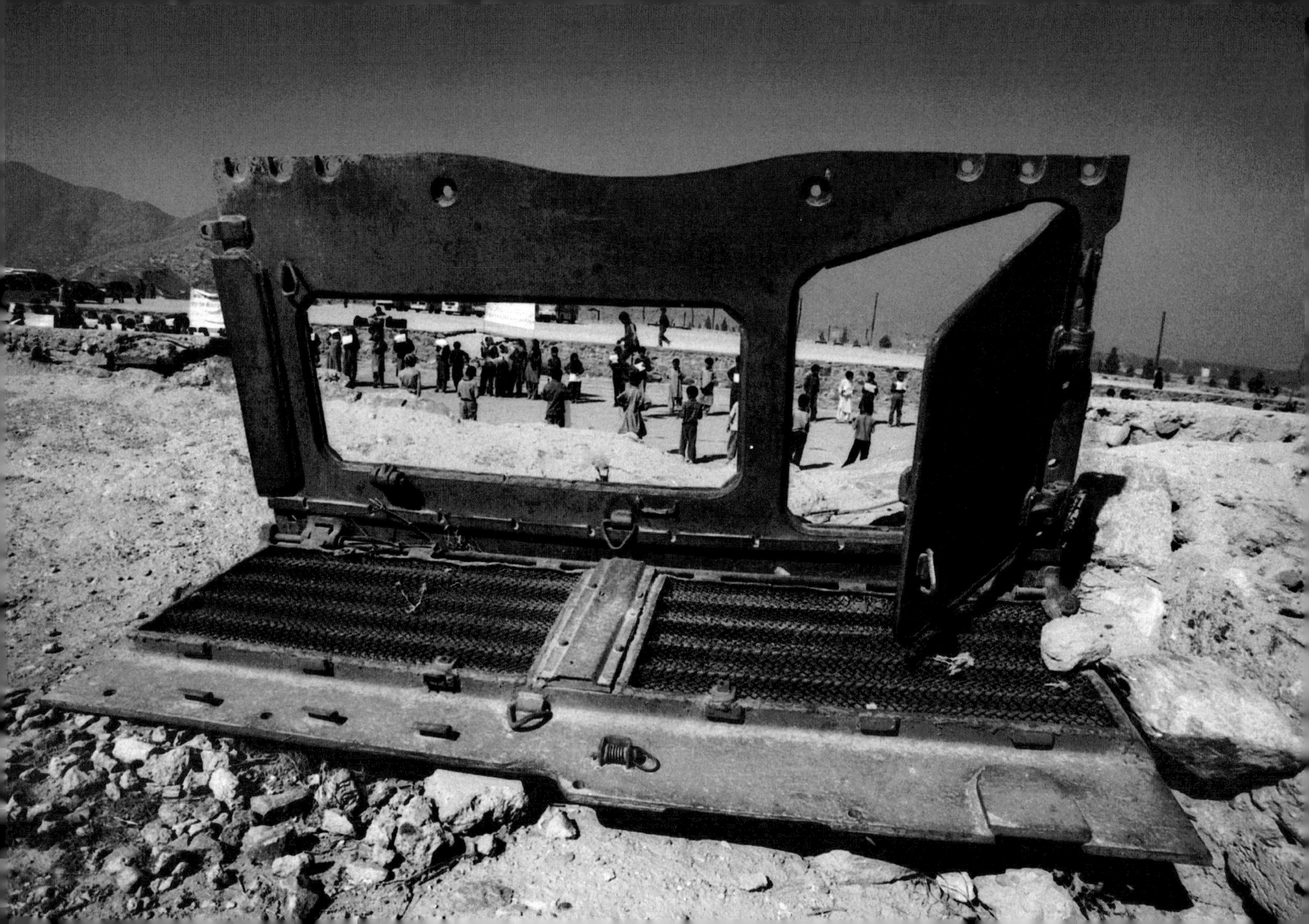

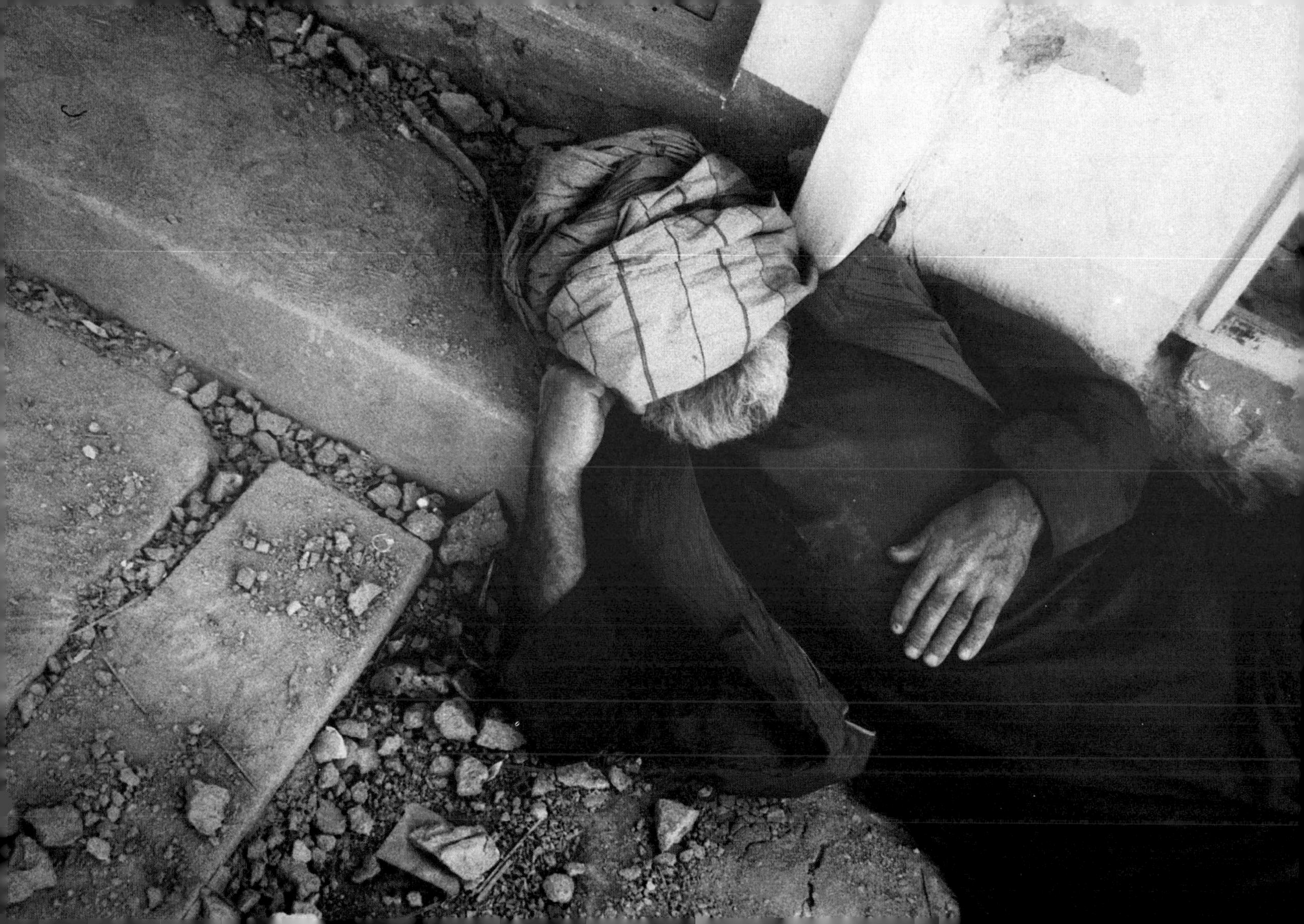

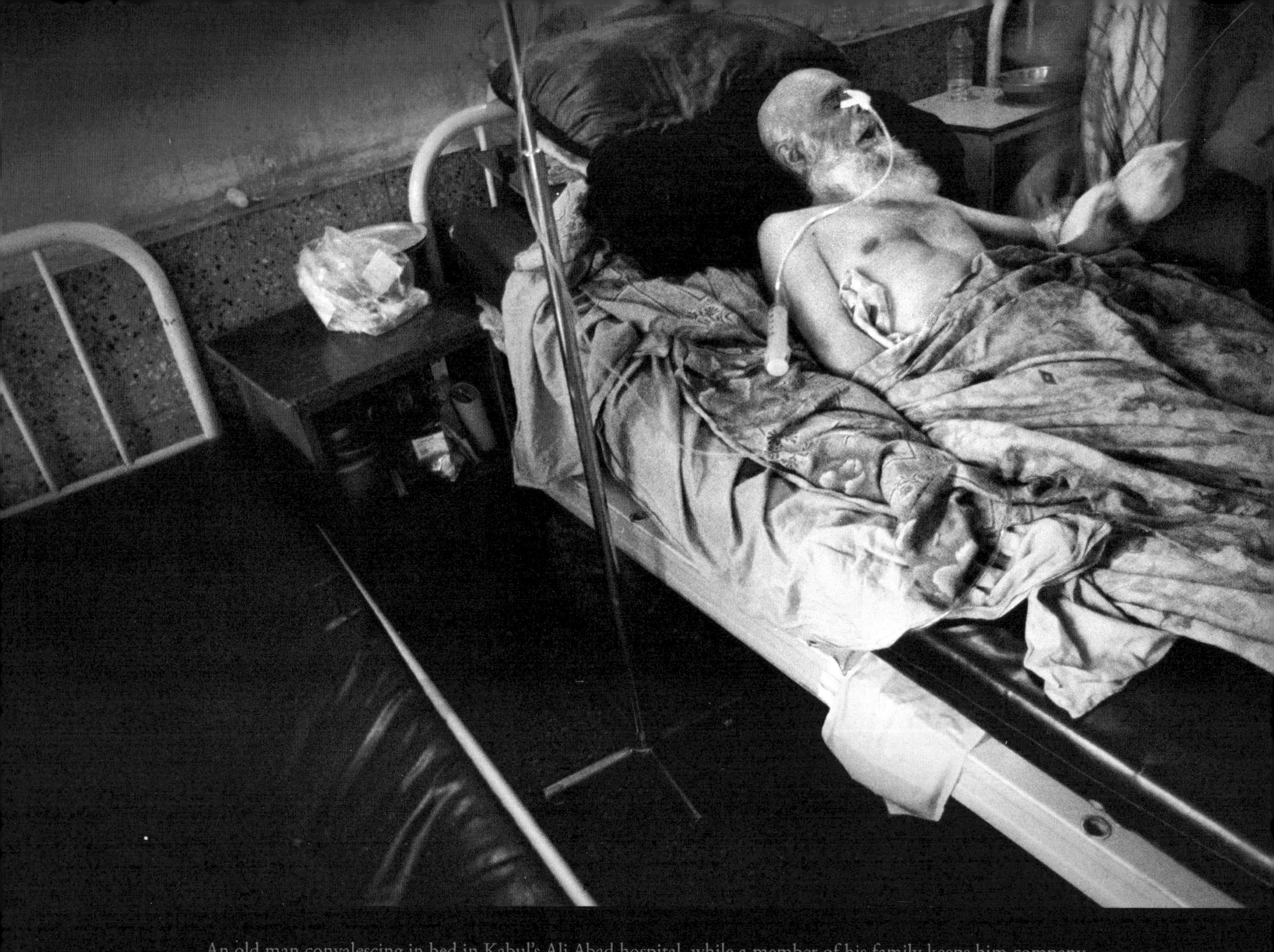

An old man convalescing in bed in Kabul's Ali Abad hospital, while a member of his family keeps him company. With limited means, the hospital workers do what they can to meet the needs of the local people. Yet the unluckiest are those who have no chance of being cared for, those who live in the street.

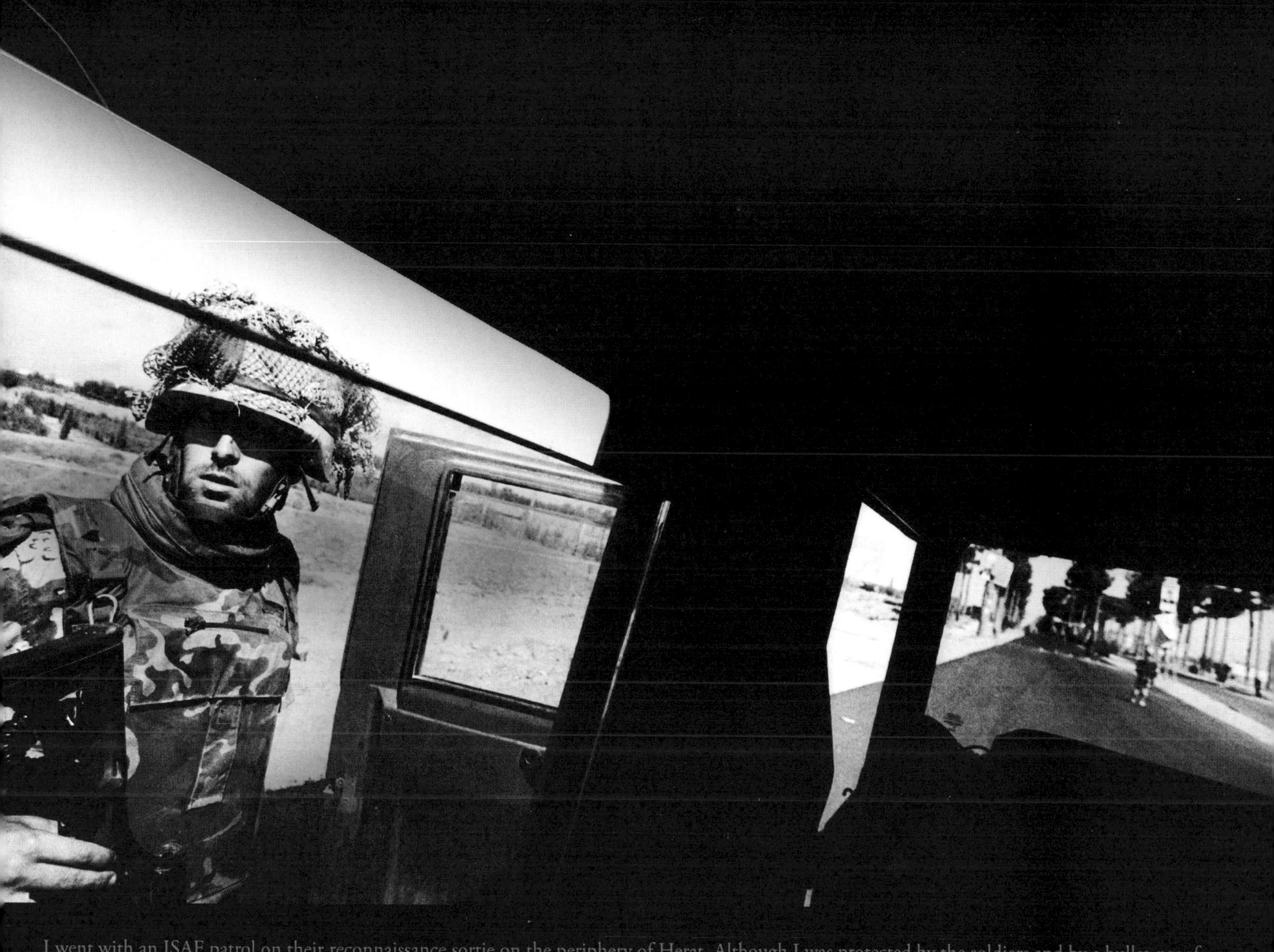

I went with an ISAF patrol on their reconnaissance sortie on the periphery of Herat. Although I was protected by the soldiers and by a bullet-proof vest, ironically this was one of the few times I didn't feel safe in Afghanistan.

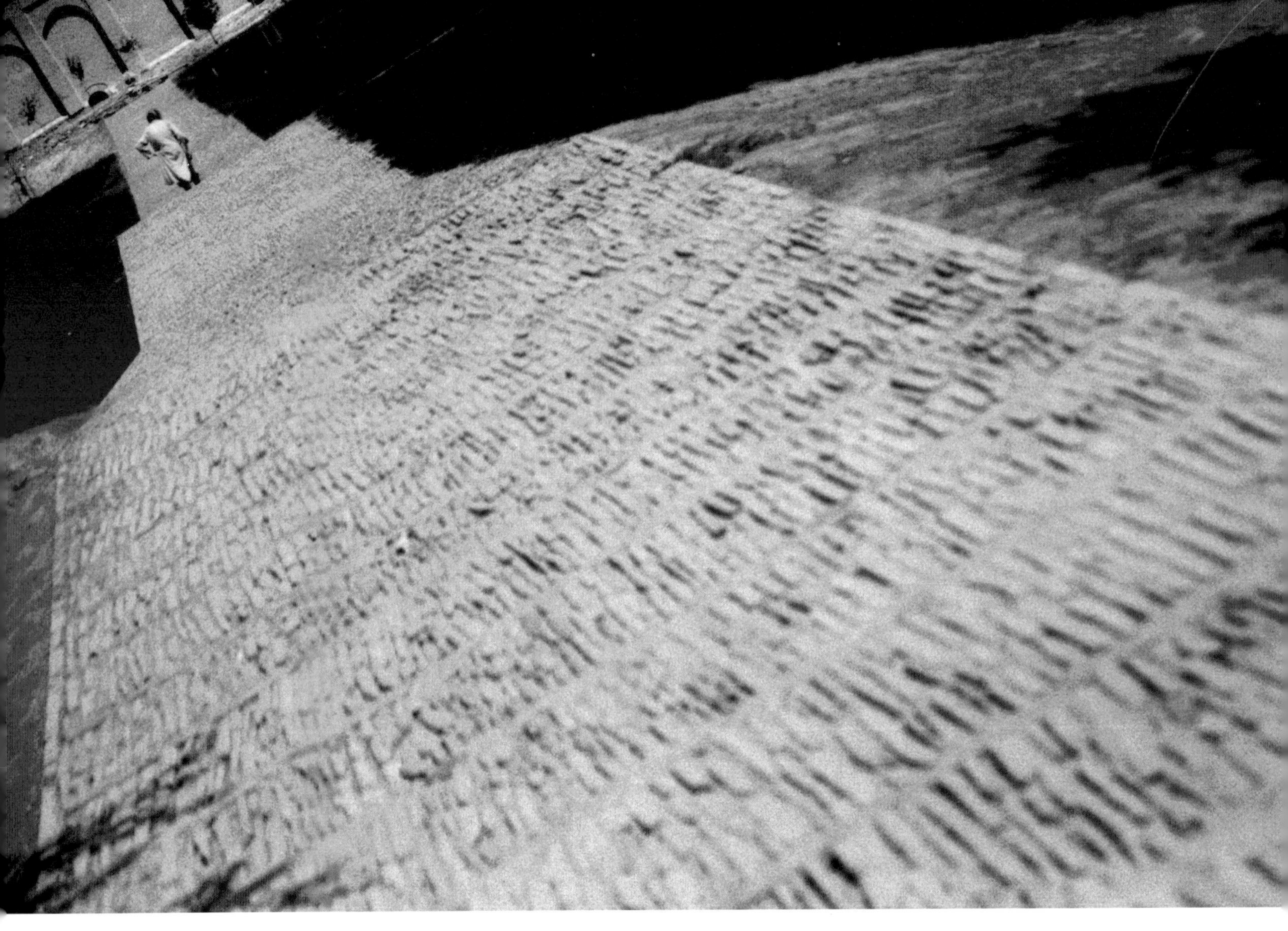

The road to peace.

WHERE AM I STANDING

Bahman Ghobadi

Worn out feet
Waiting to leave
A wait as vast as earthly roads
At last
Take you to the sky

Where is the end of this destiny?
A peace of bread in a bowl
And a place to rest

***

I can remember it well
There were fireworks
And a dance of evasive balloons
In my motherland's blue sky
And now
This monster of darkness
Who burns my house,
Which part of my land does he want to swallow?

***

No horizon to my window
No sky to my roof
No pillar to my home
Where am I standing on earth?

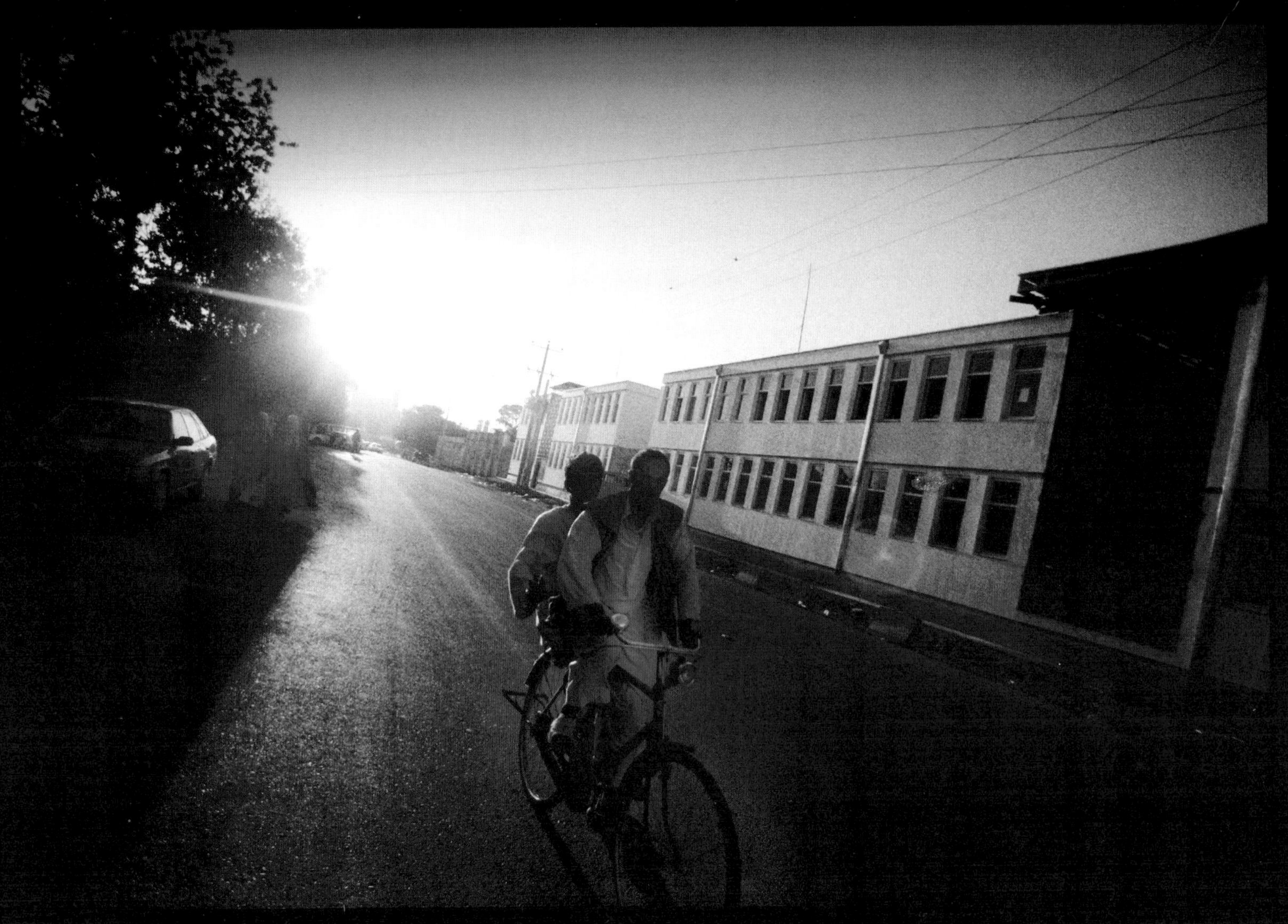

Two men approach on a bicycle at dusk in a street of Mazar-e Sharif, while two women in burkas pass on the other side. At the end of the street is the silhouette of the Persian-style blue mosque, the "Noble Shrine" that gives the city its name.

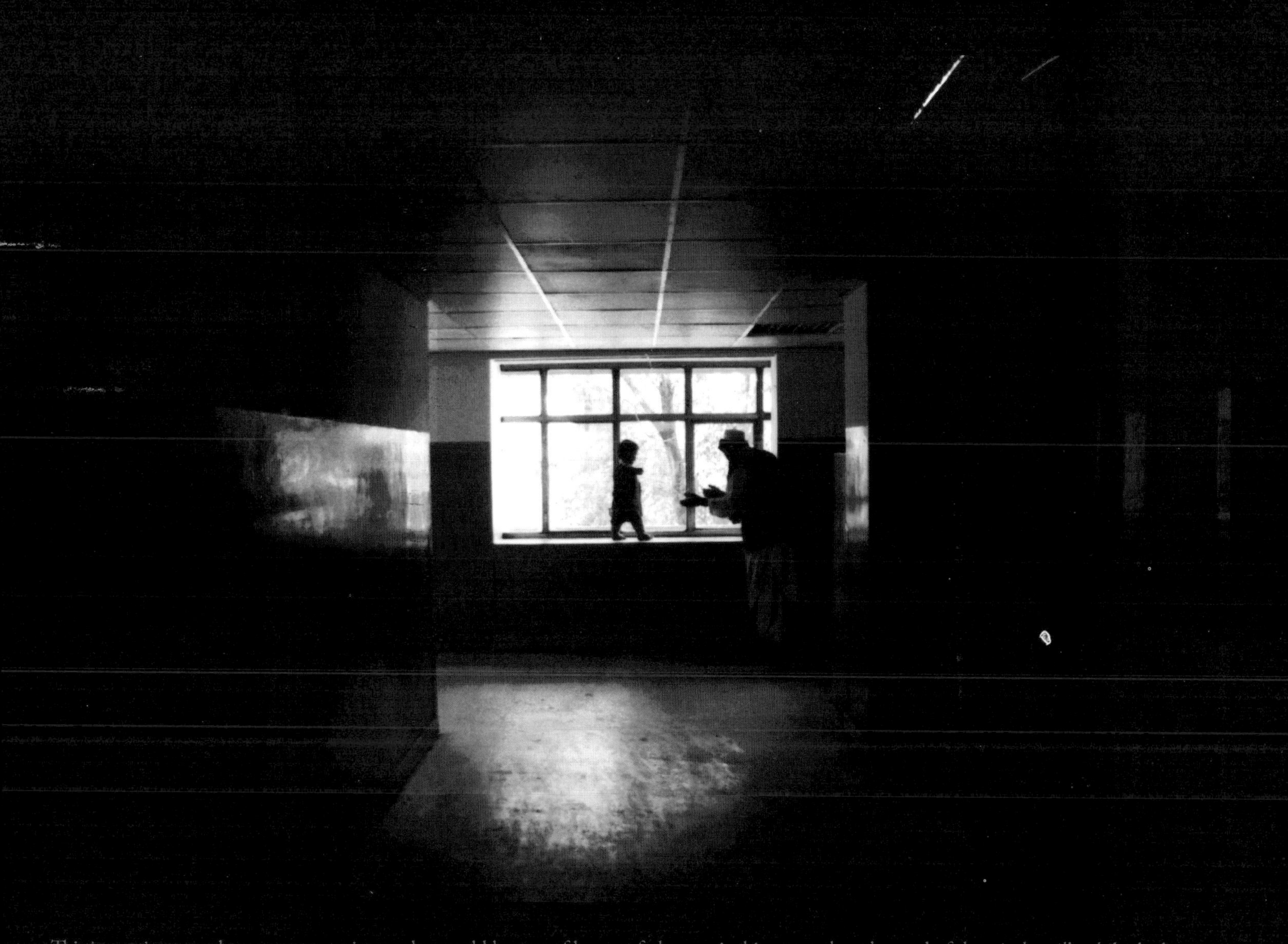

This image impressed me at once, an image that could be one of hope: a father awaits his son at the other end of the windowsill, while the boy is learning to make his first steps. I had the feeling this image could be emblematic of Afghanistan itself.

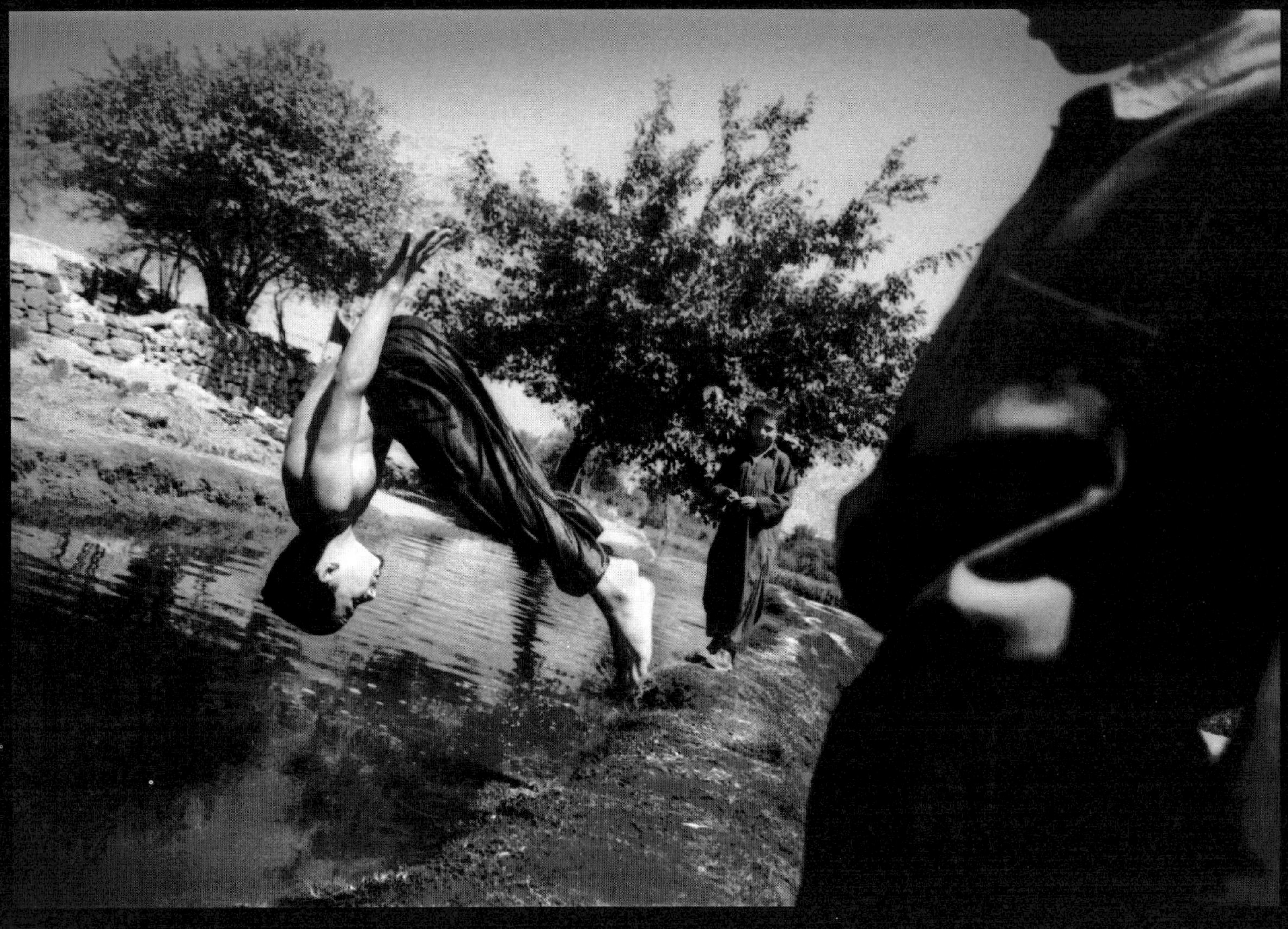

Near Kunduz we made a stop at the request of the passengers in order to buy fruit at some stands along the road. A few meters away some boys were playing in an irrigation ditch, enjoying the beautiful weather of the September days.

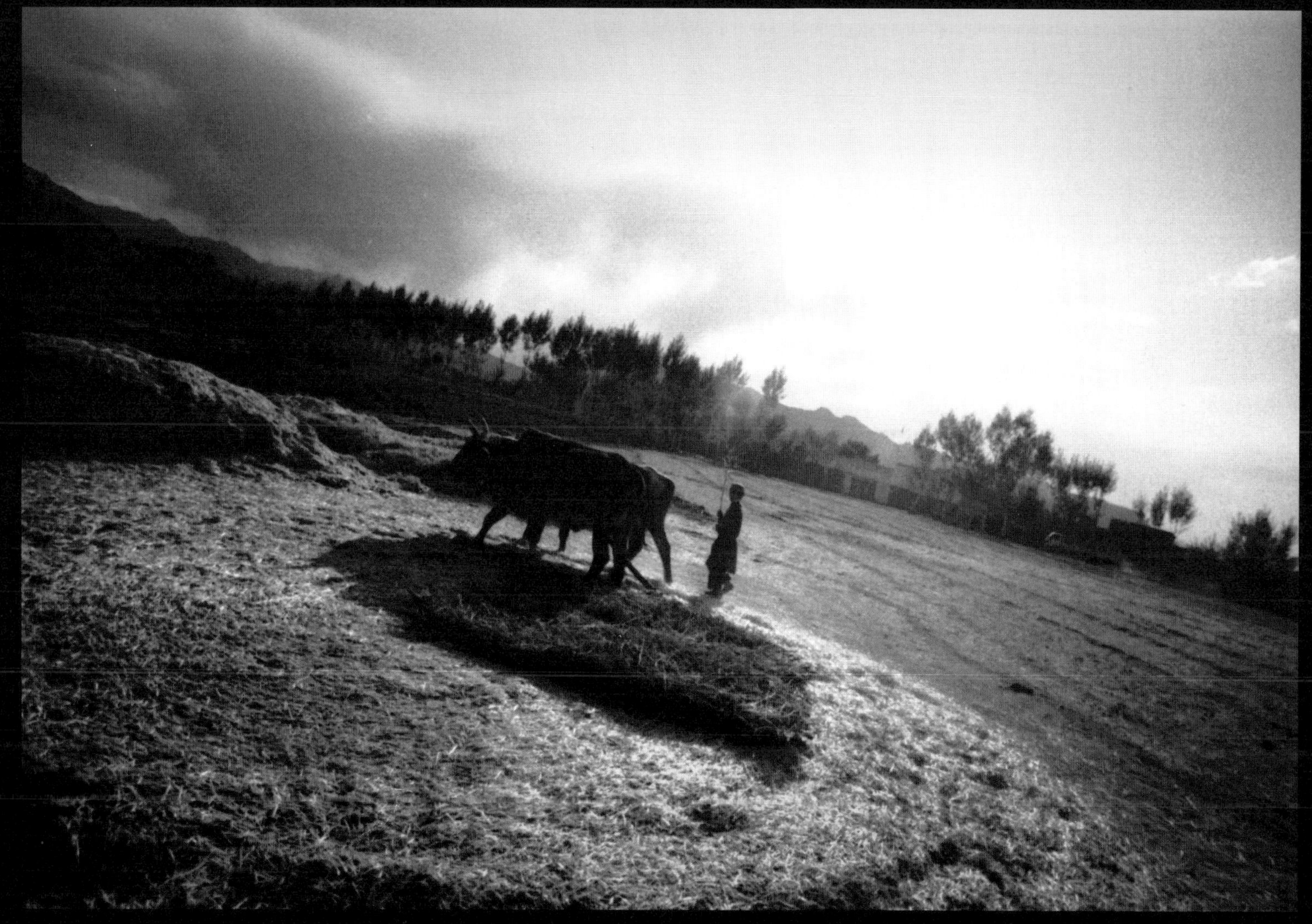

The end of the workday nears for this boy who is cultivating the fields with two oxen.
Out of necessity many children cannot go to school, and have to start working at a very early age instead. The illiteracy rate in the country is 80%.

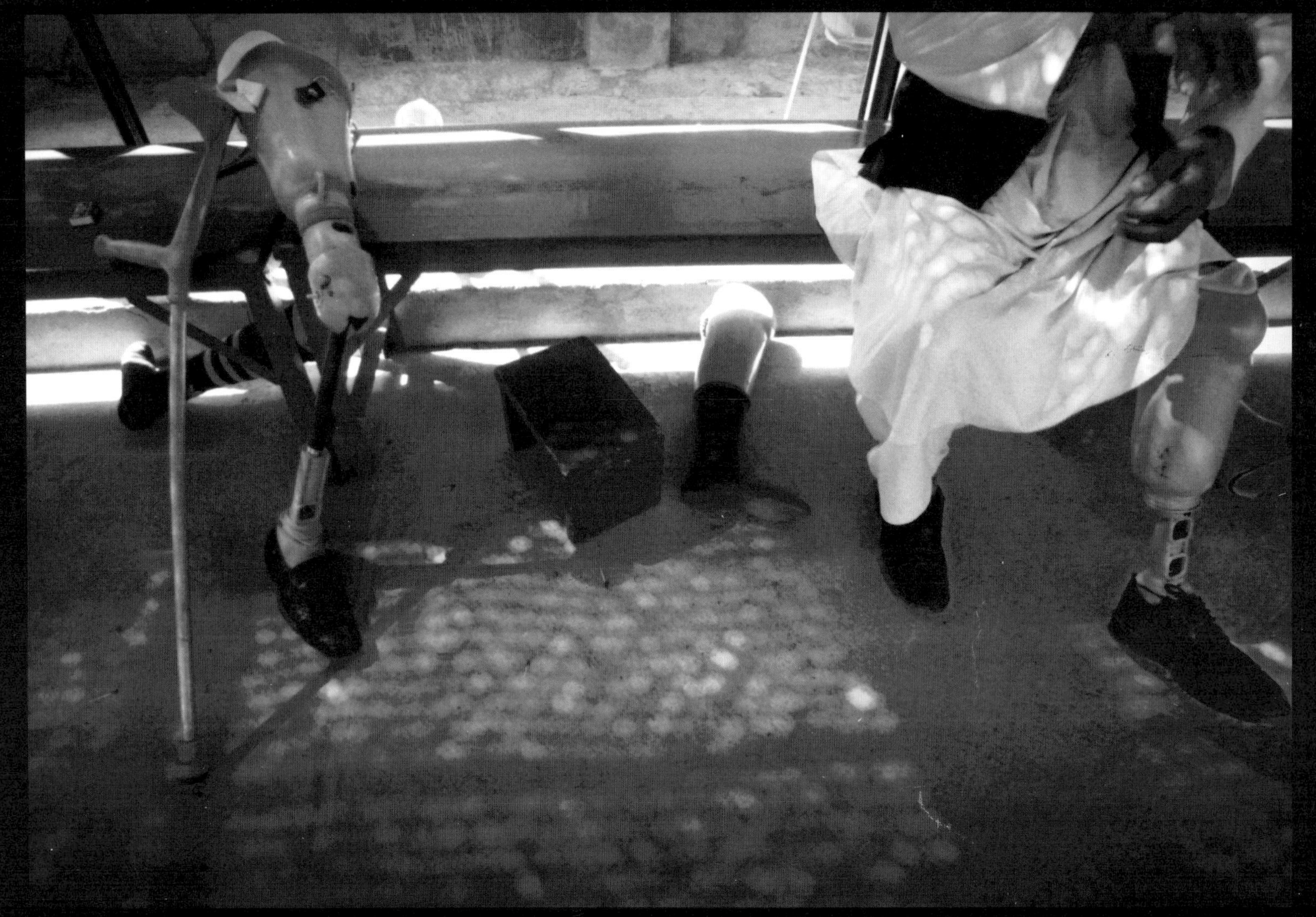

The Orthopedic Center of Kabul.

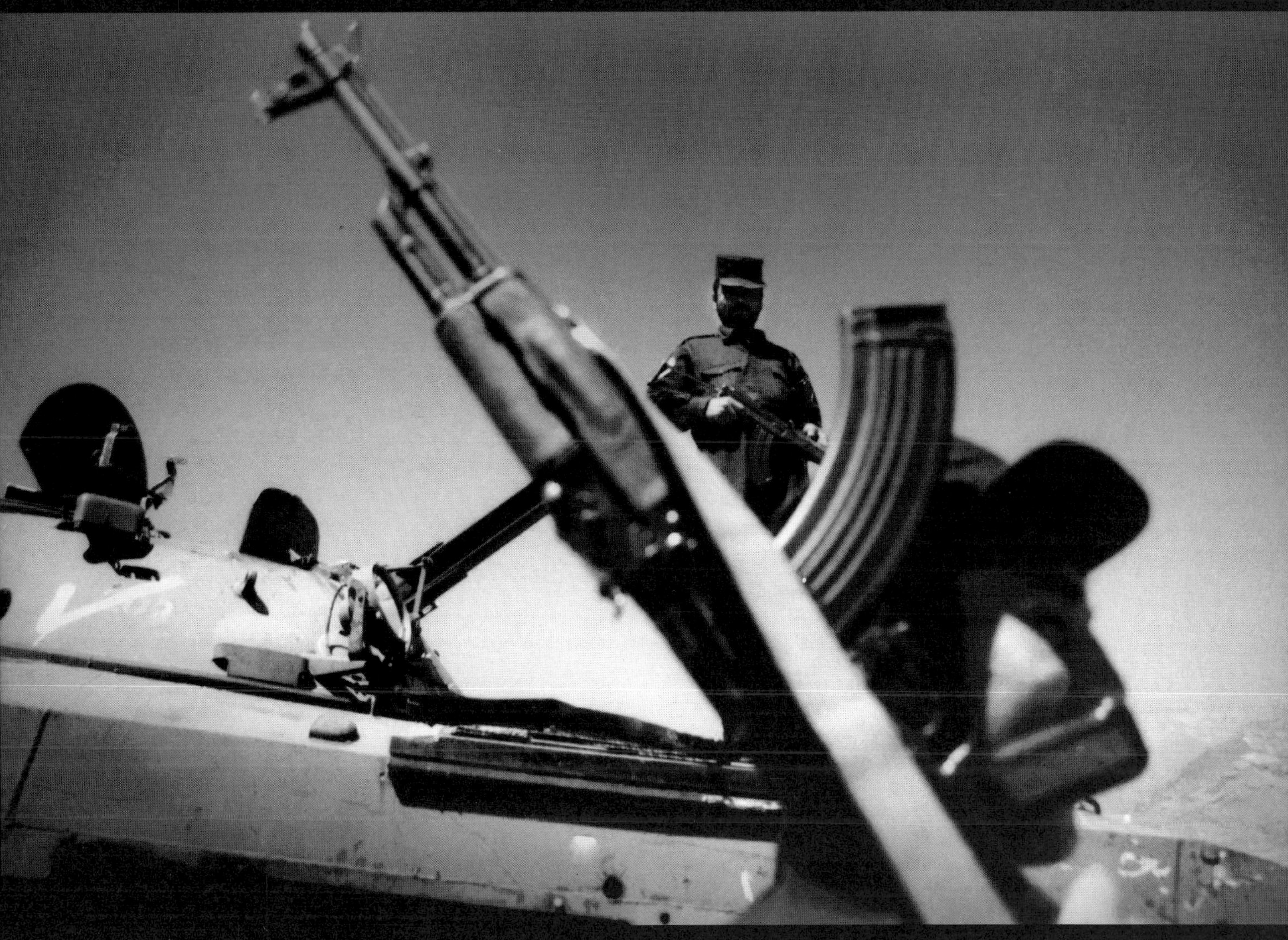

Two Afghan soldiers guarding a security post near Panjshir, where they told me proudly that they are going to bring peace to Afghanistan.

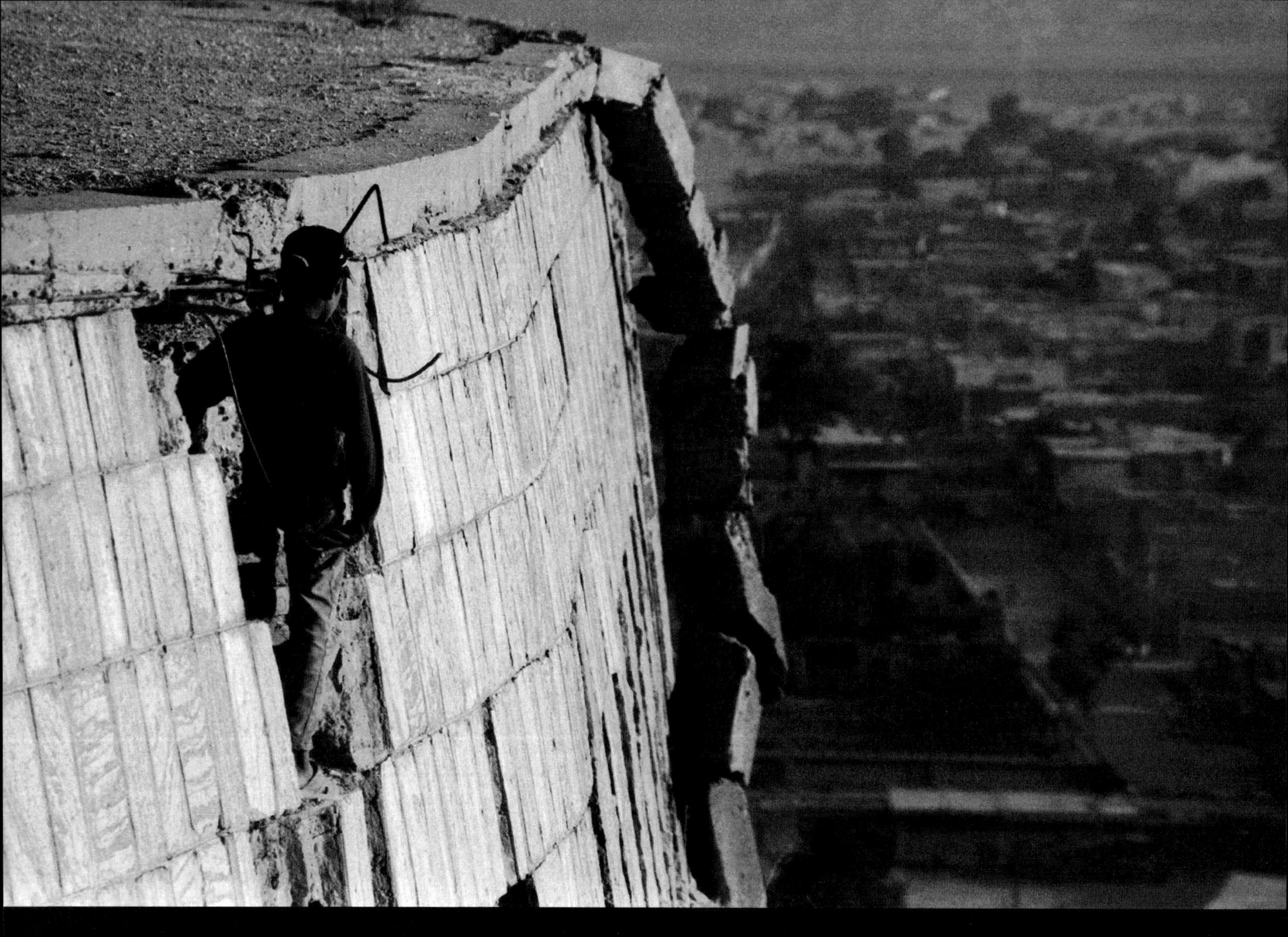

A view of Kabul from one of the mountains surrounding it.
In the 18th century, Kabul was considered to be one the most beautiful and civilized cities of the world.

THE LAND BECOME A SHADOW OF ITSELF

Michael Ratner

Silva's Afghanistan photographs were shot in what is known as black and white; but you will see almost no white. Blacks, shades of gray and deep blacks dominate as do black shadows—shadows of people. The Afghans you do see are rarely shown in their entirety; sometimes you see only the feet, or a hand or part of a profile or half of a face or a blurred face or an out-of-focus arm. There are many photographs of empty or desolate spaces where the Afghans seem almost an afterthought.

This is not because the photographer thinks the Afghans are unimportant, but because those who make war on and occupy Afghanistan have treated the lives of the Afghans as dispensable.

There is some white in a few photographs, but it is not a white of purity or hope. It is the white of sheets on a hospital bed, of bandages, or of a surgeon washing in a white sink; it is the white of injury and death. A few photographs have a white of hope, and when you come upon them, you are surprised. Scores of white doves bring to mind images of peace, but among the doves and almost unnoticed sits an Afghan on his haunches in what could easily be an image of despair. Another photograph shows white balloons in the air at a children's festival, but there are no children and no joy.

The feeling you have is that Afghanistan has become a place of darkness, desolation and shadows; its people traverse a country that has been destroyed.

We know so little about Afghanistan in the United States, even those of us who try to keep up with the news. We almost never see photographs. That is why Silva's photographs are so important. To most Americans Afghanistan was the good war; Iraq was the bad war, the mistake. But most Americans have it wrong. I do not know of a good war. Even if you accept that some wars are justified, this one was not. I and a few others opposed the war which began in October 2001, shortly after 9/11. (There was, of course, an earlier war with the Soviet Union.) We did not think the American war was justified. Afghanistan had not attacked the United States; nor had the United Nations given the authority to the United States to make war. The U.S. refused to negotiate and insisted on an imperial display of power. Now look, as these photographs demonstrate, at what the United States has wrought. The war is called Operation Enduring Freedom; it should be called Operation Enduring War—for this war is a war of killing and maiming without end.

The war in Afghanistan is a central part and was the first step of what the United States calls its "global war on terror." And a disastrous step it has been. Afghanistan has been destroyed, and now the war has carried over and destabilized Pakistan. Today, Afghanistan is a country ruled by warlords. It is again the major supplier of poppies for opium—and how many has that killed? The Taliban had banned their

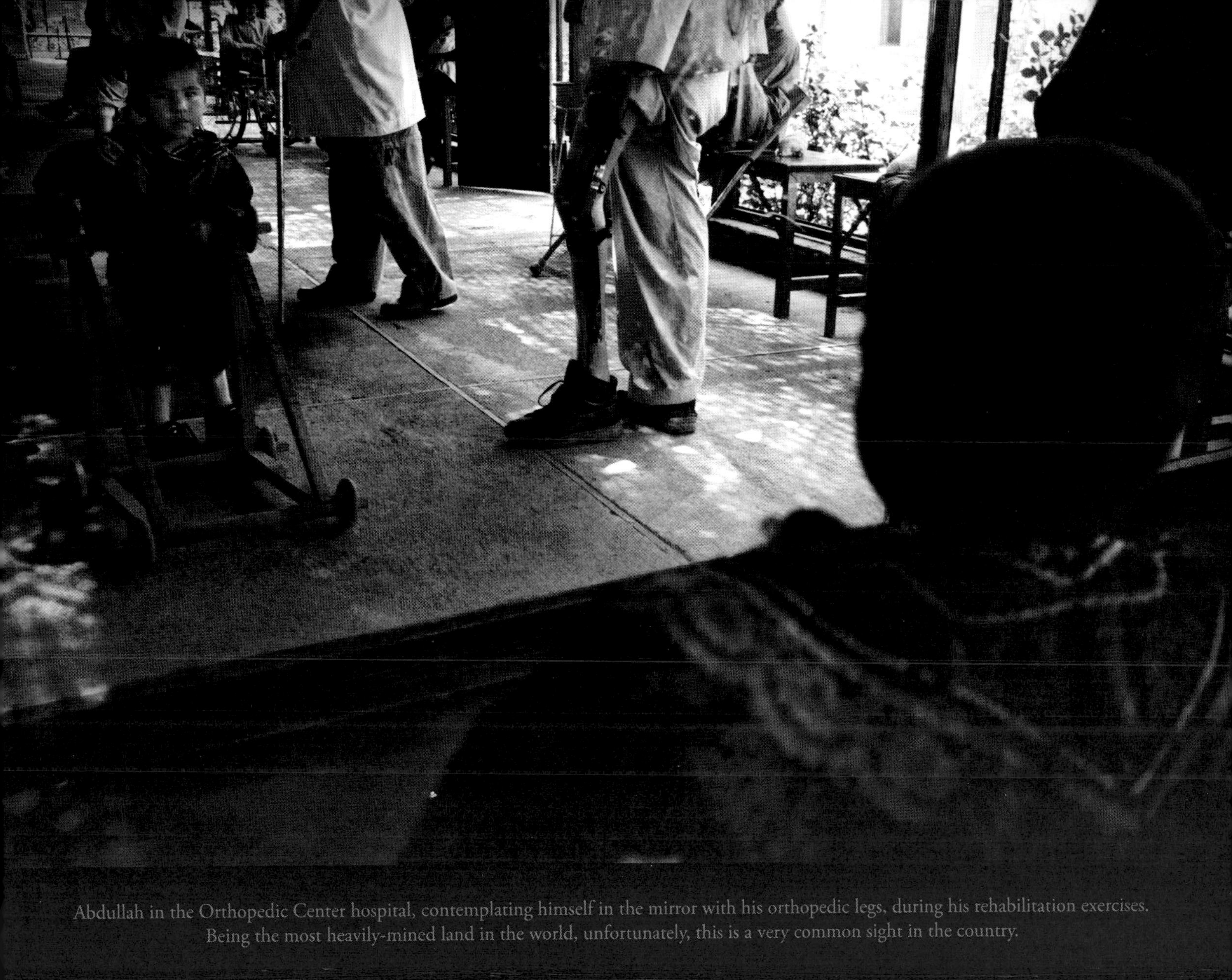

Abdullah in the Orthopedic Center hospital, contemplating himself in the mirror with his orthopedic legs, during his rehabilitation exercises. Being the most heavily-mined land in the world, unfortunately, this is a very common sight in the country.

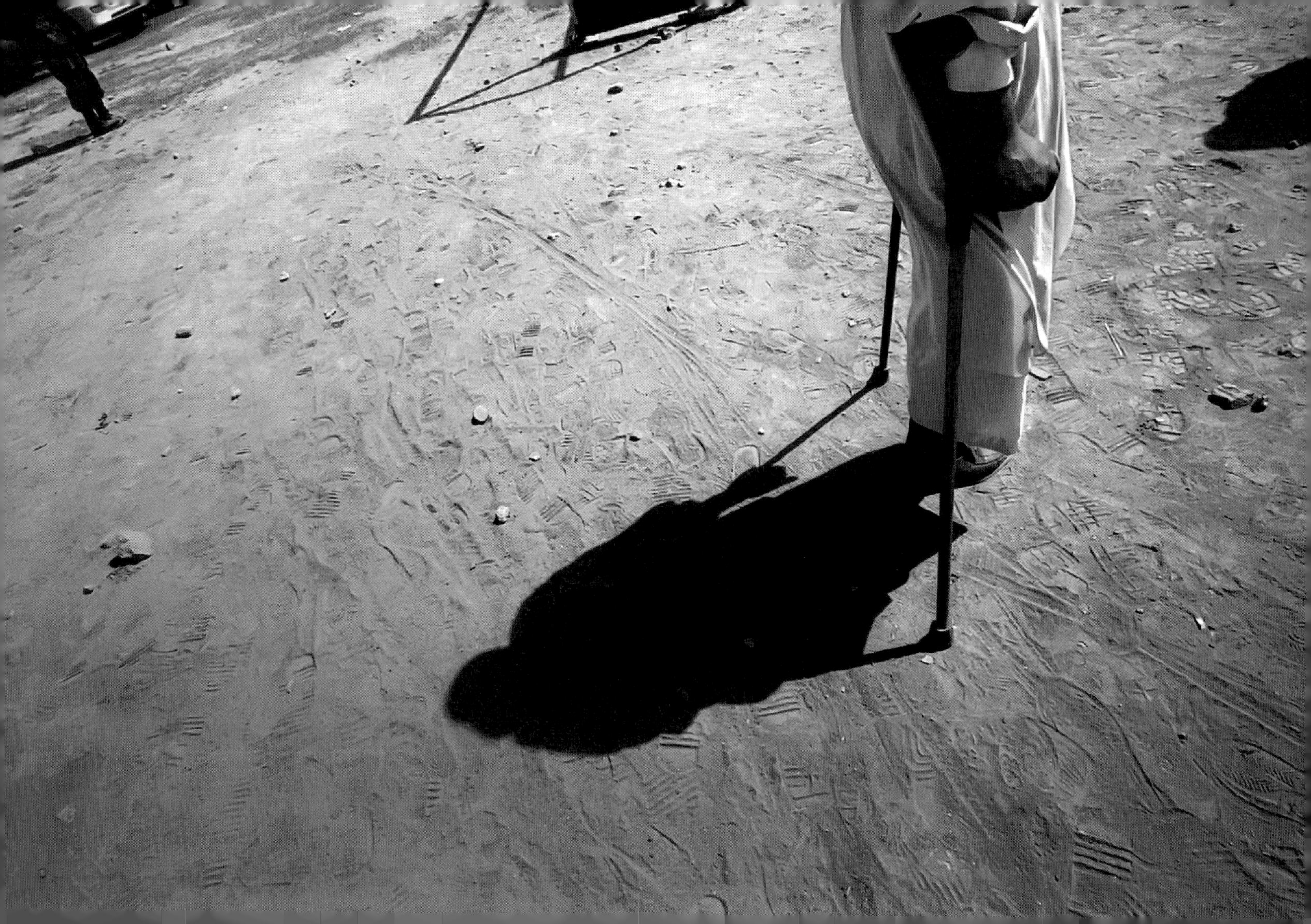

Next page
Thousands of men come to the stadium to attend a sporting event. It was here in the football stadium that the Taliban executed those who had violated the sharia law, by hanging, shooting or stoning.

planting. The Bush administration called Afghanistan a failed state, and claimed it did not need to apply the Geneva Conventions and its humane protections to the Taliban or al Qaeda, or anyone else kidnapped or captured in the country. Thus the Bush administration claimed that nothing protected those detained from being tortured, and torture was carried out systematically in Bagram—where it still continues.

That torture was exported, exported to Abu Ghraib and to Guantánamo. Many of those sent to Guantánamo were snatched from Afghanistan, and sent to other countries for torture or taken to secret CIA torture sites.

Sadly, these photographs show Afghanistan as it is today and as it will be tomorrow and as it will be for a very long time. Perhaps Silva's photos will awaken in all of us an outrage to end this nightmare.

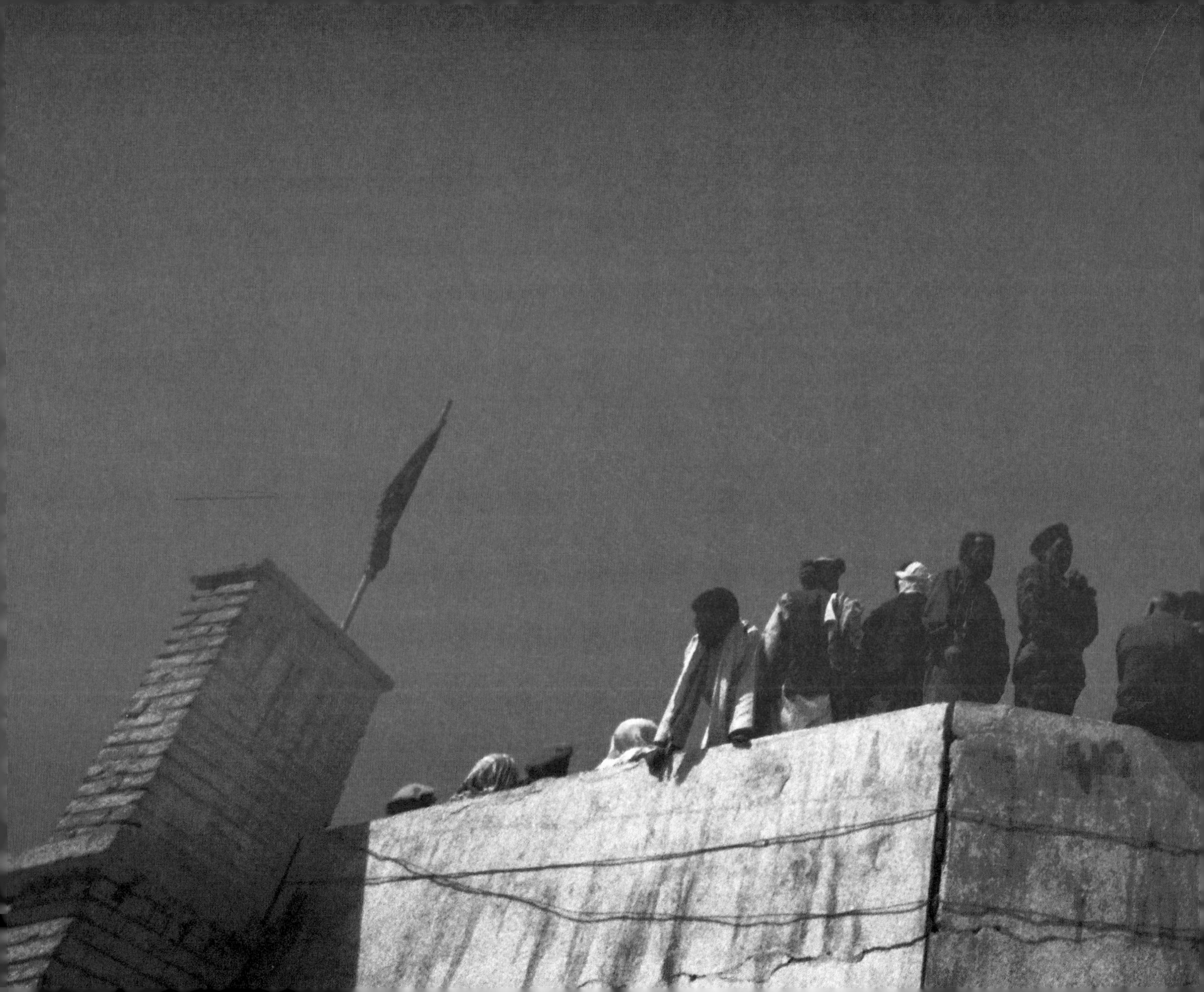

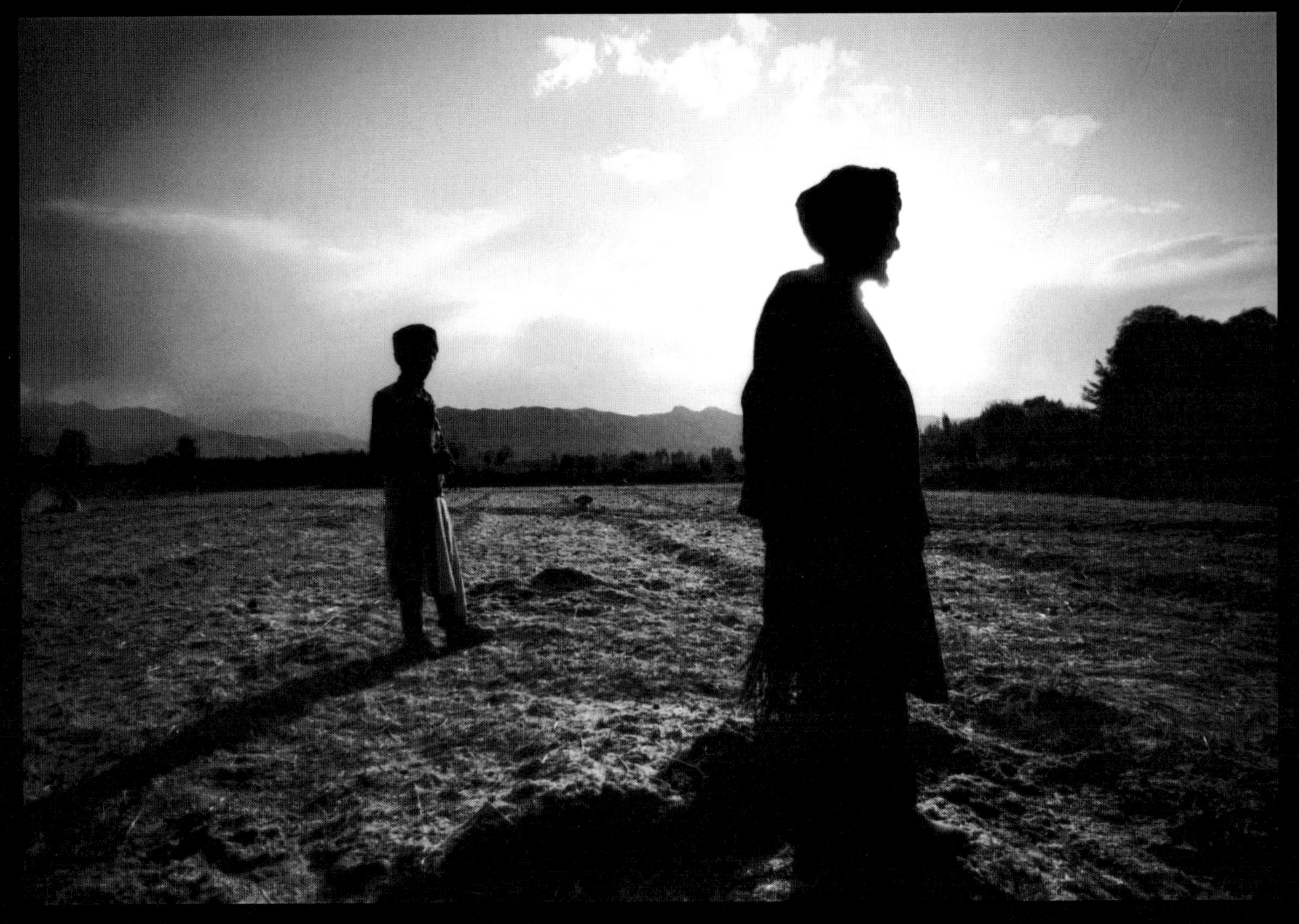

Dusk brings an end for the day to work in the fields in a Hazarajat province.
The next morning they will rise at 6:00 to continue with the tasks of working the land.

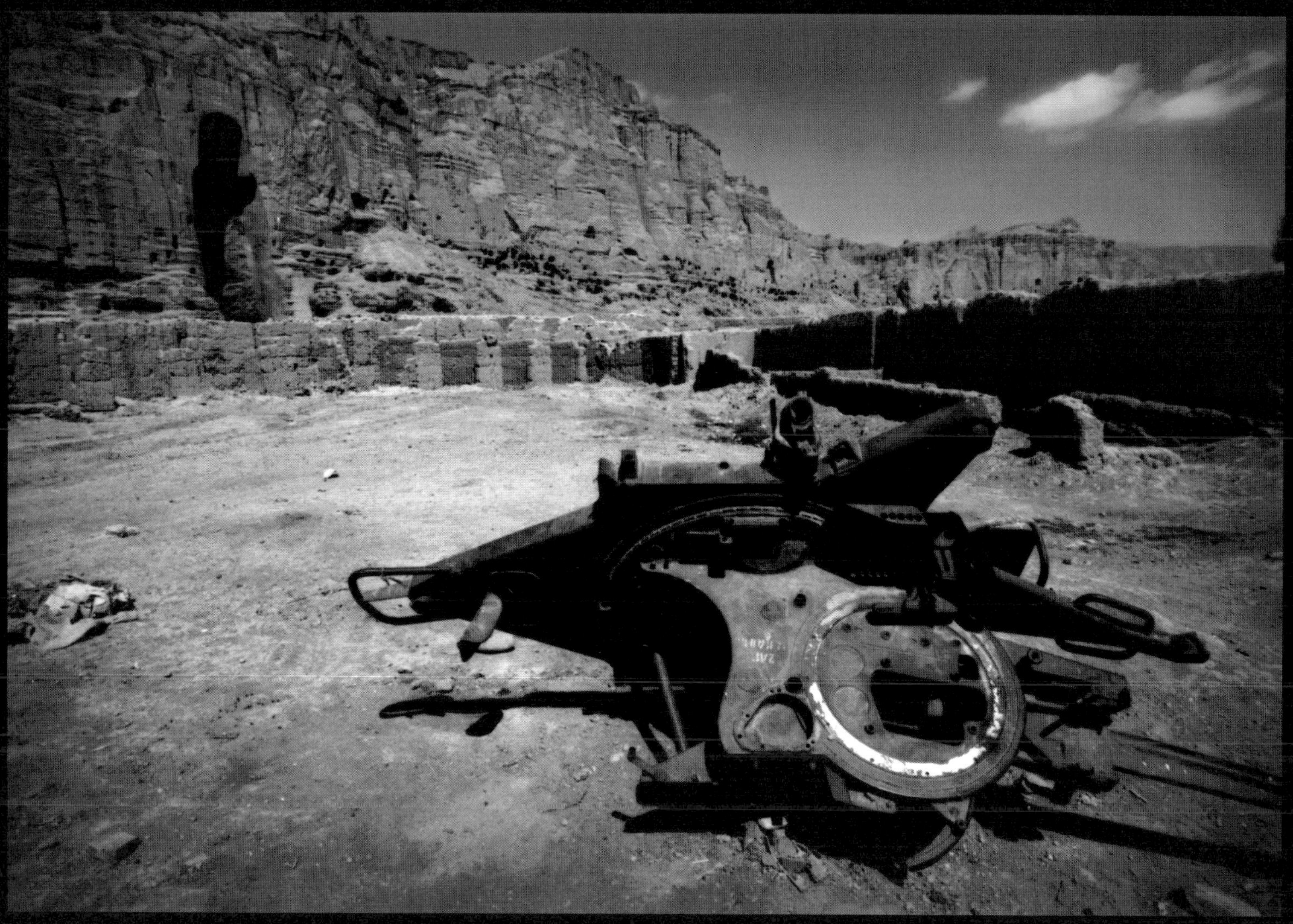

There are ruins of war all over Afghanistan. The wrecks of tanks are everywhere, like symbols of the tragic dismemberment suffered by the Afghan people, who are resigned to the hope that peace shall come one day.
In the background can be seen one of the Buddhas of Bamiyan that were blown up by the Taliban in 2001.

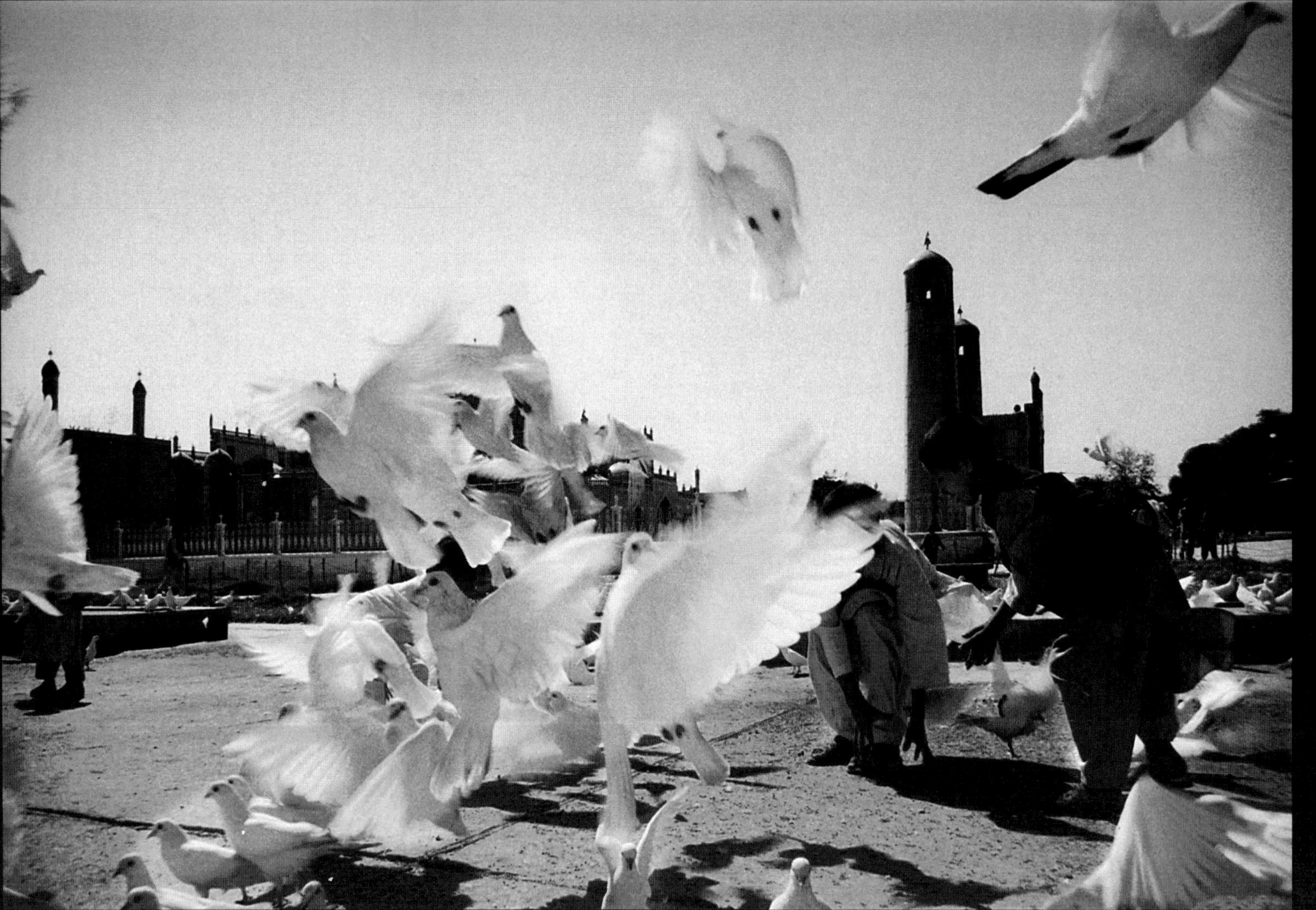

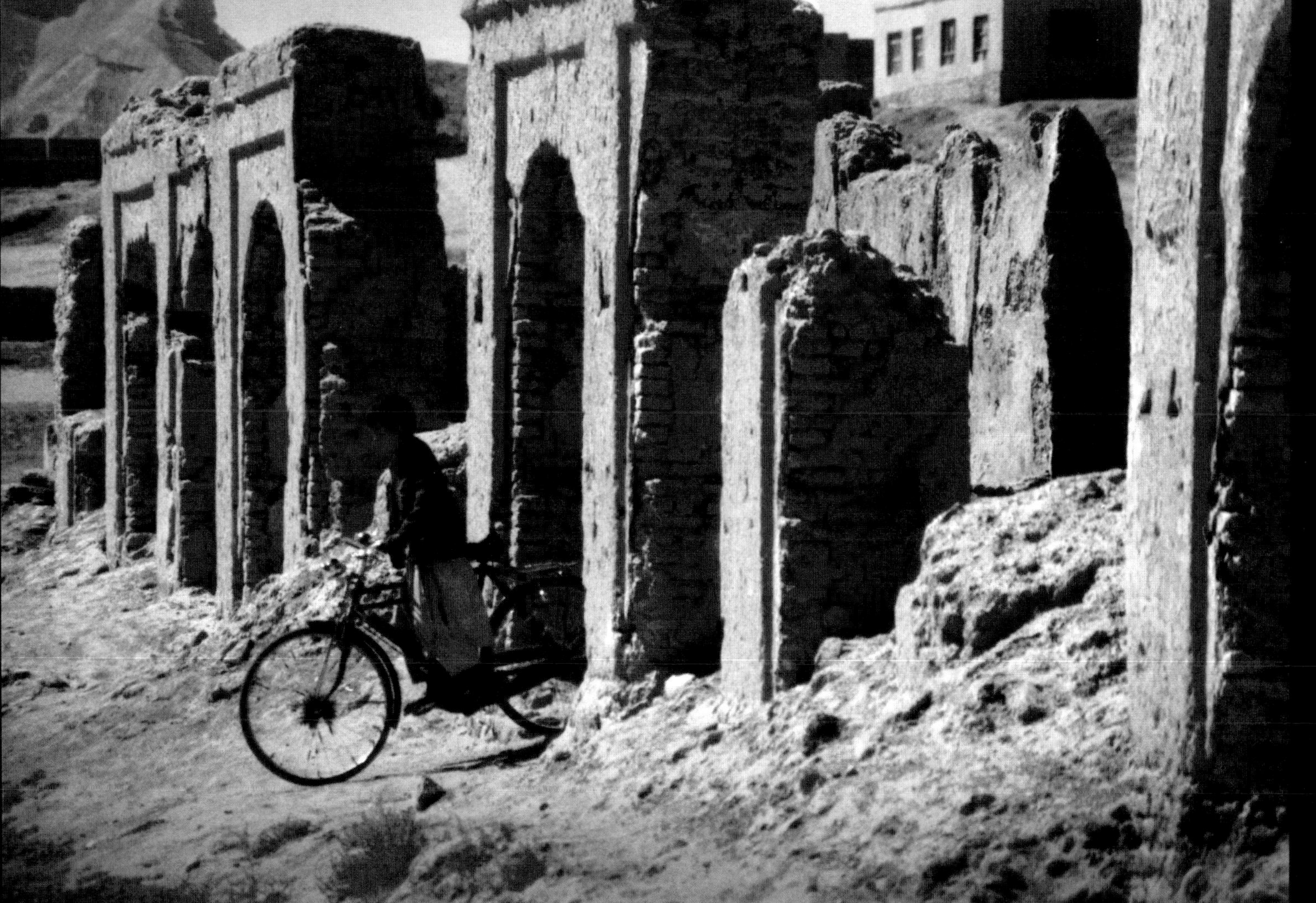

BREAK

Suheir Hammad

(nyc)

humidity condenses breath

bodies stick and stones gather in a lower
back

gray thick moving slow and alone

i am looking for my body

for my form in the foreign
in translation
what am i trying

to say i sit in this body dream
in this body expel
in this body inherit
in this body

here is the poem

i left a long time ago
remember stubble remember unwanted
remember touch

i can't remember where i left my body

poem needs form lungs need
air memory needs loss i need
to translate my body because it is profane

what had happened was
i wrote myself out of damage

this is the body of words and spaces
i have found to re-construct

(deheisha)

my home
girl is there now the air is thick
people don't breathe well hold their
tongues against cursing all of existence
all that would carry on living during this

she wakes to news just the beginning
the same story the one which leaves bodies
behind as tokens of nothing

one family
roasting corn
now all husks
silk
spraying
wind

my home girl's body
would be called white be claimed jewish
is mother and loved by a man who sits in
a bay
by telephone and radio and reaches for his
lover's body
and finds only formless

she is witness and rage
i pray her body save her
come back with her offer lover a home
daughter a beginning and all of us testimony

the people there tell her they will survive
this

if a body can carry through you follow

(beirut)

a green body obsessed white
possessed by all male religion sword sniper
garnishes silicone radishes video radiology
vixens eastern european prostitution man-
ic depression olive oil sweat camps resorts
hair gel all that is life all that is death
the roads and bridges been hit
the airport been hit

where is a body to go

we lived there once my parents sisters and
me
i left my skin there still boiling

(tel aviv)

write your own damn poem
build a grammar with something other
than bones

(gaza)

a woman's hand cups bloodied sand bits
scalp ooze
to the camera and says this is my family

(khan younis)

yamaaaaaaaaa
yamaaaaa

(nyc)

i am waiting for a break
in weather

i am not yet broken
enough to forget
desire but i wish i would

my parents worry i will never marry
i cannot comfort them

(houston)

a family says this is the summer of sacrifice
no vacation no new car no addition to the study
but pedicures and hair relaxing and shape-ups and gyms
mandatory a body must keep up must be presentable

a husband says i wake up and sleep and wake up
and all i think about is gas prices

(bombay)

bomb bay bomb bay bomb bay bomb bay

(exactly brooklyn)

my niece sleeps light
my sister feeds her her body
my clan holds one breath

(new orleans)

there is no wading in this water
a body can be polluted inside and out

(baghdad)

the children watch from bodies roasting
by roadsides
they fall in love with the soldiers killing
them
they see soldiers are bodies with orders
they wish for something to follow

a star an idea called hope sick as it sounds

(here)

is my body

is my body
an offering to give or to receive

wait for storm
know that even this is not it
that when it comes
break will be fire baptism
and in the ashes there
is my body

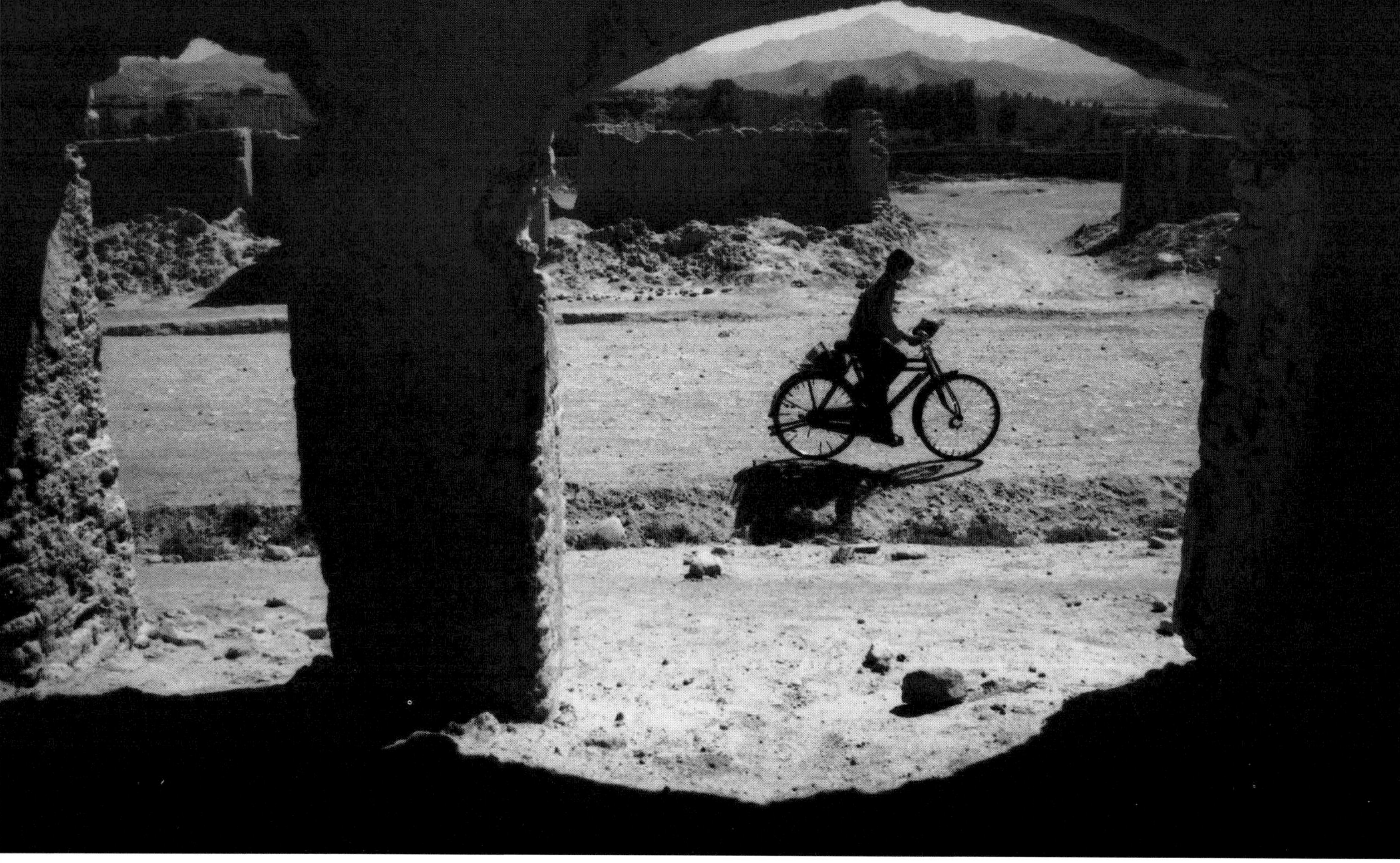

A youth on his bicycle heading home from the city of Bamiyan.

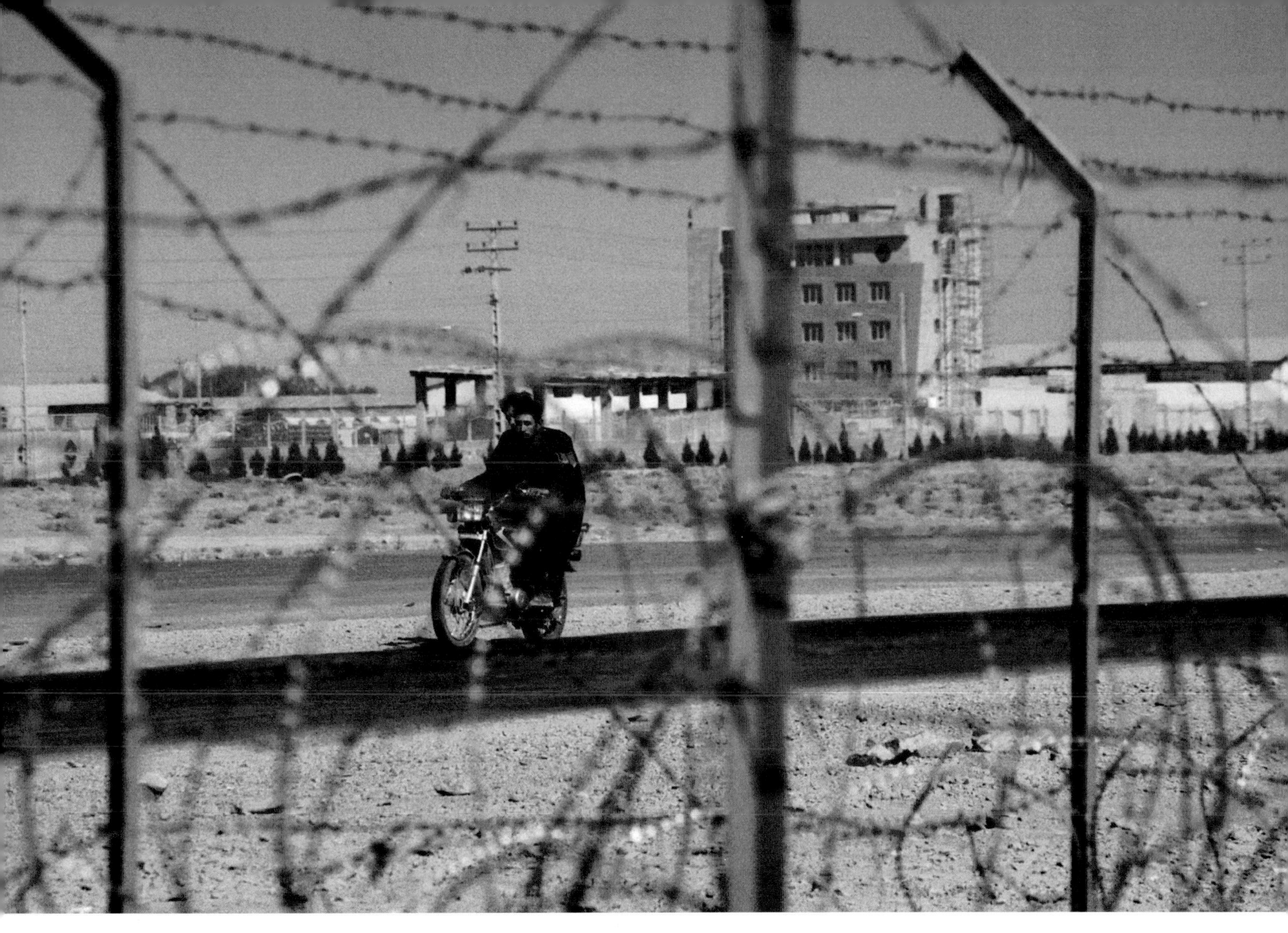

On the outskirts of Herat, a barbed-wire enclosure bars civilians from a military zone. Life for the Afghan people seems like such a fence with no exit.

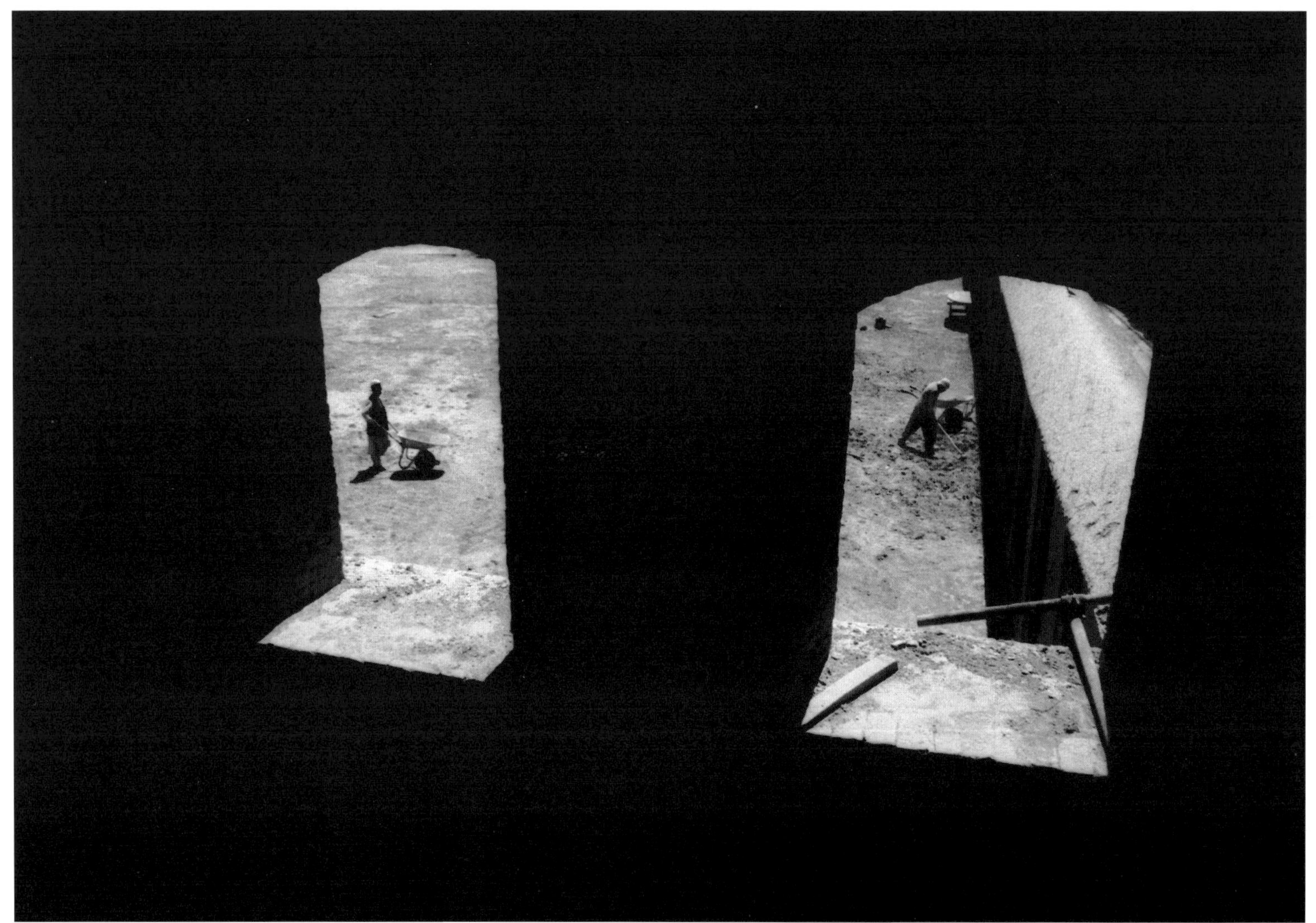

Reconstruction of a park in Kabul.

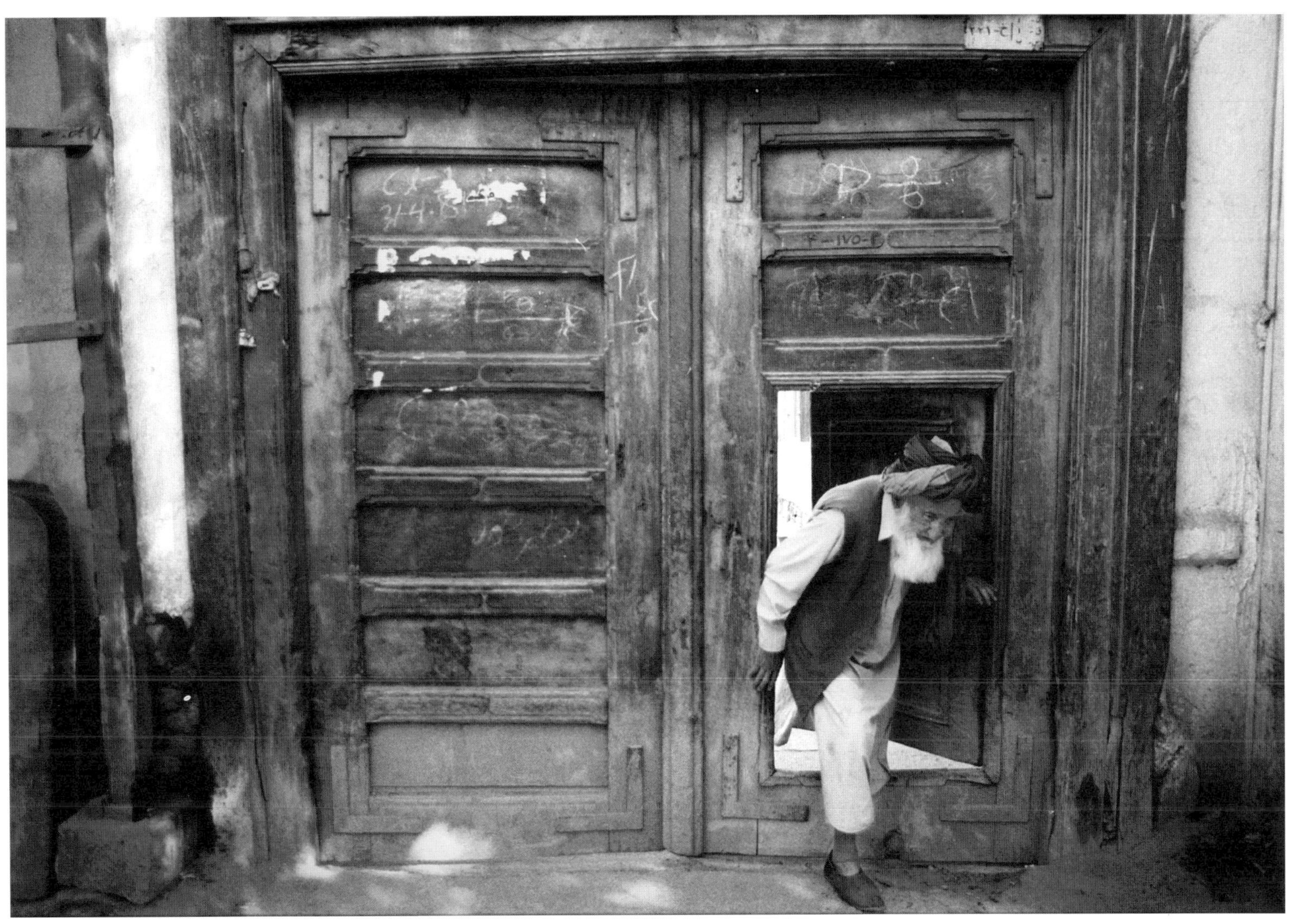

Haji is an old man who has lived all his 107 years in the center of Kabul. There he has seen the countless wars that have torn apart the country, the assassination of King Nadir Shah in 1933, the decades of peace under King Zahir Shah, the Soviet invasion and the coups d'état.

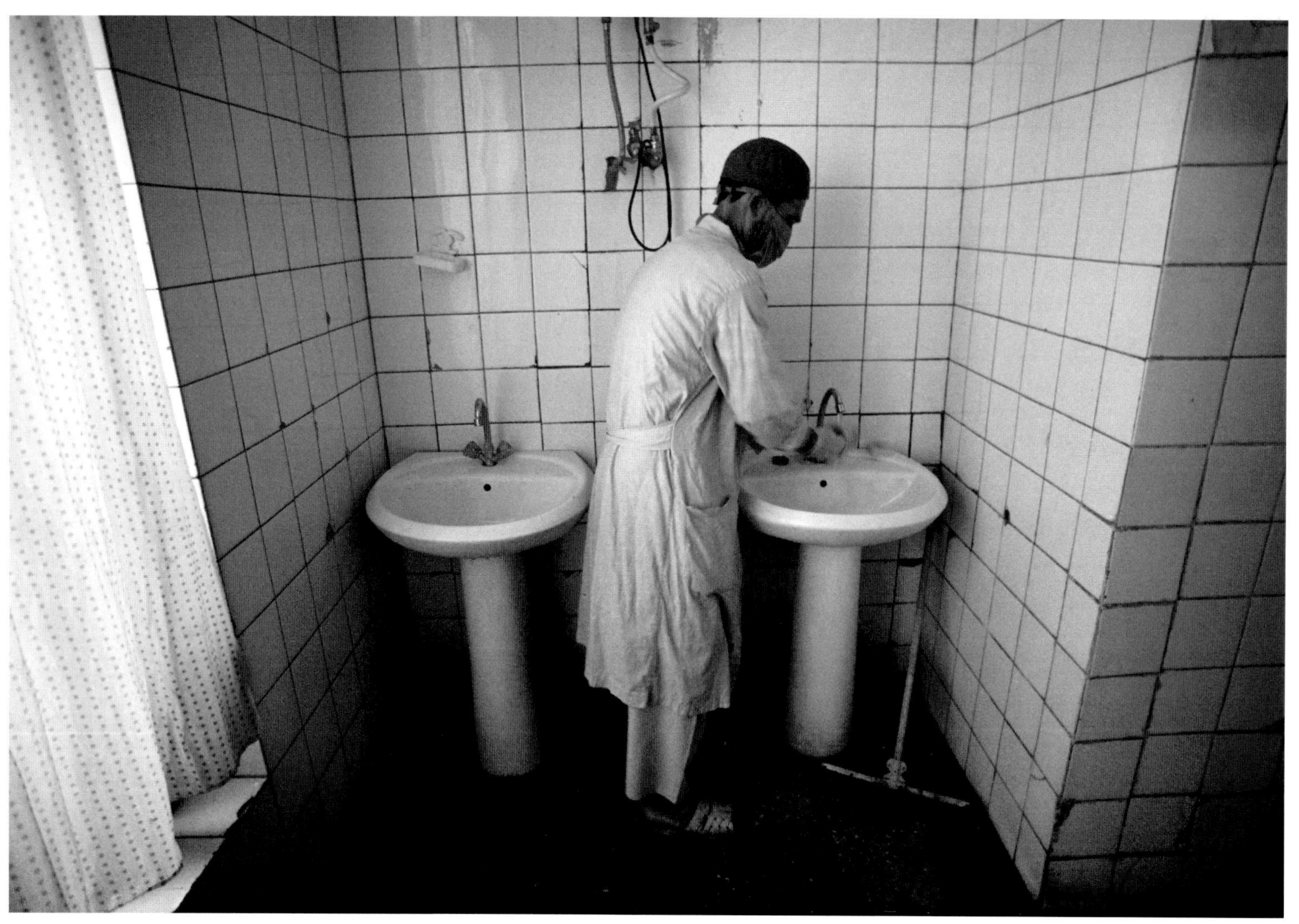

I was surprised to see what the facilities were like for surgeons to clean their hands before performing operations at Ali Abad hospital.

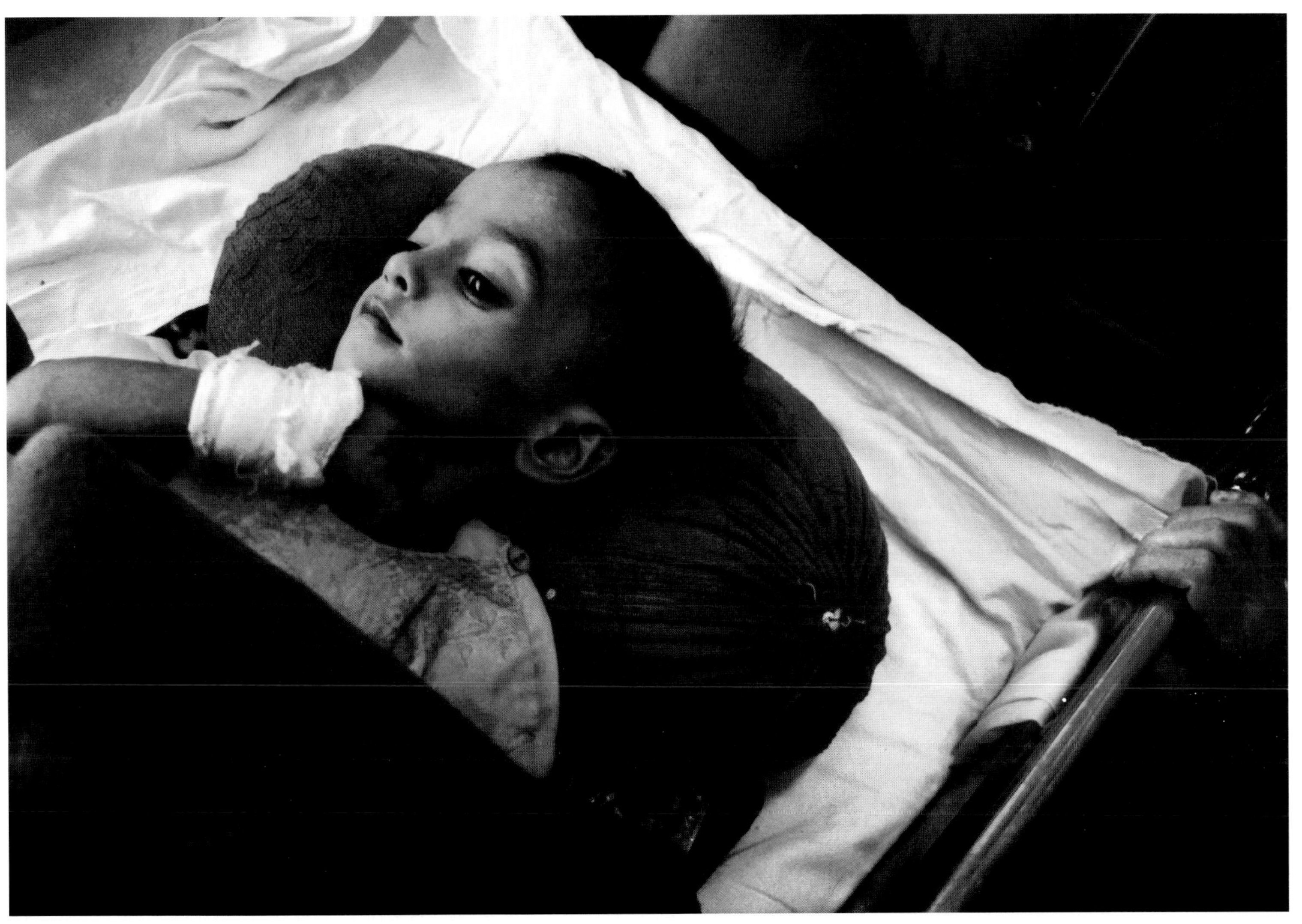

The expression on the boy's face reflects the hard life he has to live.

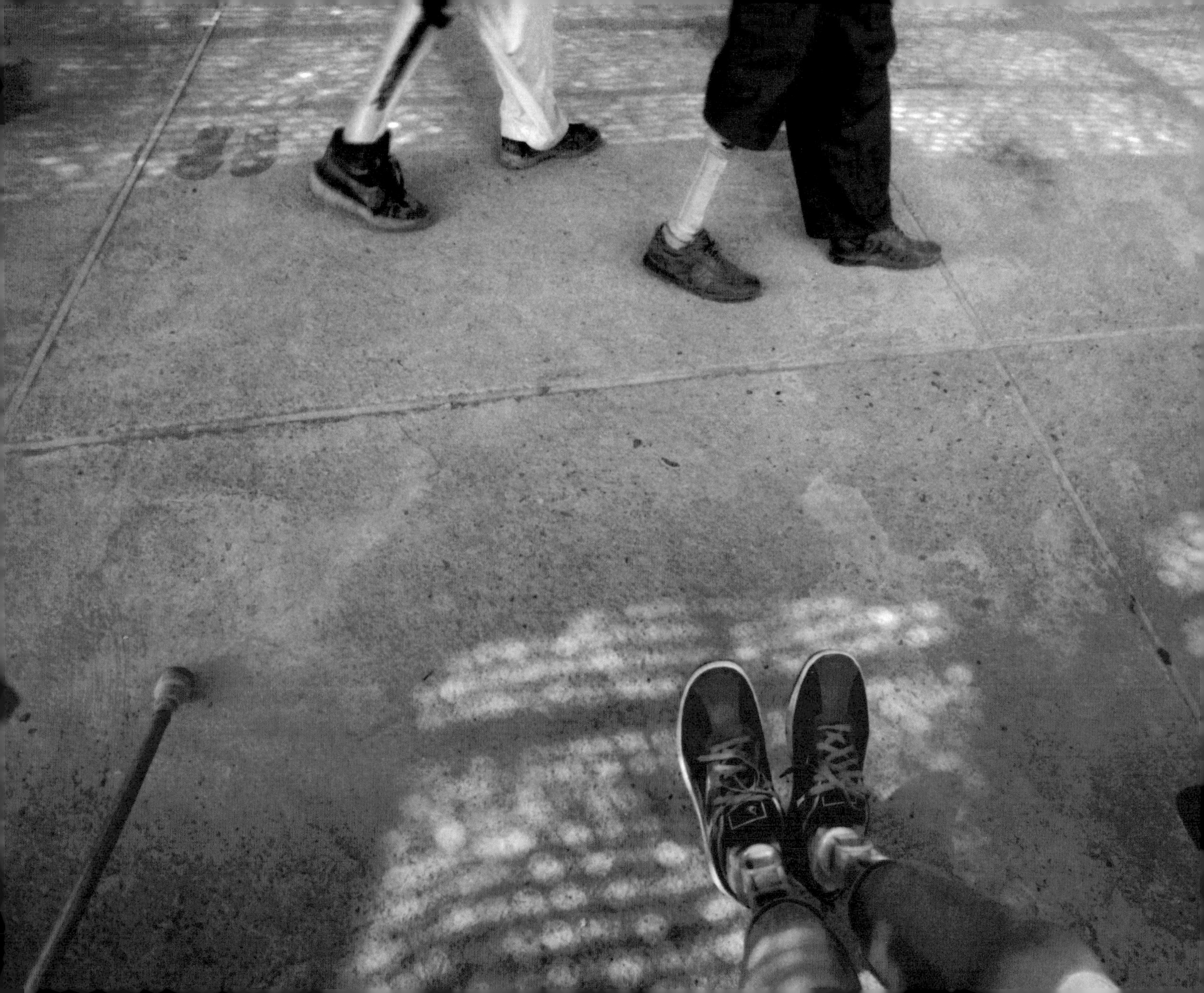

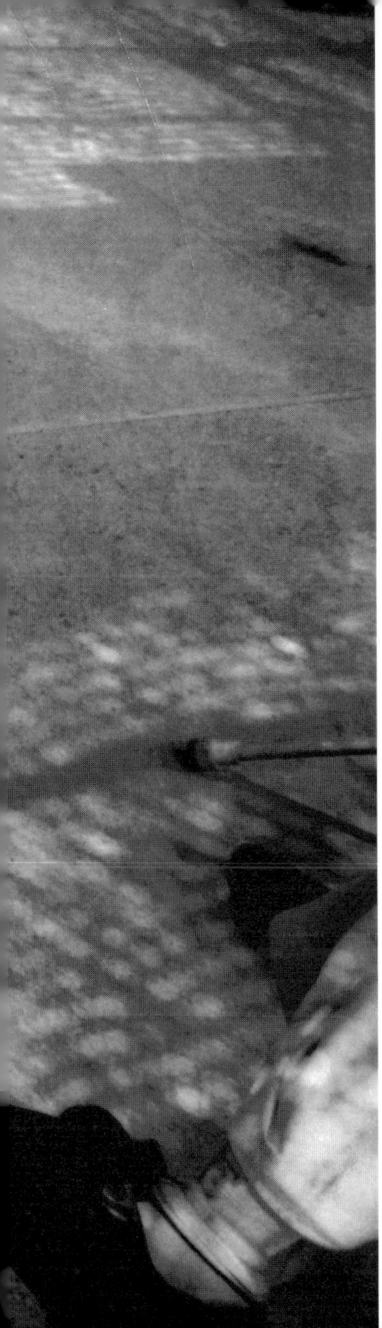

Victims of land mines. Afghanistan is the most heavily mined country in the world.

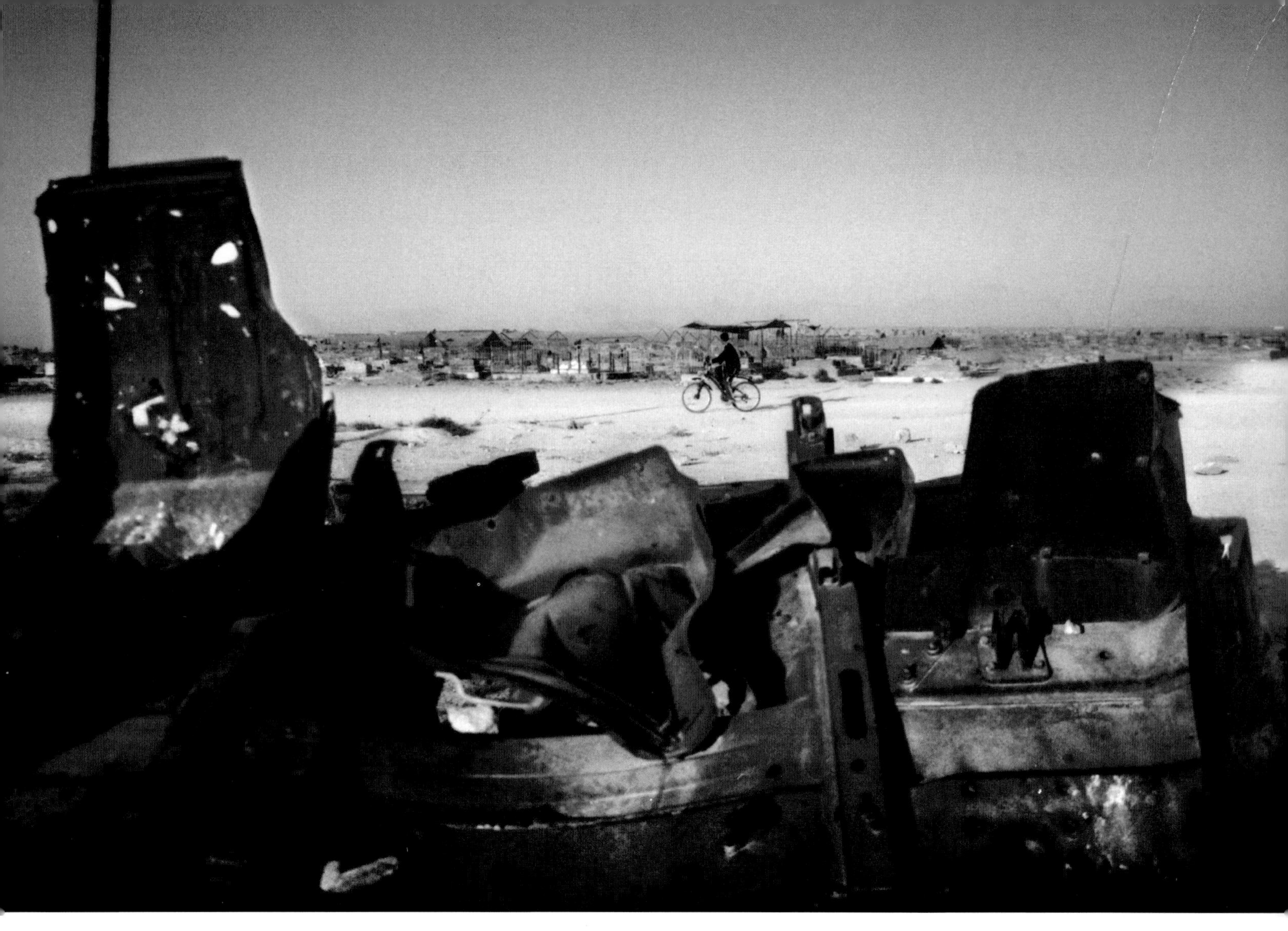

Remains of vehicles destroyed in the wars litter the periphery of a cemetery in Kabul, seen in the background.
The local people have lived among these vestiges of war for decades.

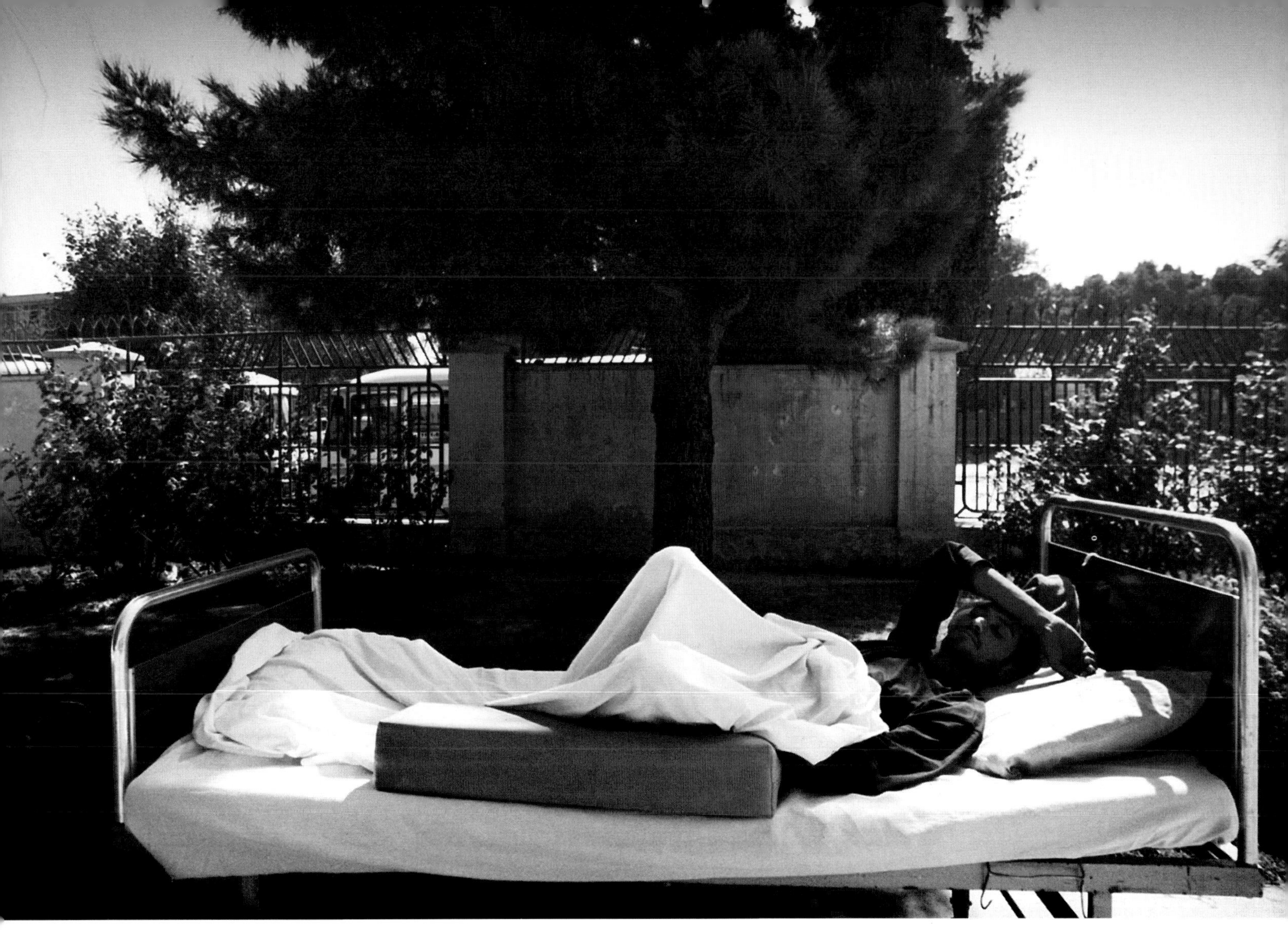

Taking advantage of the nice weather on a day in September, the hospital nurses and attendants take some patients who are in less serious condition outside, where they spend hours and hours in the open air, until it starts to get dark.

LOST SPLENDOURS

Yasmina Khadra

Jalalabad, Kandahar, Kabul... mythical names, cities of legends and fairy tales. Afghanistan, land of dreams and cosmic rapture. How many sultans have gleamed on the heights of their palaces? Odalisques are undressed by the breath of the wind. How many poets have forgotten to live due to not having arisen to sing in the morning...

When the snow fell on the summits of their peaks, all Earth's beauty is refreshed.

When the frost cracked right through to its stones, the Pashtun shepherd forbade himself from breathing on his hand to give them warmth. He wanted to be as impenetrable as his gaze, as inaccessible as his pride, and made it a point of honour not to light a fire.

When the blazing heat overcame the camels, it burned more ardently than the joy of children.

It was the country of all challenges, where it was good to live well.

What cataclysm buried the small pleasures of yesteryear? What mayhem took away reason and the spirits?

Afghanistan... How sad it is to hear clarions replace flutes, the throbbing of helicopters trouble the peaceful flight of doves... It's sad to see the empire of dreams die in nightmarish arenas!

What divides the ruined towns of today from the romances of yesteryear? The damaged gardens where not one small love is permitted, the mined esplanades where people no longer dare to stroll?

Why do suddenly, the shires which made the dreams of so many generations and inspired such happy fantasies, provoke only terror and emotion? Why is children's laughter lost in the blasphemy of machine gun fire?
Why have women become diaphanous spectres, without charm or magic, carrying around the drama of their men like a terrible curse?...

Afghanistan... I have consulted History, all the world's epic poetry, the fabulous contests, the immense spoils; nowhere have I found a answer to your chagrin or a common measure of your decay

And however, each time my heart beats under the weight of your martyrdom, I undertake to pray for when the day regains all its splendour in the eyes of your children.

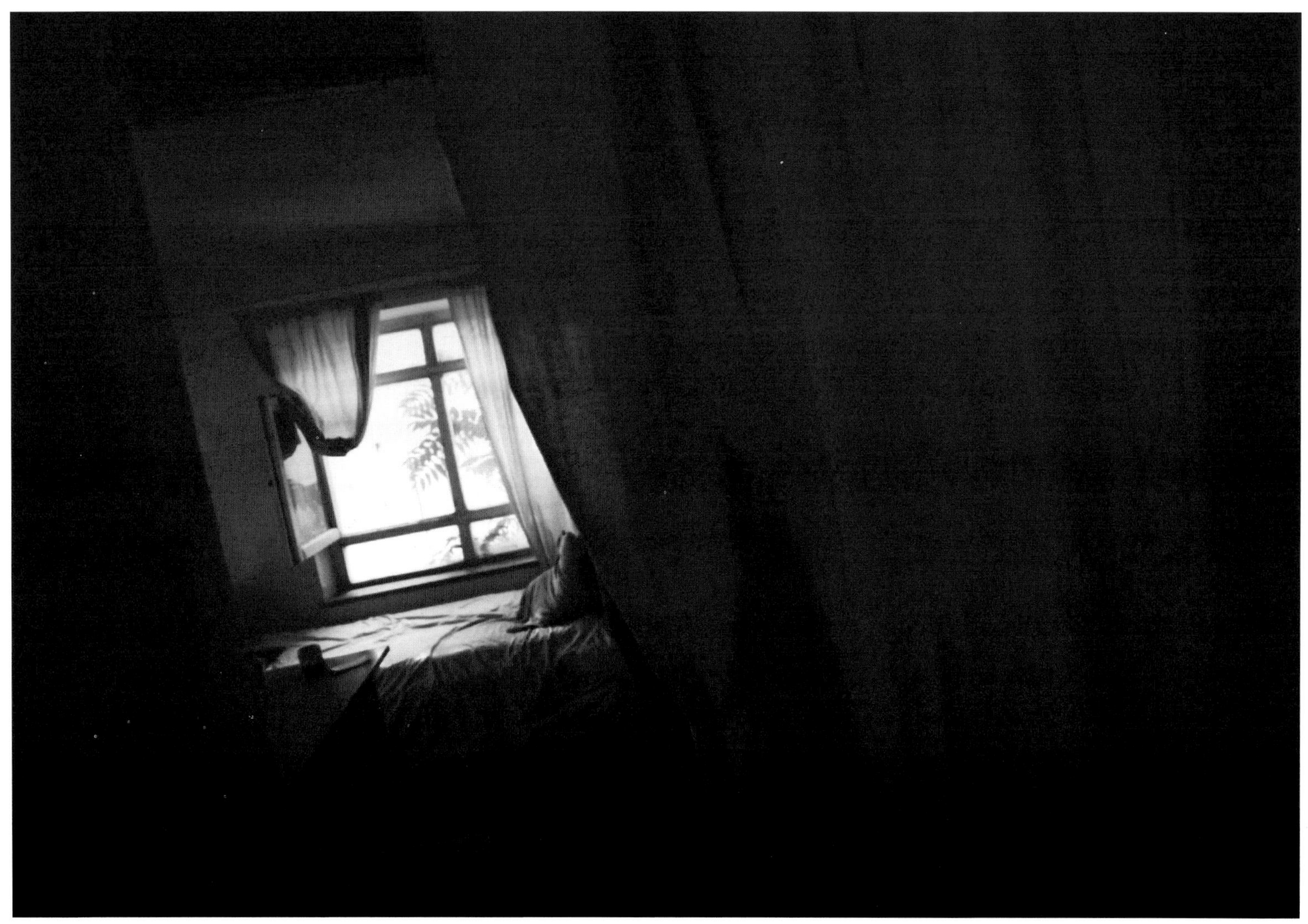

An image of an empty bed in Indira Gandhi hospital, where a patient has just passed away.

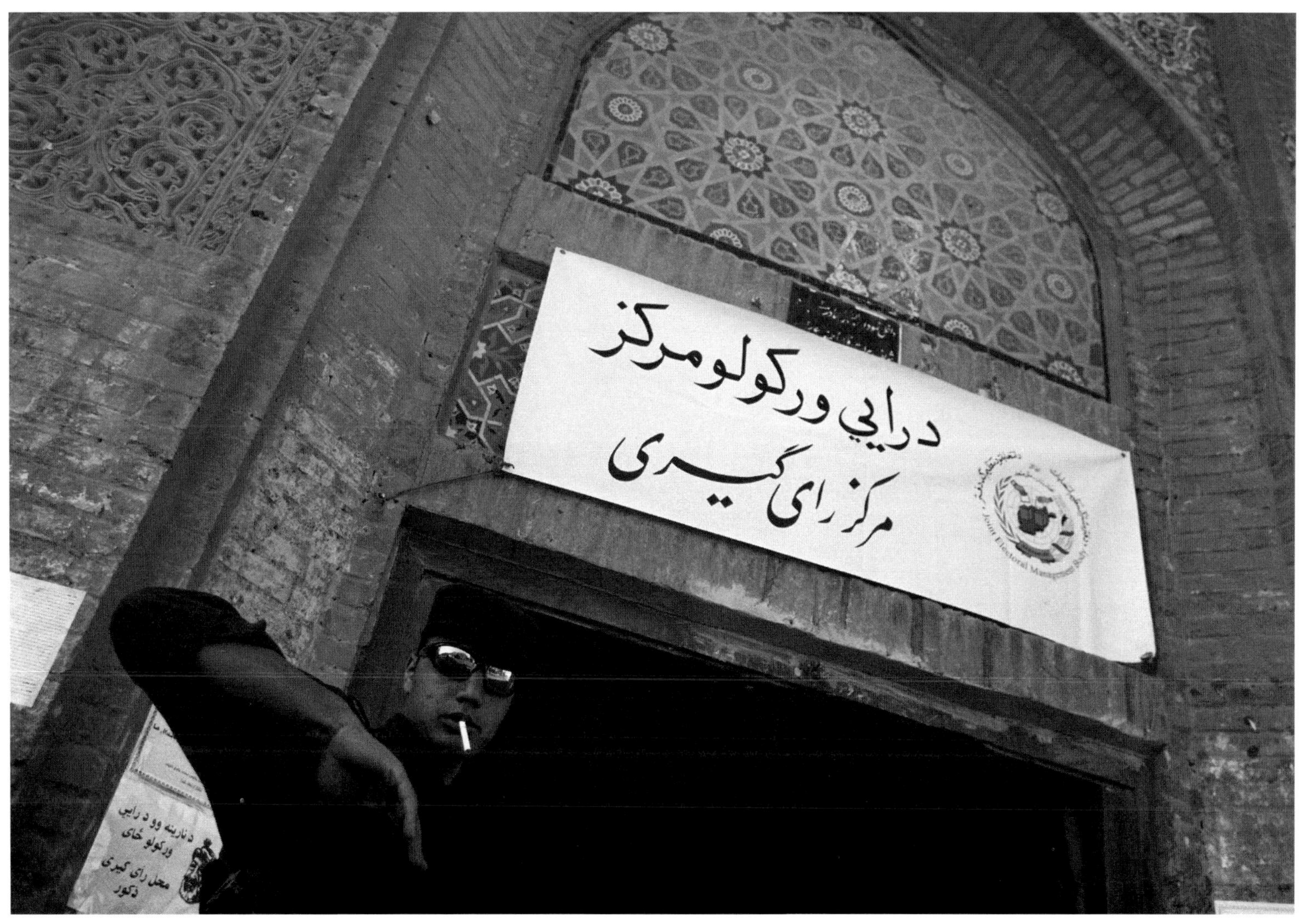

A security guard at the Blue Mosque of Herat during the presidential elections.

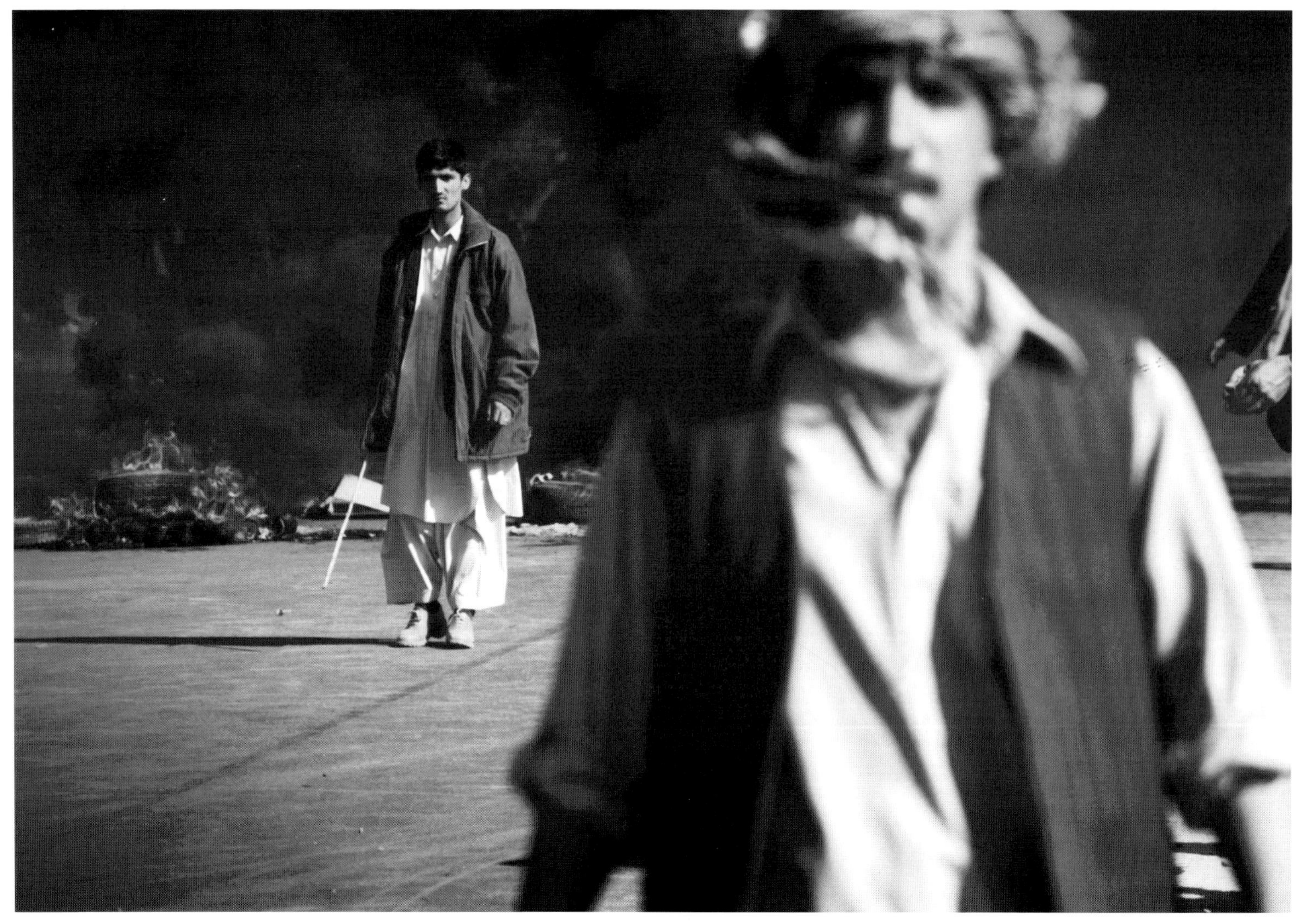

As I was making my way north, I came across an ambush where a policeman had lost his life.
Fire and pieces of vehicles were scattered all over the highway. In the bus the other passengers advised me to hide, but I got out to take a couple photographs. This was certainly my scariest moment in Afghanistan

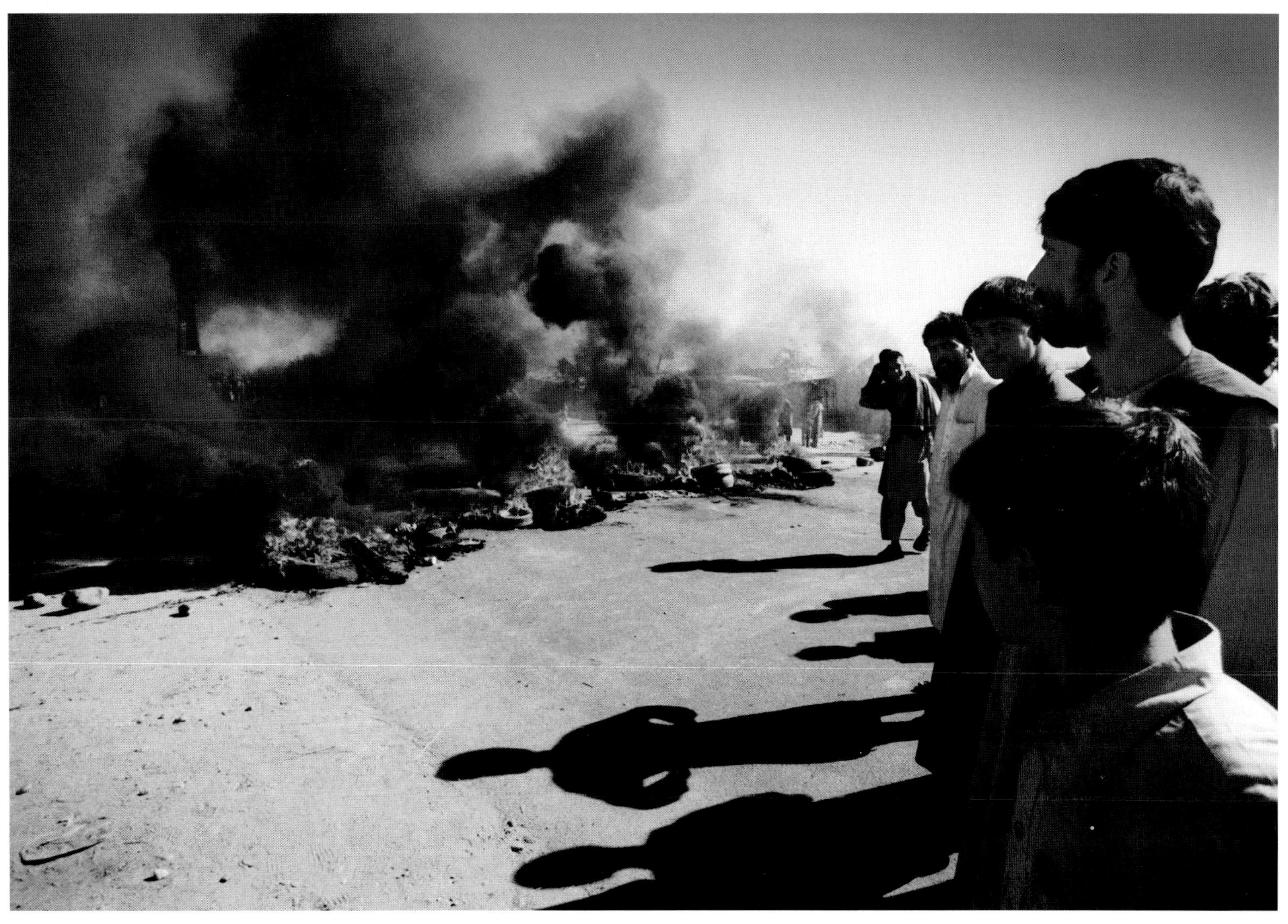

On the road north from Kabul I saw an attack on the police by the Taliban. One of the policemen was killed. Around Kabul a series of attacks began, as the Taliban laid siege to the capital in an attempt to regain it.

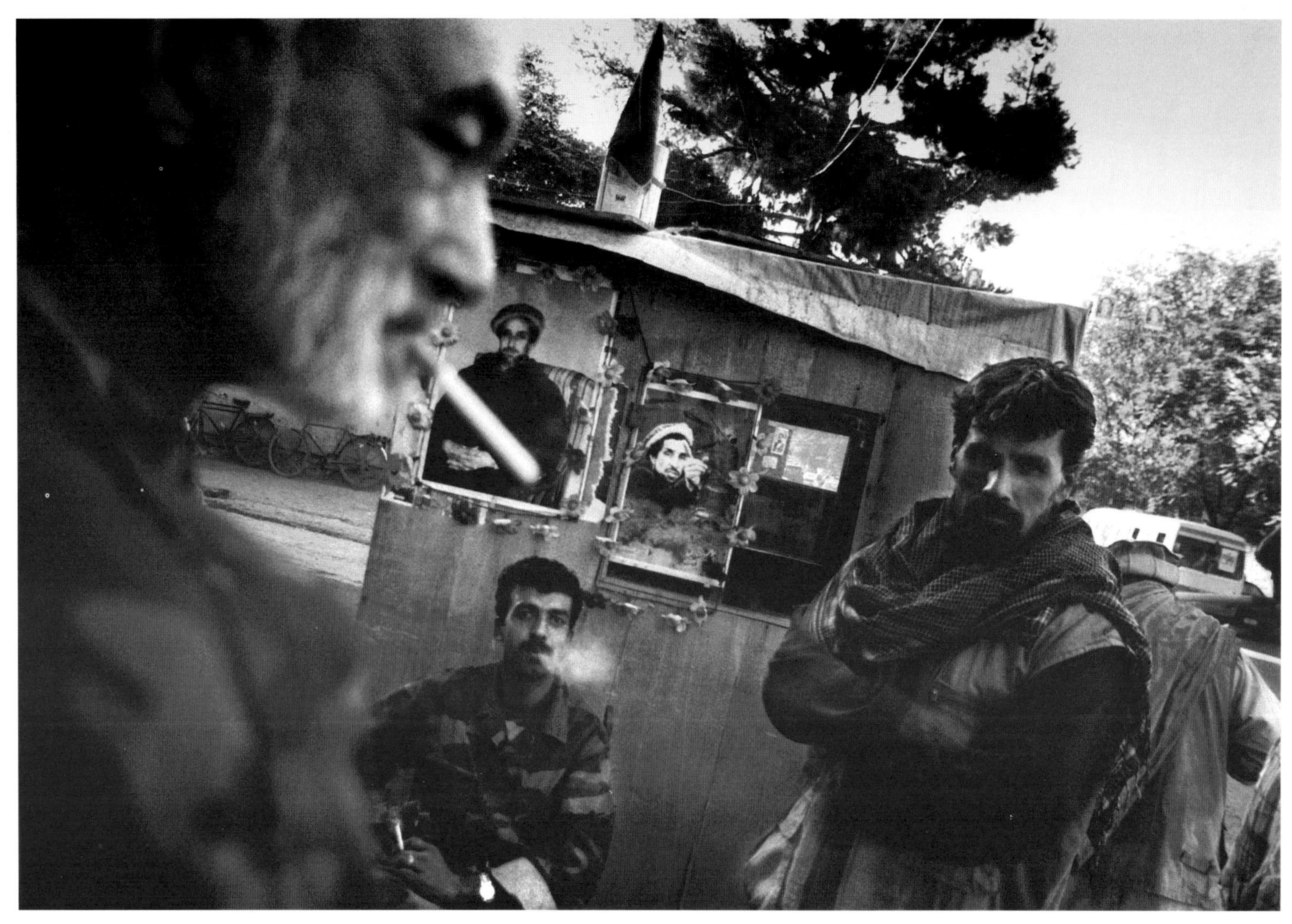

In a Kabul street, a few policeman enjoy a moment of conversation at a police post, with a photo of Ahmed Shah Massoud presiding over the discussion. For many, Massoud has become an anti-Taliban hero, while to others he was just a warlord. I spent hours with these policemen having tea, the favorite way for Afghans to spend time together.

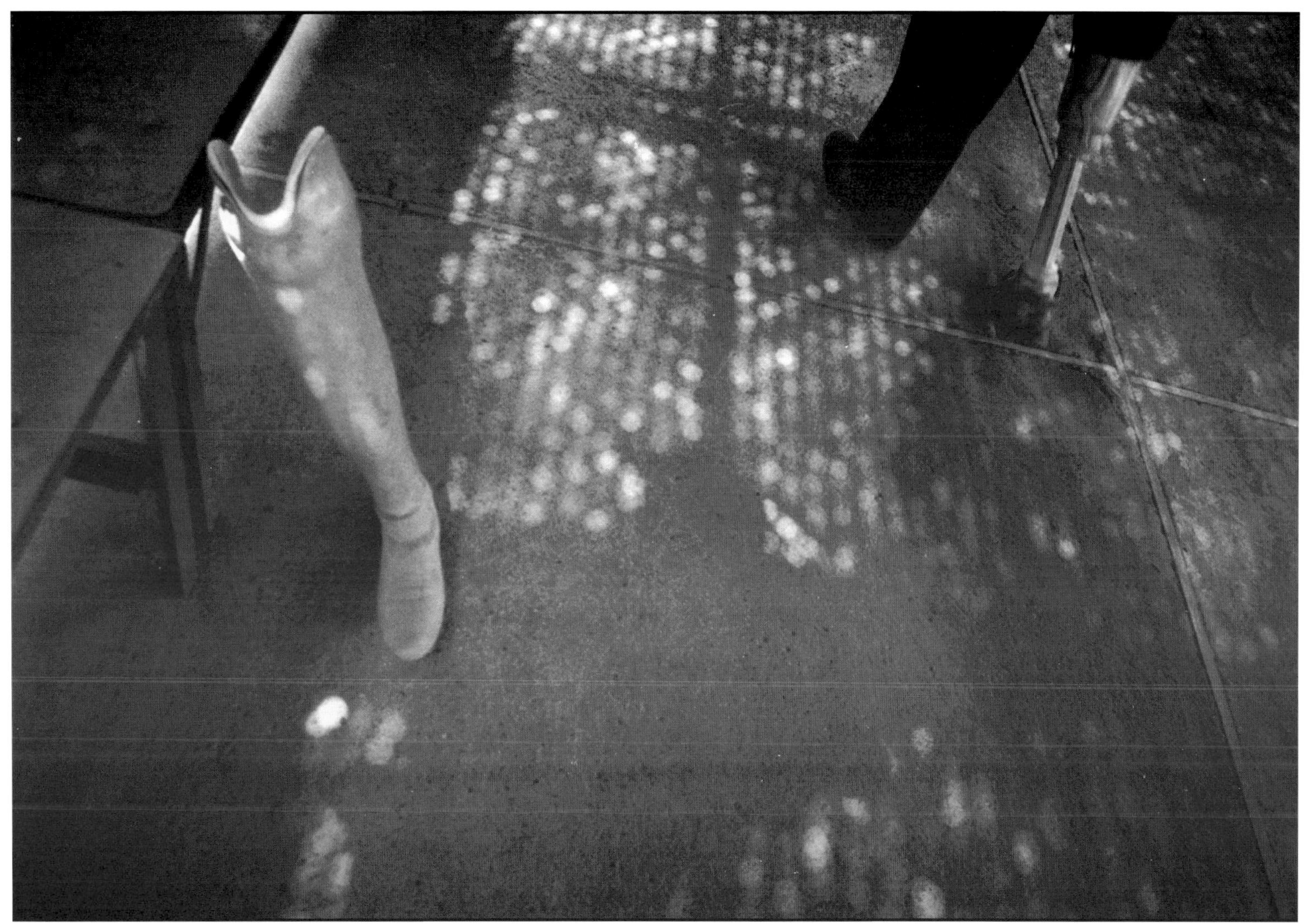

Orthopedic Center Hospital in Kabul.

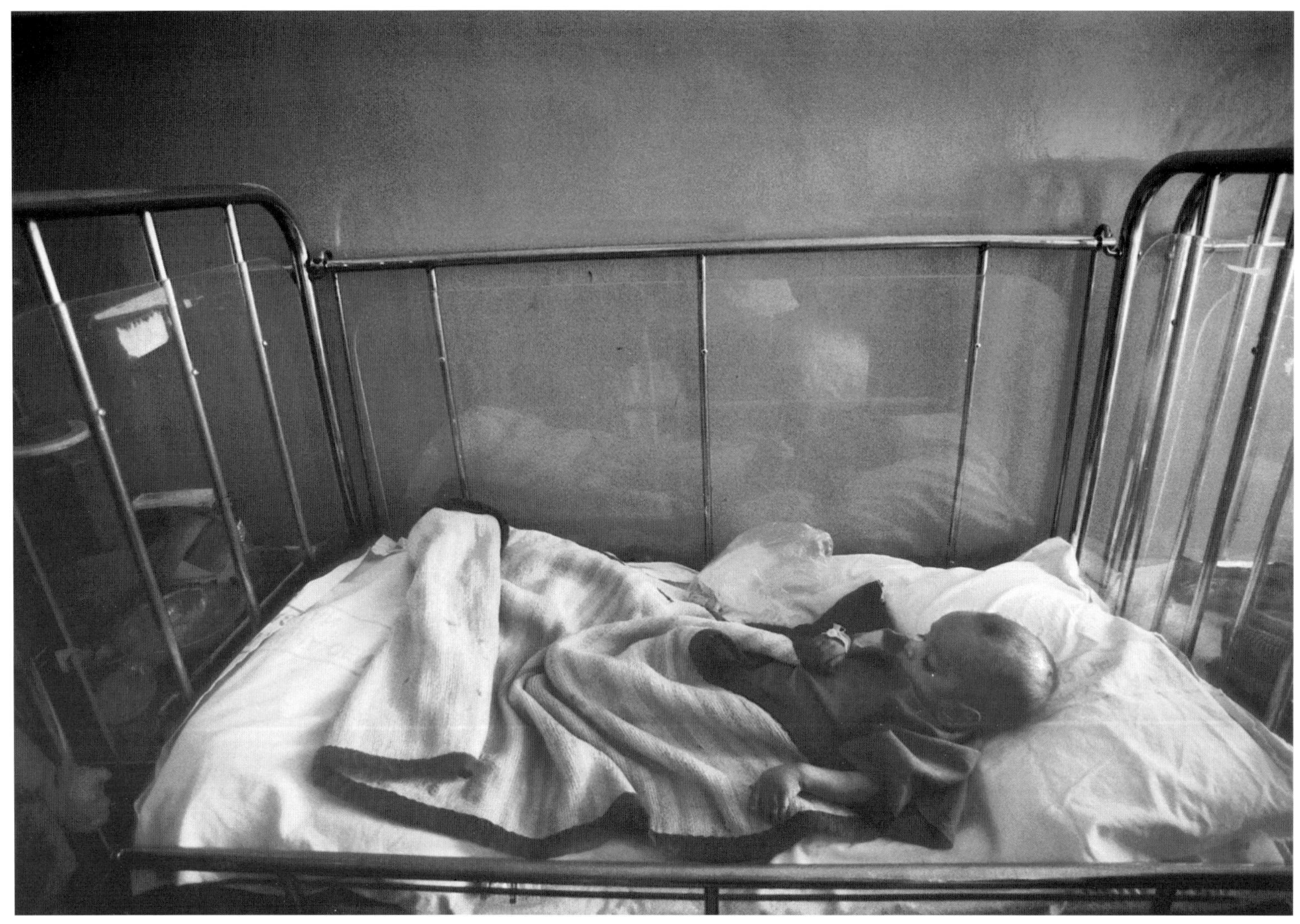

Said was admitted to the hospital with malnutrition, and remained hospitalized for three weeks.
Since Western troops led by the United States invaded the country, the situation has deteriorated, and there is a constant increase in the number of children suffering from symptoms of malnutrition.

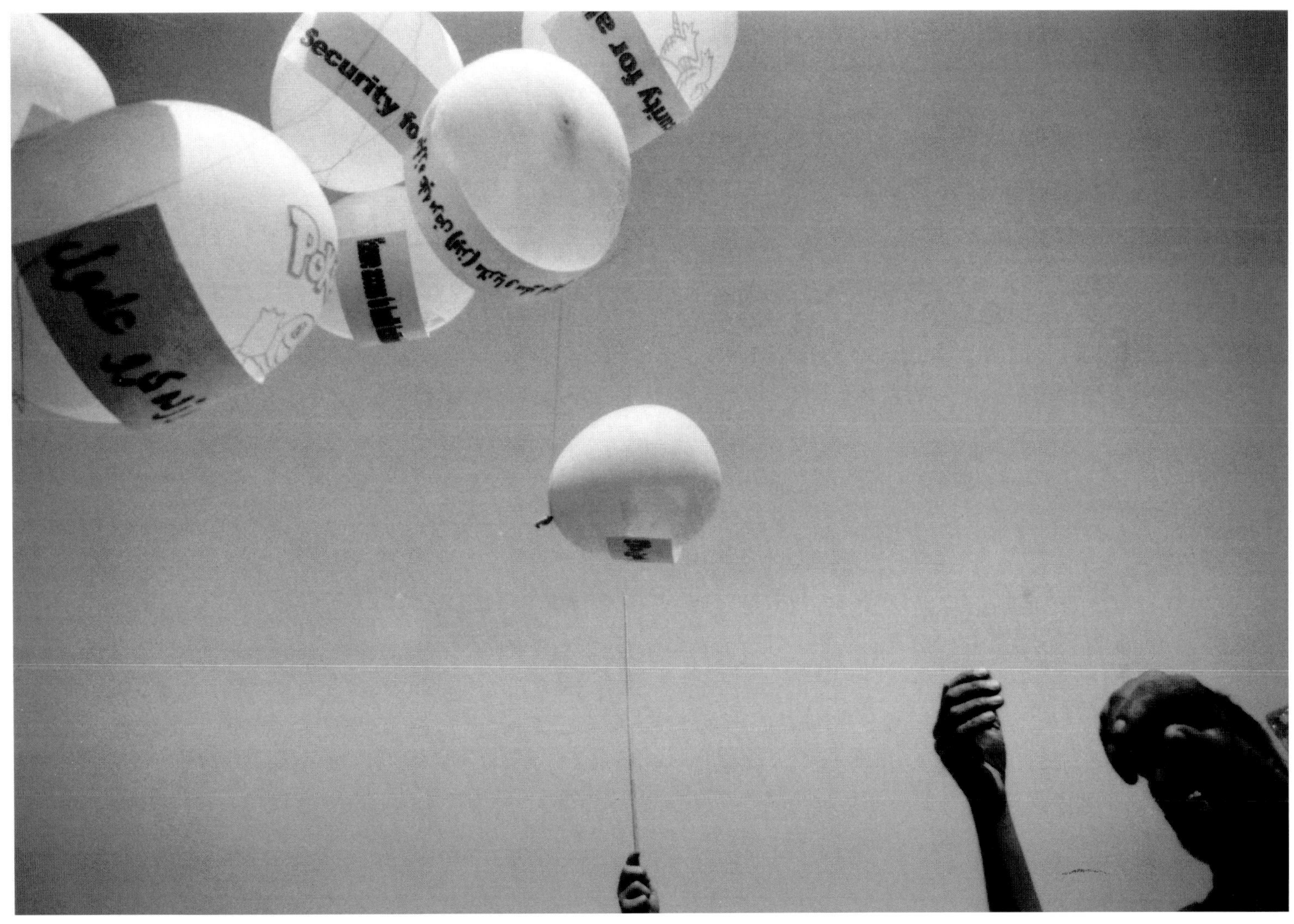

At a children's festival in the suburbs of Kabul, kites are given out and balloons are launched.
Flying kites is the national pastime for children, yet they were prohibited by the Taliban regime.

THREE EYES

Alen Silva

I never knew where my journey was taking me. In the light of the days and miles and meetings, I realized how unusual was the voyage from the beginning, and how it called to be captured on film.

All the legacy I wanted to leave of my nine-month journey round Asia was just a subjective truth of my experience with the people, who hardly feel able to raise their voices for everybody to hear their plea for a peace they long for. The Silk Road felt like a blank journal which had to be written to give sense to a pilgrimage into one's self, to find oneself; and that resulted in a photographic work which tries to show the nature of the people flogged by the most heart-rending sadness.

In the 90 photographs I collected in

the book, to summarize my stay in Afghanistan, I tried to cover all contexts that, to my understanding, were necessary so this project would have a tacit interpretation. To do so I forged documents in order to get journalist credentials that a posteriori allowed me to get into hospitals, to contact the military and to live the elections on 18th September 2005 very closely. So closely, in fact, did I want to live my experience (there had been a terrorist attack in which a policeman was killed on his way to the North from Kabul), that I was nearly killed by a group of men with AK-47s, who chased me until I was able to escape in extremis on a motorcycle. Or when I had no choice but to come back home to the Basque Country (weighing only 50 kilos) because of respiratory problems, which almost cost me my life.

To see these photographs again makes my mind wander. There are in this book many clashing memories of sadness and high moments shepherding my solitude with the insuppressible experience of the contact with their people. I clearly remember a seven-year-old boy called Omar in the Victims of War hospital in Kabul, where he spent a long time dependent on meters of tubes that ran into his little body and kept him alive. Two weeks later I came back to ask how he was, but no one knew what had become of him. In the same way I can remember the stillness of the moment in the Ali Abad hospital where a man looked through a window at an ailing relative, perhaps his father. Or Abdula, a five-year-old who lost both his legs to a land mine, whom I photographed among orthopaedic legs, looking at himself in a mirror in the Orthopaedic Centre of Kabul, and gazing without full realization of his name the uncertain future he will have to live.

With the infinitely inconsolable times of war, I still remember the starving poverty when I was taking photographs in the hospitals of Kabul, the penetrating smells of urine and old illnesses that loaded the atmosphere, their withered patients dying because of inhuman life conditions, their war cripples suffering on the floor of the halls, the children, victims of the barbarism. And the warmth with which they greeted the intrusion of a person

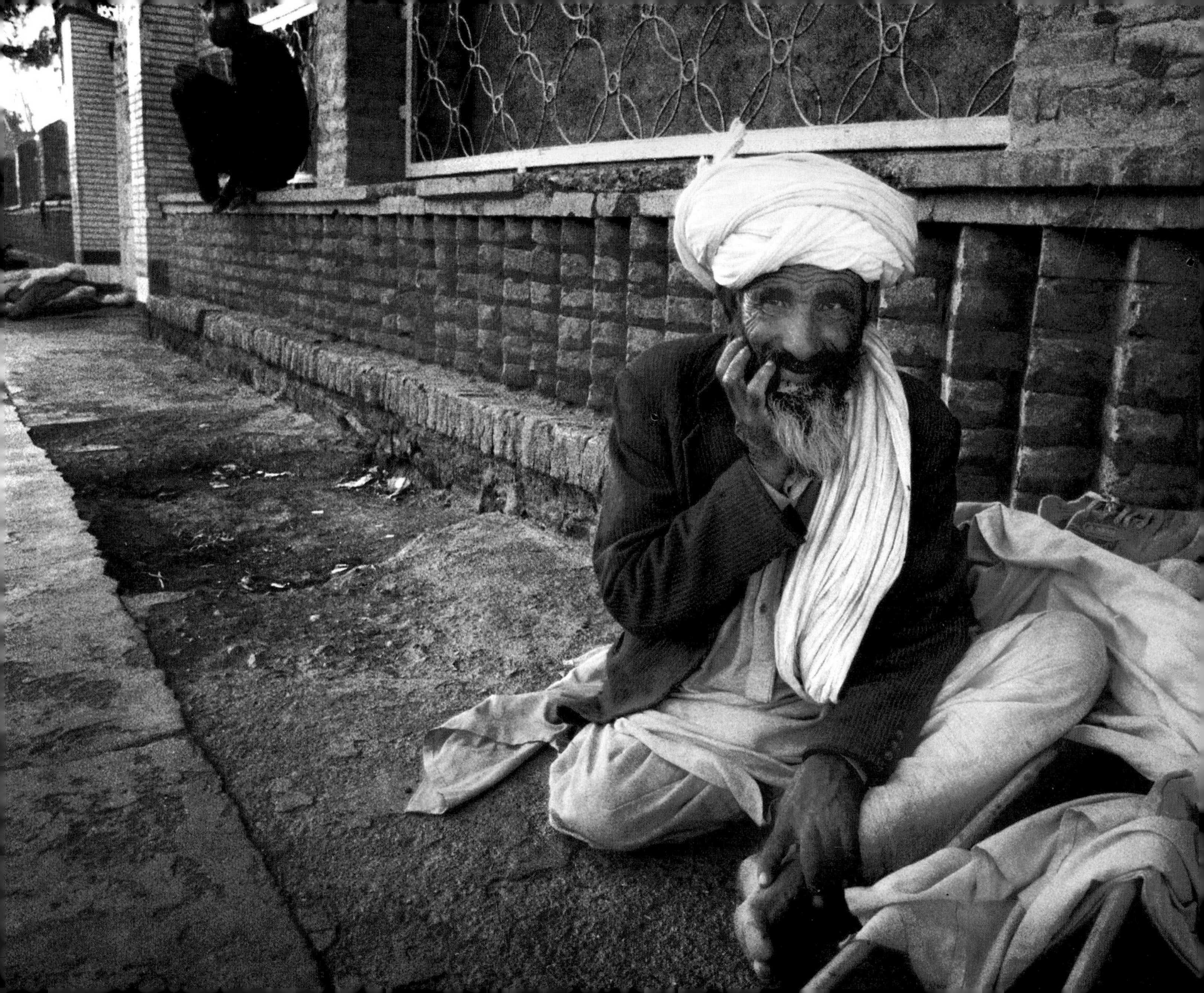

In Mazar-e Sharif, as in all the cities of Afghanistan, there are hundreds of poverty-stricken people who live in the streets from the alms of their neighbors. I took this photograph along the street that leads to the Blue Mosque, in the city center. It was fascinating to see the people come out in the evening to give food to all the beggars posted around the walls. In Mazar-e Sharif I wanted to pay for a cataract operation for a blind one-legged beggar, but he refused. Later, people told me the reason: "If the townspeople knew that he could see with one eye, perhaps they might stop giving him food."
So he preferred to go on without seeing, rather than die of hunger.

trying to take fleeting snapshots.
Having resorted to all kind of tricks and a fake press pass to be able to catch the truth with my camera, I also had the chance to see other parts of the Afghan situation, as I was in touch with the international armed forces that control the country. I saw the arrogance of some and incomprehension of others. I felt that contact with the people was almost impossible for the few who had come in peace, or the even fewer who even wanted to get to know the local culture. One is isolated in a military base, just giving and receiving orders.
I was in Herat, covering the elections of September 18th, 2005, and with access to the polling stations, and seeing faces illuminated by the uncertainty of one who does something for the first time, and throws himself into a situation that could change his stagnant life for ever. It was a separate and contradictory chapter of my journey; a crucial day yet uneventful, with just one lonely foreign soldier keeping the peace. It was a day of and for the Afghans, and they took the honors of carrying it out, and the criticism for letting the men vote in the name of their wives. I remember how for days all those men wore the blackness of the ink on their finger, showing off how they had exercised their right to vote. They wanted to look for the truth, and they found Hamid Karzai and the warlords.
I remember Ahmed, who did me the priceless favor of interpreting with the governor of Herat, in an interview in his palace of sky-high halls. The next day, I asked Ahmed himself about the women's situation, and he kept giving evasive answers, dragging a veil over his ideas, like the veil most of the women in the country have to wear.
In such a dry land, with such a lunar landscape, such a strange and distant place, even when I finally recognize it in the deepest recesses of my mind, it all seems written to be erased, leaving only an immense and inconsolable sadness. Kabul, ravaged by acts of madness, is all dried up and injured in solemnity; with all its debris of necrotic dust embracing what is left of a city teeming with nightmares and people crippled by the war. Wandering around its streets, one is aware of the raging decay of the soul, reflecting the

advanced state of decomposition that much of the country lies in. I realize this on remembering those countless ranks of dispossessed piling up in aged poverty. Among those proud men defeated by the dictatorship of luck, I see one, blind and missing both eyes, who refused to let me pay for him to get a cataract operation. He feared he would lose his status as totally crippled, and be slighted by those who distribute free portions of food in the blaze of evening. His case was no sadder than that of the woman I met in Chicken Street, where she was known for begging from all those who give, with a baby in her arms whom she drugged with opium, to give an impression of incurable illness. Poor Kabul lives in parallel with the rich part, where English is spoken and French food is dined. Where since late 2001, consignments of Chinese prostitutes have arrived to satisfy occidental cravings, where alcohol adorns the pillars of a marginalized Afghan society, sunk in resignation.

From the very beginning of my stay in the country, I had to learn to say that I did not belong to an NGO, so I could get a cheaper price for things: "I am no NGO". Chatting in the streets, I heard that everyone believed the NGOs kept their distance from the people, and this was confirmed when just then I saw a staffer in a chauffeur-driven Lexus SUV on her way to her 70-dollar-a-night room.

I could spend lines and more lines giving testimony of these undiluted truths.

Without naming what to my eye was an anthology of occidental insolence, without leaving aside in this presentation so many collaborators, who live like kings and queens at the expense of human tragedy.

Remembering that English expatriate who, when I asked what he thought of the hygienic condition of Kabul's streets, literally answered, "If an Afghan wants a crap, let him go to the river".

"People" who with thousands of dollars a month may not be seen outside the capital. It's a hard job for the hundreds of NGOs who are there to reform a country, and they do not leave the palace door of their comfort.

A boy at play in the Blue Mosque of Mazar-e Sharif. The future, his culture and the hope of attaining peace after so many years of war are in the hands of a generation born amidst the conflict of war. Perhaps the time has come for them to preserve their identity as a people, putting an end to ethnic hatreds and power politics, striving together for once towards a vision of living in peace.

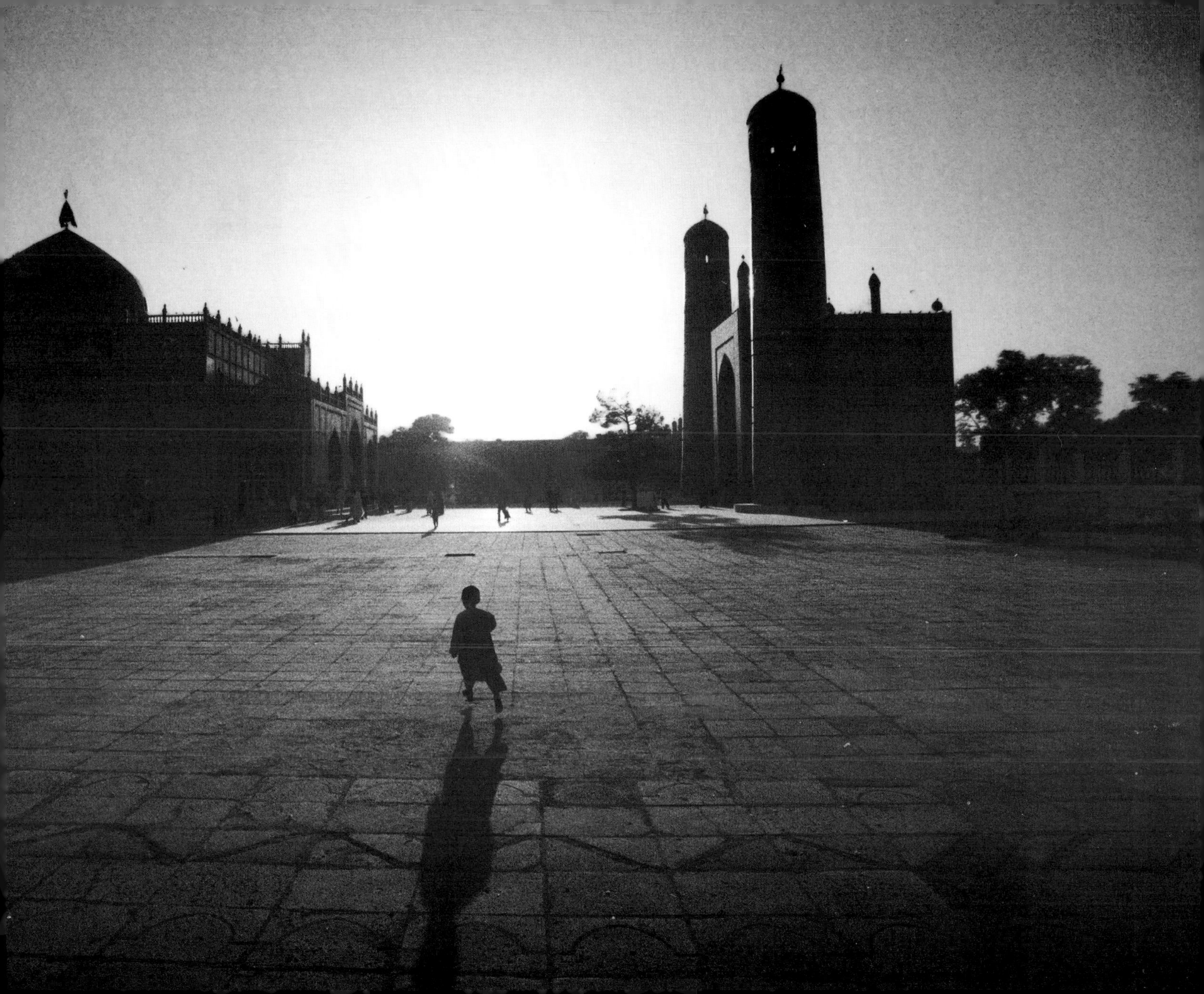

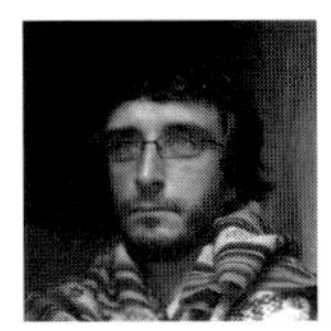

Alen Silva
Photographer, Journalist
Basque Country
Spain

Alen Silva is a 37-year-old photographer from the Basque Country, Spain. He works as a photographer for Basque newspapers. Alen has been travelling across Latin America and Asia the last 14 years. He is now planning to return to Asia and make a documentary film about the Afghan refugee camps near Peshawar in Pakistan.

Malalai Joya
Ex-Member of the Afghan Parliament
Human Rights Activist
Afghanistan

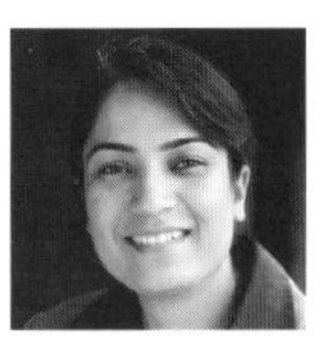

Yasmina Khadra
Novelist
Algeria

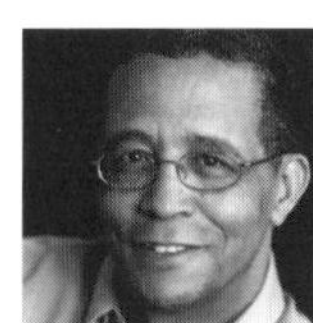

Michael Ratner
Human Rights Activist, Lawyer,
President of the Center for Constitutional Rights
USA

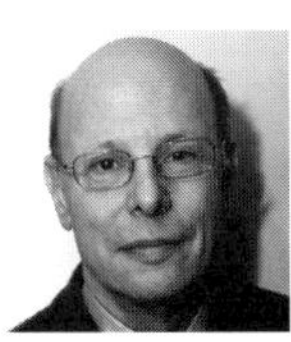

Ezzat Goushegir
Novelist
Iran

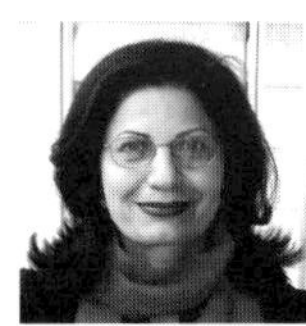

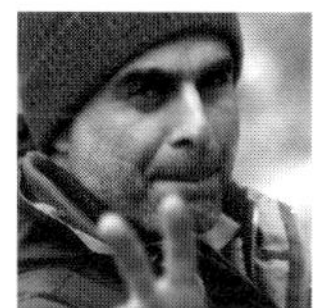

Bahman Ghobadi
Filmmaker
Iran

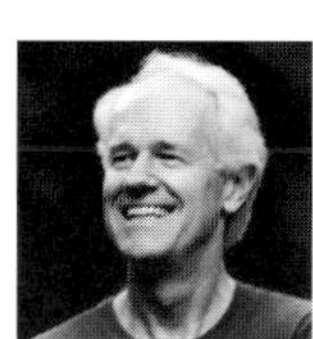

Mike Farrell
Actor
Human Rights Activist
USA

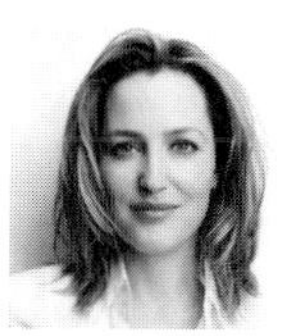

Gillian Anderson
Actress
Human Rights Activist
Canada

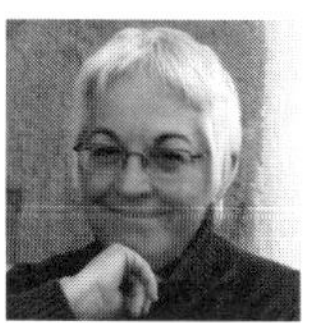

Toti Martinez de Lezea
Novelist
Basque Country, Spain

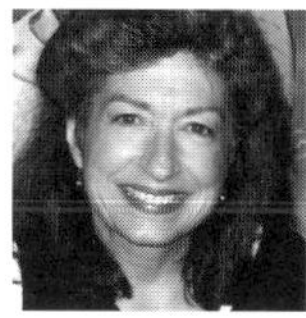

Susan Kelly-DeWitt
Novelist, Poet
USA

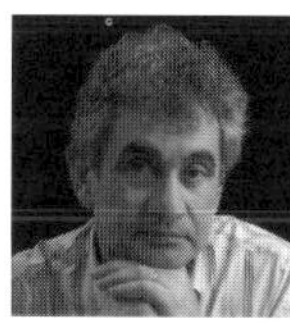

Bernardo Atxaga
Novelist and Poet
Basque Country, Spain

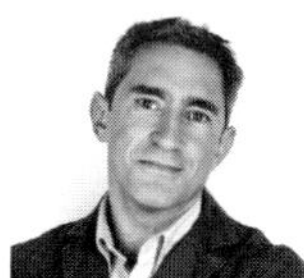

Jon Sistiaga
Journalist and Novelist
Spain

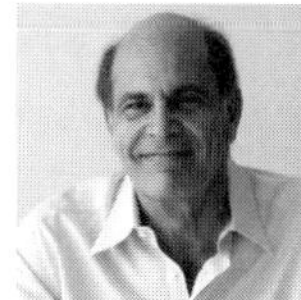

Alan Rachlns
Actor
USA

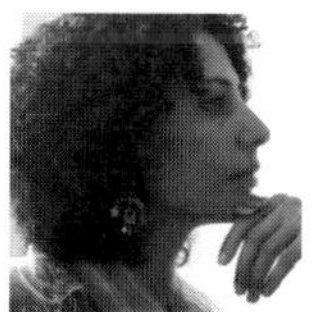

Suheir Hammad
Poet
Palestine/USA